PARTY IN A BOX

PARTY IN A BOX

THE STORY OF THE SUNDANCE FILM FESTIVAL

Lory Smith

SALT LAKE CITY

To my daughters,
Ariel and Andrea:
May all of your dreams come true, too.

First Edition
01 00 99 3 2 1

Published by
Gibbs Smith, Publisher
P.O. Box 667
Layton, Utah 84041

Printed and bound in the United States of America

Library of Congress Cataloging-in-Publication Data
Smith, Lory, 1952–
Party in a box : the story of the Sundance Film Festival/Lory Smith
p. cm.
ISBN 0-87905-861-7
1. Sundance Film Festival—History. I. Title.
PN1993.4.S55 1999
791.43'079'792258—dc21 98-3895
CIP

PHOTOGRAPHIC CREDITS

Photographs on pages 5, 7, 9, 20, 22, 24, 92, 193, 197, 198, 204, and 218 are by John Schaefer. Photographs on pages 49, 175, and 195 are by Fred Hayes. All other photographs, with the exception of the television and movie stills, are by and courtesy of Sandria Miller.

Edited by Gail Yngve

Designed by Kinde Nebeker

Contents

Introduction

"I decided to be a movie director at about age fourteen, without really knowing what it meant. All I knew was this amazing rectangle inside a box of bonbons—the movie theater."

— HECTOR BABENCO
Brazilian film director at the 1986 United States Film Festival

People have been very curious about the title of this book. Filmmakers are by nature sociable people. They have to be to marshal all the physical, financial, and human resources necessary to communicate an idea successfully on film. They need to be part poet and part shoe salesman—part scourge and part cheerleader, and they'll talk to anyone who will listen about their films, projects, and scripts, or daydreams of what they want to do. They are full of ideas and film, art, music, and literary references. They love to compare notes, share lessons, and generally commiserate about almost everything under the sun, and they are some of the most intelligent, hardworking, completely engaged, driven people I have ever met. A roomful of filmmakers with a refrigerator full of libations will create an instant party in a box.

I've spent the last twenty years watching films that arrive in boxes, either on the rectangle of a big screen in some darkened, Egyptian-motif temple or at the squeezed drama of the usually sloggy Park City Holiday Cinemas in January. These films sometimes come in anonymous black cassettes with handwritten notes. Others are calculatingly made to capitalize on the names of the actors on the video box to entice people to rent them and take them home to their own little boxes, where they can have their own little party. We're all looking for a party in a box and movies increasingly satisfy that craving.

Those who have been to the Sundance Film Festival know a big part of the drill is attending as many late-night parties as a person can handle, parties sponsored by talent agencies, public-relations firms, and distributors or perhaps wine or champagne labels. All are standing room only and held in boxy condominiums. Life in Park City becomes a party in a box, and filmmakers do like to party. All one needs to do is look to Hollywood for confirmation. A person can find it even closer to home any Friday night at any beer bar within walking distance of a film department on any campus in the world.

Finally, there's the ultimate party in a box, the one the producers and distributors have when the numbers in the box-office reports far exceed their wildest expectations, and they realize everybody is going to make money. These parties are few and far between, are often not attended by one side or the other, and are generally overreported in the press. That makes the success stories seem commonplace—a deadly illusion for first-time filmmakers.

The next question I'm asked is what gave you the idea for the book? Since its inception in 1978, I have been at the center of development for arguably one of the most influential film festivals in the world. I have been both participant and witness to what started as a small event and blossomed into an international success story. The festival has had a profound effect on our national cinema and our cultural life. I've kicked myself for the past twenty years for not having the insight to shoot my own home movies of the behind-the-scenes people and stories that have made it all possible.

This book is, in a sense, my home movie of the festival's first twenty years. I've seen it all, lived it all. I want to get it down the way it actually happened, and I think with twenty years of reflection, many lessons can be learned from this history. So party on and just think of me as the designated driver.

EARLY FILM FESTIVAL TICKET OFFICE.

Chapter One

Blame It All on Dan Quayle

In the past twenty years, Utah has seen nearly three-quarters of a billion dollars enter its economy from film and television production. The synergy between the U.S. Film Festival, the Utah Film Commission, and Sundance was no accident. It is the residue of design and is now the envy of every film commission in the country, but there were plenty of times early on when it didn't feel so visionary.

I never planned to work in the movie business even though I'd taken every film-appreciation course my liberal-arts education allowed, and had also signed up for several of Mort Rosenfeld's now-legendary film courses at the University of Utah.

Among Rosenfeld's other students was my good friend and cult filmmaker Trent Harris, whose experiences in Hollywood after two years at the American Film Institute finally allowed him to make the whacked-out *Rubin and Ed*, produced by Paul Webster and London-based Working Title Films. The movie starred Crispin Glover as Rubin—he was actually in the Rubin character the infamous night he nearly karate-kicked off David Letterman's nose before a national television audience—and Howard Hesseman as Ed. He was a last-minute replacement for Peter Boyle who had suffered a minor stroke after two weeks of shooting. Thankfully he recovered, but not soon enough to finish the movie.

Trent Harris also made the low-budget, underground *Plan 10 from Outer Space,* starring Stefene Russell and Karen Black. It premiered at the 1995 Sundance Film Festival as a midnight screening complete with a Tongan marching band.

CULT FILMMAKER TRENT HARRIS, PARTYING ON.

Another of Rosenfeld's students was Mike Cassidy, who died of AIDs after making the local cult classic of all time *Attack of the Giant Brine Shrimp*; Bryan Clifton, who went on to co-own and manage one of Salt Lake City's best and most-experienced grip and electrical houses; C. Larry Roberts, who was a brilliant filmmaker and recipient of a Guggenheim; and his filmmaking partner, Diane Orr. Roberts and Orr made several films that played in early film festivals, including the eerie Mormon documentary *The Plan* and *SL-1*, the astonishing film about the first nuclear accident in Idaho that happened in 1962 and may have been caused by a jealous husband involved in a love triangle.

Although I've gone on to make my own films, back then I never had the money to finish even one of my 8 mm efforts. Rosenfeld, who was sadly and mysteriously murdered in 1979 while writing a script, always liked my little scripts. I'd start shooting and quickly run out of the few hundred dollars I had to spend, but I've kept some of the footage. In hindsight, perhaps this was for the best. Still, never in my rather-active imagination had I ever considered working in the film business.

By 1978, after more odd jobs than one person should have to endure in a lifetime, including working as a fry cook, shoe salesman, deliveryman, fruit picker, speechwriter, waiter, substitute teacher, freelance writer, telephone solicitor, paperboy, laborer, gardener, factory worker, housepainter, librarian, and visual artist, and after the obligatory 1960s ritual of a stint on a farm, I found myself chronically underemployed, living with my lovely ex-wife, Victoria Taylor Smith, in a small Salt Lake City apartment. Along with my artistic collaborator and childhood friend, Briant Matheson, I was preoccupied with creating junk sculpture. We had done the farm stint together in southern Idaho, and during that year we amassed quite a collection of old, rusted farm implements in a workshop behind the apartment house. We used to spend every idle moment out there, drinking, smoking, and making sculptures. Because we were self-taught, we considered ourselves more attuned to folk artists than formally trained fine artists, although we had a strong allegiance

FIRST FILM-FESTIVAL DIRECTOR, STERLING VAN WAGENEN IN 1978.

to Alexander Calder, Picasso, of course, all the Dadaists, and the box maker Joseph Cornell.

Bri knew Hal Cannon, then the coordinator of Folk Arts for the Utah Arts Council, so we invited him over to our workshop to see our work. Hal Cannon is a burly old-time musician and a tenor with the Deseret String Band who organizes the Elko, Nevada, Cowboy Poetry Gathering every January. He loved our creations but politely informed us we were way too young to be considered folk artists. Breaking the news to us gently, he said, "You guys are just plain artists." We were crestfallen. He asked me what I was doing, and I said, "I guess I'm going to have to find a job." This led Hal to mention a new film festival that was just getting started and operating out of the carriage house behind the governor's mansion. In his high-pitched nasal voice, he spoke words that were emblazoned into my psyche, "You snooze, you lose."

I called the office of the fledgling film festival the next day. As it turned out, the office manager had once been a waitress in a funky canyon cafe where I used to be the breakfast cook. Her name was Linda Moore, and she set up an appointment for me with the director of the first film festival, Sterling Van Wagenen.

Sterling was a bundle of youthful exuberance, a kind of whirling dervish of ideas. A lover of films and a filmmaker himself, he was a graduate of Brigham Young University, which also had a reputation for producing some interesting filmmakers, many of whom are still working, such as cinematographers Reed Smoot, Brian Sullivan, and director Keith Merrill who was nominated his second time for an Oscar in 1998 for his IMAX film *Amazon*.

I admired the intelligence of Sterling, a Mormon intellectual with an ability to rally people to his vision and to beat a hasty retreat when it suited his purposes. He had charisma, an idea for a film festival and some sponsors, and his cousin Lola was married to a blond-headed actor who might prove useful and who had a little place up Provo Canyon called Sundance.

The purpose for the film festival was threefold—the first was to put on a national event to attract the film industry to Utah and have the support of one of the other key players in the early years, the stalwart state film commissioner, John Earle, another Brigham Young University film graduate. The Utah Film Commission deserves much credit for showing leadership from the early years of the festival to the present. The commission could have easily abandoned the festival but continued to support it with a substantial cash contribution each year. They eventually became great allies in attracting attention to Utah and helping filmmakers realize the potential for filmmaking within its borders using its experienced actors and crew.

Enhancing the film-going public's appreciation of film by selecting a retrospective program built around themes was the second reason for the film festival, then known as U.S. Film. These films could be discussed by a high-profile panel of thinkers, writers, filmmakers, critics, and even an occasional actor. This was to be the big draw of the film festival—to show old movies and have famous people talk about them.

As Sterling outlined it for me, the third objective was to start a competition for what could be described in the parlance of the time as "small regional films being made outside the Hollywood system, mostly in 16 mm." His explanation was diagramed onto a cocktail napkin he'd used for note taking during a Los Angeles luncheon with famed film scholar Arthur Knight, author of the quintessential film-studies book *The Liveliest Art*. Sterling told me, "We're looking for someone to start this competition." Somehow I convinced him I was the guy who could do this job, based on my extensive collegiate debating background—I was the recipient of the state Sterling Scholar Award in debate and drama, a local tradition of some prestige—and my basic film education, which I actually credited to Bernie Calderwood and the *Big Money Movie*, the late afternoon KSL broadcast of old classic films. I also gave credit to the Friday-night ritual of my youth, *Nightmare Theater*, another of my obsessions, all of which Sterling found funny. I had the necessary good communication and organizational skills, my extensive film-studies courses probably helped, my sense of humor was apparent from the onset, I had long hair and looked the artist/rebel sort, and, last but not least, I was immediately available.

BERNIE CALDERWOOD, HOST OF THE *BIG MONEY MOVIE*.

Sterling suggested working for the festival had only one hitch. Because they'd been able to get some kind of federal employment grant called the Comprehensive Employment Training Act, or CETA to the uninitiated, to pay the salary for the position, I would have to prove I had been unemployed for a long period over the past two years. I assured him this wouldn't be a problem. As it turned out, Senator Dan Quayle was one of the cosponsors of CETA, so in some kind of perverse way, I suppose I owe something of my career to him. Since as an artist I was the very definition of chronically unemployed, I qualified on the spot. The next day I was sitting at a desk in the carriage house behind the governor's mansion, trying desperately to figure out how to track down some of these vaguely mentioned filmmakers. The luncheon napkin had some partial titles like *Shooting Match* with leads as nebulous as "somewhere in Texas."

TALENTED TEXAS FILMMAKER EAGLE PENNELL IN ATTENDANCE IN 1978.

I spoke with old roommates, ex-wives, friends, relatives, people with mailing lists from the American Film Institute, the Association of Independent Video and Film, and a man in New York who was trying to put together a program called American Mavericks. His name was Sam Kitt. Now the president of Spike Lee's Forty Acres and a Mule, for a time he was also an executive at Universal.

Sam and I hit it off immediately on the phone, our mutual enthusiasm fueling each other as we talked about the potential of such an event for these independent films. We still run into each other at Sundance, knowing we share a unique perspective: we were there in the beginning. It is rewarding to know we are both still in there pitching, advocating the kinds of movies we like, and we have proven that others, too, respond in sufficient numbers to make this sort of specialized film a viable force in the commercial marketplace.

Despite all my efforts and with the American Film Institute unable to submit any of its uncleared films, I was only able to attract twenty-six official entries to the competition. I had to talk most of them into it. First thing I discovered, besides the festival's having no real organization or network, was that seventies filmmakers didn't like the idea of a competition. They'd all lived through the sixties, and the idea of competing against each other was antithetical to their life philosophy.

I had to explain long and hard—and not always successfully—to the person on the other end of the line that I thought the idea of a competition would translate to the press in a way that a mere program never would. It would create a newsworthy event that would give a handle to the media and the public so they could understand what we were trying to do. Otherwise, it would end up being just a small program of new unknown films, made by unknowns, in a festival full of classic films with many famous people in attendance. A competition was the only way to create the sense of expectation and urgency.

In many ways, this same dynamic is still at work today. Only now the independent films may or may not be made by unknowns. If they are receiving distribution, chances are most people will recognize the film, if not the filmmakers and actors. Still, these films compete for audience attention with movies made by well-known filmmakers who employ publicists to exploit their relationship with the media and public when it suits the filmmakers' purposes. However, most independent films now at Sundance arrive with a retinue of publicists in tow since the independents have caught on to how the game is played in Hollywood to maximum advantage.

To this day, the idea of a competition raises the level of anticipation at the festival. I credit Tony Safford with seizing the opportunity to expand the competition awards to include the prestigious Audience Award, whereby audiences actually vote for their favorite films screened during each festival. Safford was program director of the festival from 1986 until 1992, when he left first to join New Line, then Miramax, and now Twentieth Century Fox. The Audience Award has turned out to be one of the most important at Sundance, perhaps even more influential than the often more difficult and problematic grand prizewinner for distributors and the press because it is an indicator of box-office potential.

TONY SAFFORD AND AUSTRALIAN DOCUMENTARY FILMMAKER DENNIS O'ROARKE.

Back in 1978, the mood was very different, simply because no one knew what in the hell we were talking about. The idea of independent film had yet to be defined and articulated. People only had a cursory understanding of the difference between movies and films. In fact, it took us a year to catch on to the term "art" because we described the movement as "regional cinema." I know this has gone out of fashion, but I believe, as Arthur Knight did before me, that the real revolution in our national cinema was in fact a regional phenomenon. It sprouted up out of unlikely places like Florida, Texas, the Bay Area, the Northeast, and the Northwest, Los Angeles, and New York, but with a different sensibility than what had been traditionally displayed in the movies. These tended to be character-driven, intimate portraits of regional situations and people Hollywood normally wouldn't touch with a ten-foot pole. As Arthur Knight suggested in *The Liveliest Art*, these regional films represented "the kind of individualism that has recently been cropping up in the field of short films, and has also, in the past few years, begun to creep into feature production. And this is a change of no small significance. American films have long been criticized as being overly standardized and routine, lacking the style and personality of the better European pictures." They were accomplished on smaller budgets and with scaled-down ambitions, but they also represented what would become a profound shift in the national gestalt of how and why movies get made. They were films of the people, for the people, and by the people.

The other thing filmmakers wondered was why they should send me their films; after all, I wasn't able to pay a rental fee, nor could I afford to pay for their ship-

A REFLECTIVE ROBERT REDFORD IN ATTENDANCE AT INAUGURAL FESTIVAL IN 1978.

ping, except the return costs. This was before cassettes had been invented, and actual prints had to be shipped for preview purposes. Simply put, filmmakers wondered what, if anything, they would receive for submitting their film and having it play in some little festival in Utah. Many people wondered where Utah even was. I politely explained that Utah was west of Colorado but east of Nevada, that the festival expected to generate substantial coverage by actively soliciting press involvement and attendance, and that Robert Redford, who was chairman of the board of directors of the fledgling event, would attend and participate. That usually did the trick. Call it charisma or his public and personal persona as gifted actor and concerned environmentalist, but Redford also seems to have a native intelligence combined with a sense of humor and an understanding of irony, a distrust of institutions, and a subtle glint in his eye. He has a power with people, like many great actors. When he is in front of someone, that person commands his utter attention. He has a level of concentration that is short but intense. He was a famous movie star who was tangentially attached to the film festival and whose tenuous relationship I was all too happy to mercilessly exploit. I had a significant amount of pressure to deliver some kind of first-time event that could generate national publicity for unknown films made by people no one had ever heard of, often on budgets that wouldn't pay for the catering on most Hollywood films, usually in 16 mm and, technically speaking, just one step ahead of student films. I had to use everything I could think of. I also recognized quickly what seemed to work and what didn't. The Redford angle and the press angle worked. Other than that, I think filmmakers assumed I was just a nice Mormon kid trying to start a little film festival in Utah. I took to cussing a lot on the phone, a habit I still enjoy to this day. Most figured out pretty quickly I wasn't a Mormon, or if I was, I was a particularly foul-mouthed one.

The first U.S. Film Festival was set in Salt Lake City in September 1978, which meant that by mid-July I had to assemble a collection of local film scholars, writers, and buffs to prescreen all the submissions and then select the films included in the competition. The local screening committee was composed of many people who have remained involved to this day, including the rumpled Park City icon Rick Brough, a kind of sleuthing cinematic Columbo, replete with overcoat. An insightful writer and reporter, Rick is now a mainstay at Park City's public radio station, KPCW, and one of my favorite personalities and friends at the festival. The committee also consisted of two then-married film-theory professors from the

University of Utah, Vivian and Tom Sobchak, who had good insights, sharp wits, and yet failed to support David Lynch's seminal weirdness *Eraserhead*, which was submitted the first year but wasn't appreciated by the committee. This may have been in part because we were screening the prints in Ed Brinn's dingy, postage-stamp-sized screening room, which was also used by the Salt Lake Vice Squad to screen possibly lewd or pornographic material, on a dual 35 mm set of projectors named Gog and Magog. It was a wonderfully creepy place located at 1212 South State Street.

Ed was also a subdistributor with a warehouse full of prints, mostly the kind of stuff that ended up at drive-ins or was four-walled, where someone would rent the theater, advertise heavily on local television, and then move on to the next regional market. Ed had worked at MGM in Culver City and had an original poster-sized photograph of the famous players, a virtual who's who of Hollywood royalty from the 1930s, hanging proudly in his office. He was always reasonable in what he charged, and he always tried to be professional, allowing us to bring food and wine into the place.

The last member of the local screening jury was the legendary local film critic and editor of the successful magazine *Utah Holiday*, one of the most astute writers on film I have ever read, the amazing Paul Swenson. Paul came from a family of writers, his sister being the nationally acclaimed poet May Swenson, and he was also married to the film festival's main programmer and booker, Sharon Swenson, who was pulling together the massive collection of retrospective films. Paul is one of those writers who always looks like he just rolled out of bed. Slightly eccentric, but usually on the cinematic mark, Paul would often, during the two weeks of screenings, get up from his seat, stretch out on the floor, and watch from a reclining position. I only caught him asleep once when his snoring almost overwhelmed the soundtrack, but he snapped right back to attention. He continues as a writer, editor, and film critic for the *Salt Lake Observer* and is capable of writing in any major market in the country, so long as he stays awake. I must confess to one additional juror, my best friend from the eighth grade, fellow junk-sculpture enthusiast Briant Matheson. We lived in the same apartment house, actually across the street from Paul and Sharon Swenson on 100 South. We had worked together on the farm in Idaho with our wives and had been championship debate partners through high school and college. I asked him to sit on the screening committee because we had both taken film classes from Mort Rosenfeld, and Briant's footage always looked better than mine.

EARLY FESTIVAL SUPPORTER, THEN A VICE PRESIDENT AT WARNER BROTHERS, MARK ROSENBERG.

I also knew that if I needed to, which I later did, I could ask him to revise his score.

Because there was some hesitancy in turning over such a subjective exercise to a guy who had been determined by the federal government to be hardcore unemployable, I was asked to devise some sort of mathematical scoring system in case someone ever asked how we decided what films to include in competition. Fair enough, I thought, but I should at least hold some sort of ace up my sleeve. Bri was my ace.

I've never really trusted committees. The first two years of the film festival solidified that suspicion as have the last two years. I realize it is easy now, in hindsight, to go over decisions made in the heat of battle, but over the years I know I've made more than my share of mistakes on films I should have played but intellectually missed. In our first year, what we failed to play was almost as significant as what we included. Mostly because I was given just six slots in the film festival—after our prescreening, I was able to plead for two additional honorable-mention slots—we had to pass on the groundbreaking illegal immigrant film *Alambrista* by the master-bearded member of the Du Art filmmaking clan, Robert Young. To this day, it makes me heartsick we didn't play that film. When I screened it, I knew it was a remarkable experience, many scenes I still remember. It had won the Camera d'Or Award at Cannes, for Christ's sake! I'd had the opportunity to interview Bob, in the backseat of a car, on the way to the Salt Lake airport from Sundance. This is the remarkable man who made one of the quintessential American New Wave films of the sixties with Michael Roemer, *Nothing but a Man*. A committed individualist, Bob also made one of the early success stories in the independent-film world with the amazing Edward James Olmos, *The Ballad of Gregorio Cortez*, which we did play in 1983 to rave reviews. I apologized profusely for not having been able to play *Alambrista*.

In our inaugural year, we also missed the petite spitfire Maxi Cohen's excellent documentary about her relationship with her yard-dog father, *Joe and Maxie*. In this film about a gruff father and his irascible daughter, it is revealed he has cancer. It was one of the early personal documentaries that could've broken through. Because it was a documentary, it threw off all our damned mathematical calculations. We should have played the film. To this day, I try to support Maxi's work. She continues to work in New York, an original voice that deserves more support, having been forced into video by budget constraints.

Besides David Lynch's *Eraserhead*, we also did not play Pat Russell's *Reaching Out*, which was funded, as so many independent films are, by inheritance. The film was about a young woman coming into her own, standing up to her family. It was largely autobiographical, and Pat played the central character. Pat has attended many of the subsequent film festivals despite the fact she hasn't been able to make another film in twenty years. But she did attend the first year, which proved to be a fateful decision.

We also passed on a film called *Damien* from Hawaii about the legendary Hawaiian priest who served the outcast lepers of one of the outer islands, only to succumb to the bacteria himself. I remember there was some argument that we should include this film, though in my mind it was more appropriate for cable television than a film festival, even though cable television was really in its infancy. But *Eraserhead* made everyone squeamish. I love committees.

Another of the films we passed on was by Kenneth Campbell from Virginia, called *Stockcar!*, a documentary or maybe a promotional film about stockcar racing. Rick Brough still enjoys tweaking me about this unlikely submission. The title sequence alone had us all hooting when the exclamation point came up like the star of the movie. I've never heard again from Kenneth Campbell, but I hope he is doing well. In 1978, I was only too happy to receive the submission.

The films we did include in the first festival competition still stand out as representative examples of some of the earliest forays into independent filmmaking. They included San Francisco filmmaker and musician David Schickele's *Bushman;* David is the brother of Peter Schickele, most famous for his PDQ Bach performances. *Bushman* was actually made in 1968, but it was so textural in its black-and-white images, so divergent in its tone and, finally, so amusing, intelligent, and moving we felt compelled to play it. The film begins as a fictional portrait of an African living in San Francisco but evolves into an unanticipated documentary of real events when the film's star, Paul Eyam Nzie Okpokam, playing Gabriel, is arrested during filming. Sentenced to a year in San Quentin, Okpokam is ultimately deported, a catch-22 that the filmmakers incorporate into the work. The fluidity of the narrative line combined with the skilled camera and soundtrack, and Okpokam's intelligence and charisma, made *Bushman* a bemused and painful examination of an encounter with American life. It represented an inclination on my part toward politically tinged films, something the festival is still known for to this day. A goal I had early on was to promote a politically progressive event and perspective in a culturally conservative climate and state. I guess it was my subversive side coming out.

Claudia Weill's *Girlfriends,* which was the first grand prizewinner, was the funny and compassionate story of two girlfriends (Melanie Mayron and Anita Skinner), each making her marginal way in New York, as a bar mitzvah photographer and a would-be poet, respectively, when one's sudden marriage changes their relationship. Their misconceptions about each other's lives after the marriage finally bring the friends back together as they come to see each other through a clearer lens. It was perhaps the most recognizable of the films in competition, ultimately distributed on a limited basis by Warner Brothers, and it launched the career of Melanie Mayron who practically disappeared into the part. Claudia Weill went on to make *It's My Turn* in 1980 with Jill Clayburgh, Michael Douglas, and Charles Grodin. In what might be one of the first cautionary tales of independents venturing into Hollywood, *It's My Turn* was nominated for the infamous Razzie Award as one of the worst screenplays of the year. Claudia Weill continues to work, mostly in television, having directed episodes of *Chicago Hope* and *My So-Called Life.*

New York–based Mark Rappaport was another story entirely. He had submitted two films, *Local Color* and *Scenic Route*, and we loved both of them, but decided, as fascinating as each film was, with such limited screenings, we could only select one. *Local Color* was Mark's strange and wonderful construction, in black and white, about simple confrontations among a small group of people: two married couples, a gay couple, and two women, one of whom may write a novel about the others. A gun turns up periodically and serves as the link between the characters. In this low-budget surreal world, two characters talk beneath photographs of themselves that change to reflect their state of mind. Loosely based on a comic opera that is introduced early in the film, *Local Color* was as eclectic as any film in the program. Between the two films, one could sense a mature and committed artist at work. Mark has been a mainstay of the New York underground film scene, with his most recent films, *Rock Hudson's Home Movies* and *The Journals of Jean Seberg,* which premiered at the 1996 Telluride Film Festival. Mark is truly an original in the world of filmmaking, an aesthetic innovator. He continues to push the envelope, at both edges simultaneously—technically and dramatically—by creating worlds of his own construction, integrating tidbits of popular culture, and using characters to express his deepest ideas. Over the past couple of decades, Mark has created a consistent and unique body of work. I remain one of his biggest fans.

George Romero's follow-up to his cult classic *Night of the Living Dead* was the creepy yet utterly believable *Martin,* a modern-day vampire story. Trapped in the legends and superstition of centuries of family vampire lore, young Martin does his dreadful bloodletting out of a compulsion that may be part of his genes, but also may just be in his head. The film is infused with wit and suspense, making Martin's father confessor an exploitative radio talk-show host who raises his ratings through midnight conversations with "the Count," as he calls Martin. Martin has a more practical approach to his calling: using hypodermic needles to sedate his victims to make the bloodletting as painless as possible for them and himself if not for the viewer. George Romero, despite his cinematic reputation for gore, terror, and biting social commentary, is a teddy bear of a guy, closer to the part he played in *Martin* as a priest than to a schlock meister. It was apparent that one of George's great strengths was his ability to edit. *Martin,* and so many other horror films to follow, used the smash cut to elicit pure shock, the kind that could get viewers out of their seats with adrenaline. But in person, George was warm and caring. He and his business partner at the time, Richard Rubinstein, who went on to work with Stephen King, extended their friendship and support to me and the film festival.

LEGENDARY HORROR FILMMAKER GEORGE ROMERO, IN ATTENDANCE IN 1978.

Richard remains a good friend to this day and underscores practically every time I see him how valuable that exposure the first year was for George and him. Through meeting Verna Fields, vice president at Universal Studios and a member of the national jury for the festival, who recognized their talent and invited them out to Hollywood, they made their first venture into the heart of the beast. Richard still sits on the Sundance Film Festival advisory board. George Romero, who is married to actress Adrienne Barbeau, continues to live and work out of Pittsburgh, Pennsylvania, where all his films have been made. He has helped to develop an entire community of technicians and filmmakers in Pittsburgh.

One of the most memorable films from the first year, or any year for that matter, is the seldom-seen *The Whole Shootin' Match,* made by the talented, if laconic, lanky Texan Eagle Pennell. It was the black-and-white, 16 mm story of two buddies and business partners, Frank and Lloyd, who have been through numerous get-rich-quick schemes, including chinchilla raising, but this time they are ready for success. Of course, they get something far short of that but deepen their personal bond with each other and the audience. The film ends up being a surprisingly affecting, funny-without-being-condescending exploration of unpretentious, small-town Texas lives. Its warmth is won by its authenticity and the winning performances of the two leads, Sonny Davis and Lou Perry. Eagle Pennell was the big discovery at the first film festival. The film had been made for $26,000 and was full of heart. It showed considerable talent, and Verna Fields invited Eagle Pennell to Los Angeles and eventually signed a $10,000 option of one of his projects, *The King of Texas,* to be developed with Kim Henckl, friend and fellow Texan, writer of Tobe Hooper's *The Texas Chainsaw Massacre.* Eagle Pennell and I became good friends.

The next film also had some interesting crosscurrents. *Property* was from Portland, Oregon, and was made by Penny Allen. It was a first-time film shot by Eric Edwards, who would become one of Gus Van Sant's cinematographers, about a group of ragtag posthippies who attempt to rescue their crumbling Victorian neighborhood by raising money to buy it. The film was shot in a cinema-vérité style, as though a quasi documentary, with many of the actors playing themselves, including the Portland poet Walt Curtis, antihero and crab-extraordinaire; Lola, the cosmic hooker; Corky, the comic dwarf; Michael, the ex-politico; Marjorie, the red-headed Gypsy ragpicker; and Richard, the hippie piano player. The film takes on a poetic tone of irony and resignation, compromise and negotiation, but all of it is infused with a sense of humor and that Portland sense of the possible. Penny Allen returned with another film three years later called *Paydirt,* a narrative film way ahead of its time in its portrait of an Oregon community divided between wine growers and pot growers. The last I heard of Penny, she was living in Paris and writing a novel.

One of the last two films screened, out of competition but as honorable mentions from the local screening committee, was *Johnny Vik,* made by Jane Nauman in Custer, South Dakota, about a half-breed Indian who returns to Custer after his recovery in a military mental hospital that acts as his halfway house from his experiences in Vietnam, only to chafe under the domination of his mother and the indifference of white society. Vik finally makes his way into the woods to live on the edge of society in pursuit of isolation. It was an amazingly competent effort from a woman who wasn't trained as a filmmaker but who understood her community and the Native American community. She wanted to make a difference, so she made a film, hoping it might be a movie.

The other truly interesting choice as an honorable-mention film was Martha Coolidge's first effort, the remarkable *Not a Pretty Picture,* a kind of hybrid documentary with recreated footage that explores the actors' feelings as well as the filmmaker's, which is poignant because the film is autobiographical. It details the director's own experiences in a 1962 boarding school when she was date-raped. The film intercuts between re-creations and reality, past and present, and forces viewers to engage the events and examine their own responses. The film is innovative, instructive, disturbing, and, finally, deeply moving. Of course, Martha Coolidge's career veered toward Hollywood, where she has established herself as one of the truly successful women directors with films, such as *Valley Girl, Real Genius, Rambling Rose, Lost in Yonkers,* and *Angie,* and as an elected officer of the Director's Guild of America (DGA).

All in all, it was an impressive collection, but with only eight films compared to the entire retrospective program—classics such as *Midnight Cowboy, Badlands, Hester Street, McCabe and Mrs. Miller, Lonely Are the Brave, Mean Streets, The Apartment, Deliverance, Jeremiah Johnson, Cool Hand Luke, Next Stop, Greenwich Village, All the King's Men, The Clock, A Streetcar Named Desire, The Sweet Smell of Success,* and most of John Ford's classic westerns in a tribute to John Wayne—the expectations for this regional program were very low. In fact, the two honorable-mention films were relegated to single midnight screenings on Saturday and Sunday nights of the six-day event.

Yet, the focus of the first film festival was always as a retrospective event. In the first catalog, its purpose was explained as:

> The movies, and their children, are in many ways at the center of the American experience in the twentieth century. Many of the ways in which we view our lives and our possibilities are results of an art form we have invented, and in which we continue to believe. Whether we choose to admit it or not, the movies make a difference.
>
> That difference is the reason for the creation of Utah/US Film, a public event to be held yearly in Salt Lake City. Utah/US Film is an exploratory event, intended to search out and examine the ever-changing, dynamic relationship between the movies and American life. Utah/US Film is a festival event, intended to celebrate and enliven the phenomenon of going to the movies in America.

I guess the competition films were considered the children of the movies. We certainly enlivened the phenomenon of going to the movies in America, all right, but I don't think it was quite in the ways the original festival organizers had envisioned, at least not the first year.

The subtitle of the first year's film festival and its primary component was the National Film Forum. As stated in the 1978 program notes,

> Examining the relationship between American life and American film will be the on-going task of the National Film Forum. Films selected in reference to a specific theme reflecting concerns and currents in contemporary American life will be screened. Commentators drawn from public life and the motion picture industry will complement the screenings by addressing themselves to issues suggested by the films, and their consequences in our society.

Nothing like ambition to jump-start an idea!

In 1978, the inaugural theme of the National Film Forum was "Landscapes of America: Cycles of Hope and Despair—The City, the West, and the South." It was ponderous to say the least. The film program was coordinated by noted film professor and Bergman scholar Sharon Swenson with help from Paul Swenson and Barbara Bannon, who remains an able writer in the Sundance program notes and a trusted editor. The film program was as ambitious as the goals of the festival. It was a rare opportunity to see some of the classics on a large screen.

But the program went far beyond the classics. It included the 1948 documentary work of Janice Loeb Levitt and Helen Levitt, both related to the Levitts of Alta, and director Sidney Myers. *The Quiet One* was shot on the streets of Harlem as cinema-vérité about a young black boy scarred by his parents' rejection and indifference. Considered to be the first feature from the New York school, made in 16 mm for $20,000, as James Agee's commentary of the film states:

> Its aim is to make children a little better able to take care of themselves . . . a little better able to care for the children they will have than their parents were to take care of them—lest the generations of those maimed in childhood, each making the next in its own image, create upon the darkness, like mirrors locked face to face, an infinite corridor of despair.

Utah filmmakers Diane Orr and Judy Hallet also had a documentary in the first film festival. *The Longest War* was a look at what really happened at Wounded Knee, South Dakota, the site of the 1890 massacre of the Sioux nation by the U.S. Calvary. It was the story of the second confrontation between the white man and the Indians on March 8, 1973. The film introduces the viewer to the American Indian Movement and one of its leaders, Dennis Banks, even as they were under fire within the compound. It was a brave film shot under dangerous conditions, like most good documentaries. Diane Orr went on to share a Guggenheim with her friend and filmmaking partner, C. Larry Roberts, one of my favorite people who died in 1988 of AIDS.

FILMMAKERS C. LARRY ROBERTS AND DIANE ORR, 1978.

The program also included the 1937 documentary *The River,* directed by Pare Lorentz and shot by Willard Van Dyke, whom I would meet some years later in Park City and correspond with in New Mexico. Lorentz's film captures the rhythms of the mighty Mississippi and the impact of the people who live near it. He used film as would a painter, forming his materials from real life. Natural events determine and form the content of the film, giving a feeling of reality the audience finds palpable. *The River* received first prize as best documentary at the Venice International Film Festival in 1938, winning over Leni Riefenstahl's *Olympiad*.

One of the other truly interesting choices in the retrospective program, which shared more with the world of independent filmmaking, was Joan Micklin Silver's *Hester Street*. Made in 1975, with her husband Raphael Silver serving as producer, it was a turn-of-the-century drama about the assimilation of a group of Russian Jewish immigrants, set in the Lower East Side of New York. The film was accomplished on the incredible budget of only $350,000, starred a luminescent Carol Kane, and became known as one of the early crossover films. The filmmaker's daughters, Marissa and Dina Silver, would return to the festival in 1984 with their film *Old Enough,* which would become the grand prizewinner of that year and also one of the first films to generate a bidding war among distributors. So, screening *Hester Street* the inaugural year was more than appropriate.

Even in its infancy the film festival had many fine examples of the antecedents of independent film and was especially well represented by women filmmakers, something no one really noticed back then.

The panel discussions, free to the public and underwritten by the Utah Endowment for the Arts, included an impressive array of "people drawn from public life." Former mayor of New York John Lindsay spoke on a panel, which included auteur proponents and New York film critics Andrew Sarris and Molly Haskell. Cicely Tyson spoke on another panel with Professor Robert Sklar from Harvard. And screenwriter and novelist Diane Johnson, who adapted *The Shining* for Stanley Kubrick, spoke on a panel with Pulitzer Prize novelist (*House Made of Dawn*) N. Scott Momaday and the actor who lived up Provo Canyon, the chairman of the board of directors, Robert Redford.

The board of directors also included a kind of mysterious guy named Gary Allison. He was a producer in Los Angeles who had written and produced *Fraternity Row* for Paramount and was coproducing *The Hanoi Hilton* for ABC. He taught courses at several universities, including the University of Southern California, and he may or may not have had some ownership in an airline, Piedmont, as I recall. He took an active interest in the management of the festival, really an intrusive interest. It was Gary's insistence that as the festival approached and the final catalog was going to press, we should change the name from US Film, to Utah/US Film Festival, in an effort to indicate we weren't some out-of-town outfit but a homegrown event. It was one of many last-minute crises and the first of many name changes for the event. Gary also insisted on being a member of the first national jury to select the winners of the competition and award the $5,000 in prize money.

Another member of that first board of directors was Stephen Dart, a producing partner of Gary Allison. He was the son of a heavy-duty industrialist and southern California millionaire Justin Dart, a friend of Ronald Reagan. They were contract producers at Columbia Pictures Television. Another well-connected member was local guidebook author and sometime columnist Terrell Dougan, who was married to Paul Dougan, a successful Utah businessman involved in oil and banking.

Tad Danielewski, a professor at Brigham Young University, was also a helpful member of the board of directors. He had attended the Royal Academy of Dramatic Arts in London and produced and directed a variety of films, including the Emmy-winning, four-hour television special *Africa* with Gregory Peck.

Actress and friend of Robert Redford's Katharine Ross *(Butch Cassidy and the Sundance Kid)* also served on the first board of directors. Additionally, she attended as a member of the national jury.

John Earle, the film commissioner for the state of Utah, was the final member of the board. He was actually designated the special advisor to the festival, for he was the mastermind behind most of the financial contributions to get the thing started. He had cleverly approached a quasi-governmental agency known as the Four Corners Regional Commission and had been given a grant that would focus some attention on the area.

The John Ford Medallion was to be an annual award, presented in conjunction with the John Ford family and the state of Utah, which would forever commemorate the unique relationship between John Ford and Monument Valley. It was a sweet idea that was fraught with problems from the very beginning. First thing, after John Wayne was selected as the recipient, his health was failing. There had been some hope he would be able to attend, but it was finally decided that should he die while there, it would be a disaster for all concerned. He begged off on attending, and instead sent his son Michael.

The other problem was trying to get John Ford's wife, Mary McBryde Smith Ford, or his daughter Barbara on the phone to approve the image and design for the medallion, select the recipient, and be involved with the minute details, which they insisted they be informed of as the details unfolded. They lived in Palm Springs, and we discovered early on it was much better to catch Mary or Barbara early in the day rather than later. In the tradition of Mr. Ford, they could be tough-talking, cigar-chomping, whiskey-slugging tyrants with apparently way too much time on their hands. These sorts of experiences were like being allowed the first peek under the tent of Hollywood, beyond all the manufactured artifice, seeing it as it actually was. Peter Bogdanovich, in his excellent book *Who the Devil Made It?*, quotes Mary in her eighties, "If you want to stay in the movie business, Peter, never believe anything you hear; and only half of what you see!" It is sound advice, though difficult to follow.

John Earle had also been the conduit to one other local filmmaking legend, the chameleonlike Charles Sellier, or Chuck, as he was known to his friends. He was the president of Sunn Classic Pictures, a Utah-based production and distribution company with a remarkable track record of producing B movies, such as *Stories from the Bible, The Lincoln Conspiracy, Back and Beyond,* and *In Search of Noah's Ark*. Chuck was one of the early pioneers in four-walling films around the country. It was a successful strategy for self-distribution. Chuck was also one of the early advocates for test-marketing ideas, scripts, concepts, and ultimately cuts of films. He had a whole computer program dedicated to test marketing that used sensors hooked to subjects, reading perspiration, breathing, heart, and other anatomical rates and responses. It was such a novel concept at the time that he became partnered with Schick, the razor-blade people who also had a nicotine-cessation program that involved aversion therapy. They shared the same interests as Chuck—human behavior and making money. As Schick-Sunn Classics, Chuck had one enormous success story. *Grizzly Adams*, starring Dan Haggerty and Bart the Bear, was a television series on NBC. Ironically, Bart the Bear is the one still active in the business who with his handlers, my good friends, Doug and Lynn Sues, still lives in the Heber Valley, just up the road from Sundance. Bart was featured in Jean Jacque Annaud's film *The Bear* and more recently in *The Edge* with Anthony Hopkins and Alec Baldwin, where he almost stole the show. Bart also appeared as a presenter at the 1998 Academy Awards, broadcast live to over one billion people from the Dorothy

Chandler Pavilion in Los Angeles. *Grizzly Adams* was shot in and around Park City, and Sunn Classics really was the training ground for many Utah crew members who have continued to work in the business. People such as Carol Fontana, Tam Halling, Dennis Stewart, Dennis Williams, Leon Dudivoir, Henning Schellerup, Morris Chapnick, Linda English, Steve Thompson, Perry Husman, and hordes of others worked for Schick-Sunn Classics. John Earle and Sterling Van Wagenen approached Chuck to talk about this new film festival and how he might become involved. It was one of the classic meetings of all time.

EARLY FESTIVAL VISIONARY JOHN EARLE, INTRODUCING NEW YORK MAYOR JOHN LINDSAY.

Chuck was a fanciful character. He was prone to wearing turtlenecks, was something of a lady's man, had a great deal of confidence, and was highly successful, creative, and talkative. When Chuck spoke, like any good director (he directed *Killer Santa Claus*), he tended to speak to the entire room. He also had a penchant for weapons, having his isolated Park City home outfitted with a sealable hallway that sported gun turrets to capture any uninvited intruder. To my knowledge he never actually had to use those turrets, but he became so influential in Park City, he had himself deputized as a member of the local police department.

When Sterling and John were escorted into his private Salt Lake City office in the building he owned at 200 East and 600 South, he had built a virtual film factory. They outlined what was going to be a national, ongoing film festival, dedicated to independent film, showcasing Utah. Chuck immediately seized the vision, scope, and potential of such an event. They explained they were hoping for some sponsorship, in the form of contributions, and Chuck asked what they had in mind. In one of the understatements of all time, John Earle suggested, after some hemming and hawing, they were looking for maybe "twenty-five," meaning twenty-five hundred dollars. Chuck didn't flinch, saying, "That shouldn't be a problem." He said he wanted to be involved, and it was decided he should be on the national jury with some other prestigious Hollywood folks, and that sounded right to Chuck.

After about a week, a check arrived in the festival office. I was there when Sterling opened it, anxiously, because we were having severe cash-flow problems at the time. He let out a gasp. The check was for twenty-five thousand dollars, not twenty-five hundred! We all learned a valuable lesson that day. Let the other guy fill in the zeros! Chuck continued to be a significant supporter of the film festival in the early years, with cash contributions and in-kind donations. By the second year of the festival, we were using offices in Chuck's building. To this day I credit him with helping to save the festival. No matter what a person thought of his choice in material, he was a skilled filmmaker, an impressive salesman, and someone who seized initiative. He also apparently made a large sum of money and was willing to share some of it. For that the festival will always be grateful.

Charles Sellier went on to infamy in a scam perpetrated on him by someone involved in one of his CBS specials, which was really a plundering of his 1979 picture *In Search of Noah's Ark*. According to *Time* magazine, the perpetrator had done an interview with Chuck in which he had been maligned in the final version of the film. He was determined to get back at him, exposing Sellier's operation as an under-researched, loose-with-the-facts, slash-and-burn kind of program. The guy videotaped himself in his kitchen baking a piece of old railroad tie marinated in wine and soy sauce, about to be passed off as a piece of Noah's ark all the way from Mount Ararat in Turkey. Needless to say, when the con was sprung, Chuck and his producers were completely taken aback, as was CBS, which canceled his other eight hours of commitments. It didn't really seem fair, because no one really believed the wood was from Noah's ark in the first place, but the last I heard, Chuck was somewhere in Oregon making bullets. Wherever he is, I hope he knows I remember. He had the guts to support a small, uncertain Utah event.

The other members of the national jury the first year were truly luminaries in the world of Hollywood. First and foremost was the grand dame of editors, Verna Fields. She was credited with having saved Steven Spielberg's *Jaws* from disaster through her editing. She actually made them shoot some additional sequences, the spot where the body pops out of the underwater wreck, in her own swimming pool. She also had much more to her credit, having started as an apprentice to Fritz Lang in 1942 then worked as a sound editor on many television programs for Four Star Productions, including *Sky King, Death Valley Days,* and *Wanted Dead or Alive.* In 1960, she edited *Studs Lonigan,* and her career as a film editor was launched. She went on to edit over twenty-five feature films, including Haskell Wexler's *Medium Cool,* and Peter Bogdanovich's *Paper Moon, What's Up, Doc?* and *Daisy Miller.* She coedited George Lucas's *American Graffitti* and Steven Spielberg's *Sugarland Express.* In 1976, she became the vice president of production at Universal Studios, the company that had released *Jaws.* In 1978, she was the highest-ranking female executive in Hollywood.

I'll never forget being seated next to her at one of the festival dinners, when we talked about our favorite cars, and she actually got nostalgic for her BMW 2002. We bonded that night. She pledged her support to me personally and to the festival when I delivered a message to her at the Salt Lake Hilton Hotel, and she answered the door in her nightgown. It was like being taken under the wing of one of the real matriarchs of Hollywood. She personally secured $10,000 in donations

EARLY FESTIVAL SUPPORTER VERNA FIELDS, EDITOR OF *JAWS*, THEN A VICE PRESIDENT AT UNIVERSAL.

annually from Universal Studios until her death in 1986. We did a special tribute to Verna that year with her son in attendance. She was one of those rare talents in Hollywood from the old school. She meant what she said, and she followed through on her commitments. She was a great woman, and it was my privilege to be her friend.

The special-effects master Linwood Dunn was another likable Hollywood luminary. He created the special effects for such films as *King Kong; Citizen Kane; West Side Story; The Great Race; It's a Mad, Mad, Mad, Mad World; Star Trek;* and *Airport.* At the time, Linwood was the president of the American Society of Cinematographers. He attended with his lovely wife Lucille, and he, too, wanted desperately to help us create something special. He told a wonderful tale at the lunch table on our first day about a German production that was in the last two days of filming, when the leading man died of a heart attack. All the last sequences involved this actor, so the producers decided to rewrite the script so that all his remaining shots could be covered over the shoulder. They proceeded to prop up the corpse in an armchair and shot over his shoulder to complete the movie.

One other influential and immensely supportive person was the director Mark Rydell. Mark had started out as an actor, studying with Lee Strasberg at the Actor's Studio. His first film-acting job was alongside John Cassavetes in *Crime in the Street.* His first feature film as director was D. H. Lawrence's novella *The Fox.* Then he directed Steve McQueen in William Faulkner's *The Reivers.* He directed *The Cowboys,* the only film in which John Wayne dies. He also directed *Cinderella Liberty, Harry and Walter Go to New York, The Rose,* and *On Golden Pond,* which we premiered at the 1985 festival. Mark Rydell returned to the festival many times as a panelist, juror, and filmmaker. He was helpful in Los Angeles circles for our fund-raising efforts, a man who was willing to make the calls.

The other heavyweight from Hollywood was the costume designer Anthea Sylbert, who was a vice president of special projects at Warner Brothers and went on to become a producer, partnered variously with Paula Weinstein and Goldie Hawn. Anthea was stylish to say the least, having done the costume design for *Rosemary's Baby, Carnal Knowledge, Shampoo, Julia,* and *Chinatown* to name a few.

The great hope of the inaugural festival was to be able to bring together these two camps: regional independent filmmakers, who often felt they worked in a vacuum without much of a support network of their peers, and the other side of the equation, the Hollywood contingent, who had money, clout, access, and, most of all, distribution outlets. It may have been our desire to bring these two schools of filmmaking together, but we weren't quite sure what to expect when they did finally meet.

What we discovered, despite Charles Sellier arriving for the jurying session with his bodyguard, Hal Schlueter, in tow and stationed just outside the door, was that both sides wanted to make good films. Each side could learn something from the other. For the independents, Hollywood could provide financing, technical, and marketing expertise, casting options, and worldwide distribution capabilities. The independents could teach Hollywood about passion, efficiency, cleverness, and how to open up a new world of film subjects, all the while absorbing most of the financial risk.

Of course in 1978, we didn't realize the cultural depths to which all this would eventually go. No one could have predicted that this festival confluence would have such a profound effect on how movies get made, what kinds of movies get made, and how those movies get out to the public. Who could have predicted that independent filmmaking would reinvigorate Hollywood? It really was, in many ways, a marriage made in heaven. No fistfights broke out. There was no name-calling or verbal taunting. Instead, telephone numbers were exchanged along with promises of meetings in Los Angeles.

It was the beginning of a dance, which twenty years later is still going on, a dance not without controversy. Many people have been critical of Hollywood using the festival and the world of independent film merely as a proving ground. If a filmmaker runs the independent gauntlet successfully, Hollywood will scoop the filmmaker up and help him or her make Hollywood-style movies. Many independent filmmakers are only too eager to go this route because they are really a callow lot, opportunists who are only wearing the mantle of independence long enough to get their foot in the door of Hollywood until they can become the film brats they've always wanted to be. The dance goes on, with a stronger backbeat than ever.

With *Girlfriends* winning the grand prize and *The Whole Shootin' Match* taking a special jury prize, the closing-night ceremonies were held in downtown Salt Lake City at the prestigious Alta Club, which, until recently, was an exclusive private club with a rich history and membership limited to males. With all the women filmmakers in attendance, it was a collision of the past with the future.

After the dinner and awards, all of the filmmakers wanted to go out to celebrate. Most of the drinking establishments had closed for the evening, so I invited everyone over to my house, where we drank beer until the wee hours of the morning. When Eagle Pennell arrived, he took off his sports jacket, whirled it around his head, and tossed it into the bushes. He always had a sense of drama about him. We were all full of hope and possibility. Later that evening I noticed Eagle Pennell and Pat Russell making out heavily on my couch. Little did I realize that back in their hotel, they would consummate their relationship, and it would result, nine months later, in the birth of a son. Pat Russell deserves enormous credit for being a solid single parent all these years. I've met her son—a tall, lanky kid who looks just like his father.

FILMMAKER PAT RUSSELL, IN ATTENDANCE IN 1978, A FATEFUL DECISION.

By the time Eagle left my house, he couldn't remember what had happened to his sports jacket. He was convinced someone had stolen it, and he was ready to throw a few punches to drive his point home. I guess some Texans have a funny way of saying good-bye. We finally found his coat, just where he'd left it, in the bushes in front of my house.

In wrapping up the festival, we were all astonished to discover in reviewing the box-office figures that these independent films were the most widely attended of the festival, an occurrence none of us had expected. People had literally lined up around the block to see the award-winning films. We knew we were on to something. The other thing we realized was that there had been a substantial financial shortfall in the flurry of last-minute arrangements, and with disappointing box-office results from all the rather expensive retrospective films that had been booked, we ran in excess of a $40,000 deficit. This was even after Sharon Swenson, Barbara Bannon, and our first ticket coordinator, Liz Welty-Montague, had, in an effort to save money, gone out and personally picked sunflowers in the foothills of Salt Lake City at 5:00 A.M. for the closing-night dinner.

In a funny way, it was that very cost overrun that guaranteed the festival would continue. We quickly discovered there was no real way to raise money if we weren't planning to do another film festival. Planning began almost immediately. Except that Sterling Van Wagenen wasn't inclined to participate again. The large debt scared him, and although he felt somewhat responsible for it, he had some other ideas he wanted to pursue with his relative who lived up Provo Canyon. It seems this idea of independent film had captured someone else's attention, too.

ONE OF MANY LATE-NIGHT PARTIES HELD IN PARK CITY CONDOS.

CHAPTER 2

A Meeting in the Mountains

With a looming $40,000 deficit on an event budgeted at around $150,000, the staff scattered to the wind. Everyone believed it was a temporary gig, and as anyone who has ever put on a film festival knows, no matter what size or duration, it does take a toll. Festivals are all fantastic cinematic endurance tests: How many films can one see? How many parties can a body attend? How much schmoozing can one person endure? A depression settles in when the whole thing is concluded. It has been such a high-energy buzz, it is an inevitable letdown when actual life starts to intrude again.

After a few days of wrapping up, I remember heading to southern Utah with friends for a camping trip. The trip is memorable for two reasons. We were driving the 1962 Chevy Apache truck that belonged to Victoria and me and had three flat tires on the drive down. We stopped at a friend's place in an accurately named little hellhole called Fry Canyon, the only gas in seventy-five miles, and who should walk into the place but Sterling Van Wagenen. I was shocked to see him that far into the desert. We embraced, and he said he would be in touch about some interesting ideas in the next couple of weeks with which he could use my help. It was one of those funny happenstance meetings, with a 1962 truck and three flat tires in the middle of the desert, and I was desperate to hear any good news.

Of course, this was still back in the days when a person didn't need much money to get by. Rent was less than $200 a month, but the life of an artist and writer was a meager existence. I've had people read my vita and assume I came from some kind of money. I always tried to be well read, to hang around interesting people—other artists and writers—and to live like a king, but actually I never had a dime. I was determined to stick with this film festival; however, my optimism was all based on my conversations with filmmakers around the country, and I could just sense something was brewing. It was gratifying to see the general public respond so strongly to the idea of alternative cinema, and I was convinced this was culturally important. I was committed to seeing it through, and I still had a CETA grant.

REDFORD WAS CHAIRMAN OF THE FILM FESTIVAL BOARD TWO YEARS BEFORE SUNDANCE INSTITUTE WAS CREATED.

Sterling did contact me shortly thereafter about an idea Redford and he had discussed. He said Redford had been looking for a way to marry the arts community to Sundance, his mountain retreat and mom-and-pop ski resort nestled on the backside of Timpanogos, one of the most dramatic mountains in Utah. The name in Ute means "place of the sleeping princess."

Redford had started out as an artist. He'd taken art classes and a trip to Europe, and to this day has a genuine dedication and appreciation for the visual arts, and he identifies with the artists. Sterling explained, Redford had long admired what Walter Poepke had done in Aspen, modeling a small mountain community around a serious commitment to the arts.

The idea of independent film was appealing to Bob, in that he'd always been slightly embarrassed by his success, and it was important to him to give something back to the industry, but in a way that matched his own artistic leanings. Sterling thought I had done an incredible job putting together the competition and wondered if I might want to help write a grant to the National Endowment for the Arts for a planning conference at Sundance in late fall of 1979. We would talk about what Sundance might become. Of course, I was on board immediately. By the summer of 1979, the $8,000 grant had been awarded, and Sterling began to assemble the participants. In the meantime, I had another competition to pull together for the September festival.

Several people stepped forward to help make it happen. Again, principal among them was John Earle, and he helped once again to convince Chuck Sellier to help out. Between the two of them, we had about $50,000, free offices, and, if I was willing to go into the film-commission office, access to a toll-free line.

STACKS OF FESTIVAL TICKETS WAITING TO BE SOLD.

Sharon Swenson, who had written a substantial grant for the previous year's festival with the Utah Endowment for the Humanities, couldn't do it again, mainly because of exhaustion and the debt, so I was forced to come up with the program idea and write the $28,000 grant. Still, technically, none of this money could be used to retire the debt. But our hope was that with a slightly scaled-down event and slightly more realistic expectations, we might be able to make a substantial dent in the $40,000 debt while staying loyal to the original concept.

It used to get so bad when our offices were located in Chuck Sellier's Schick-Sunn Classics building that when the phone rang, we'd argue over who had to answer, because we knew the caller would be looking for money: "I got it last time; it's your turn." During the final awards ceremony at the inaugural event, I'd had to insist that we honor our pledge to give each of the finalist filmmakers a $1,000 cash prize and the winner $5,000. We also paid my friend James Fetzer, son of the Mormon temple architect, who'd labored for weeks to produce the US Film logo in a clunky wooden-framed plaque, with the winners' names silk-screened on glass. I think the ink was still wet when we handed them out. It all cost money. We decided early on that one of the few perquisites we would provide to make it a true festival was to pay the airfare and accommodations for filmmakers attending the festival. Then we would make them part of the program by having them participate in panel discussions and answer questions following their screenings.

The second year's festival in Salt Lake City, by then known as Utah/US Film Festival, was held in the fall of 1979. The retrospective theme was "The Landscapes of the Mind: FEAR AND FANTASY in American Film." Once it looked like we were definitely going forward, Sharon Swenson came back to program the retrospective films and again did an incredible job.

As Ray Bradbury said in the article accompanying the program guide:

> Ours are all hearts of darkness. In each man and woman is the hidden away need to cripple those who run swiftly, douse those who see well, deafen those

> with musical ears, smother those who sing beautifully, skin those whose beauty threatens, bludgeon those whose brains are superior. Not one of us, in the presence of excellence, though that excellence play at modesty, has not thought murder, or, at least, hamstringing.
>
> It is these elements of paradox, these boxfuls of dreadful stuff out of our genetic past and our masking present, that make many people turn away from horror films. They refuse to recognize that Buchenwald is a country within the hearts of every man of every color in every country upon earth. This is a dire notion and a dread truth, better not spoken of. . . . For only by knowing, acknowledging, feeling these terrible truths, can we grow, and grow, hopefully, toward some balance of goodness.

Apparently, Ray Bradbury never had to answer the phones for an organization that owed so many people so much money, but he got the sentiment just right for the second Utah/US Film Festival anyway.

I got back to the competition and again had to work vigorously to find two dozen films. I mailed press releases to university film departments and advertised in *American Film.* It was difficult because we only wanted feature-length films, and, frankly, there weren't that many people making them in the late 1970s. But fortunately for us, and for audiences, there were a couple of benchmark independent films in 1979. Undoubtedly, the highlight of the festival didn't turn out to be the winner, but it should have been. Described invariably as a minor masterpiece was John Hanson and Rob Nilsson's *Northern Lights* (produced by Sandra Schulberg, the niece of fabled Hollywood writer and producer, the blacklisted Budd Schulberg). This exquisite black-and-white film was set in North Dakota in 1915. Then, the grain-rich plains were owned by eastern businessmen but farmed by Scandinavian immigrants. *Northern Lights* detailed the sensitive story of Ray Sorenson and his refusal to join in the Nonpartisan League, an agrarian movement of frustrated farmers. But when the weather and greedy bankers splinter both his family and his fiancée, he becomes part of one of the most important American farm struggles of this century. The film was shot under severe winter conditions in North Dakota, where the weather was so extreme, they actually had to wrap the cameras in blankets to keep them from freezing up as they shot exterior sequences. *Northern Lights* conjured up images reminiscent of Ingmar Bergman, with its rich cinematography and lean characterizations.

INNOVATIVE BAY AREA FILMMAKER ROB NILSSON.

The film won the Camera d'Or at Cannes in May 1979, and it still stands as one of the most outstanding independent films ever made. Sandra Schulberg, John Hanson, and Rob Nilsson are still working the trenches of independent film, having between them been involved in making nearly a dozen of the best independent films of the decade. Schulberg, in particular, has become a close friend and supporter over the years. She is the only other person in the country I can think of, besides myself, who has the distinction of having attended every single Independent Feature Film Market, held each autumn in New York since 1979. She came out of the New York, Michael Hausman—protege production background, which is as good as it gets since Hausman has produced some of the greatest films of all time, especially with Milos Forman as director. They include *Hair* and *Amadeus*.

The actual grand prizewinner in 1979 was Ralph Liddle's feel-good Alaskan dog-sledding story, *Spirit in the Wind*, based on the real-life experiences of George Attla, an Inuit who as a boy was sent to live away from his family for seven years. By the time he returned, he had sustained a crippling injury that further isolated him from his native community. He had difficulty deciding where he belonged until he found solace in starting a dog-sledding team, which in the end of the movie wins the big race. The synopsis really doesn't do justice to the spirit of the film. It was a formula piece that had a couple of name actors in small parts, such as Slim Pickens of *Dr. Strangelove* and Chief Dan George of *Little Big Man* fame. It was a well-performed, well-directed effort with a rousing ending that left people buzzing out of the theater. As I recall, *Spirit in the Wind* did get some limited distribution, but Ralph Liddle was unhappy with how limited, and the film ended up entangled in some lawsuits.

PRODUCTION STILL FROM THE 1979 GRAND PRIZE WINNER, RALPH LIDDLE'S *SPIRIT IN THE WIND*.

One of the other interesting films, if not entirely successful, was Eugene Corr and Steve Wax's *Over, Under, Sideways, Down*. It was the story of a blue-collar guy who still harbors the dream of playing professional baseball until he loses his job and his dream. He has to decide what to do with his wife and his life. It was one of those understated human character studies, where the ending takes viewers by surprise—not at all formulaic.

One of the other funny discoveries at the second festival was Rick Schmidt's

Showboat 1988: The Remake. Rick came out of the Bay Area, having roomed with Wayne Wang and befriended just about every filmmaker in that part of the world. Rick is one of those rare individuals who has taken the road less traveled and successfully blended his life philosophy with his work and play. He is the author of the quintessential how-to book on independent filmmaking, *How to Make a Feature Film for Used-Car Prices.* It is a priceless educational book, which should be required reading for anyone who wants to make a film and not go bankrupt in the process. I referred to it frequently when I was making my own short films. He told me he wrote it every morning before his family woke up. Rick is one of those truly original voices out there rabble-rousing for all of us.

Showboat 1988: The Remake was a hilarious filmed tryout, ostensibly for a remake of the southern musical *Show Boat,* which made *The Gong Show* look like a church meeting. People responded to ads in the local press for the tryout, held in the heart of the Tenderloin District in San Francisco. Rick just let auditioners choose what they wanted to do, and the cameras just kept rolling. By the end, Rick had distilled the experience into a riotous examination of the whole mythical cycle, like some kind of modern-day answer to the river of life. The only problem was, after we had committed to playing the film and included it in the printed program, Rick called to inform me that he had received a nasty letter from an attorney for 20th Century Fox—a cease-and-desist order, which indicated if he continued to use the music from the original *Show Boat,* he would be sued. This immediately got Rick's attention, and he called his attorney.

In a day or so, he called me back to say he had come up with a solution because I had said I was hesitant to play the film if he was going to get sued or if he had to turn off the sound in certain sections. In the span of two weeks, Rick recut the film with a crawl at the beginning that explained on the advice of their attorney, (cut to shot of attorney), 20th Century Fox would sue his ass off if he played the original *Show Boat* song. So when the section came up where he would have played the song, the audience would now hear a gong, and the word "censored" would appear over the screen. As it turned out, it was an acceptable compromise, not quite as good as the actual song, but it still got its point across.

Rick Schmidt and I became good friends; I've always been interested in whatever he is making. One of the funniest film scenes I've ever seen is in Rick's *Emerald Cities*, in which the main character, Ed, comes to have a celebration in a restaurant just after he has learned he has cancer. Only one other person shows up for the luncheon, and then the waiter tries to tell them about a play he's seen the night before in which a guy hangs himself, and though this waiter is only trying to lighten the mood, the two men really aren't interested in his story. I cry every time I see this scene—one of those little gems that shows a filmmaker with something special to say, getting it out of his system.

Rick says he always likes to use the actual lives of his actors to help create the drama. In fact, he even uses film as some sort of catalyst for the actors to resolve personal issues. He also had a unique technique for speeding up the shooting process. He called it the Rick Schmidt "Freeze" technique; he had his actors freeze in position, then he reset the camera for a two-shot or a close-up and picked it up where he had left off. It's one of his budget-saving techniques. I've seen the results, and it actually works, though it's a bit tedious for the actors.

On the other end of the spectrum was another horror film out of Pittsburgh, made by many of the same people who had worked on George Romero's films. The film was *Effects,* made by John Harrison, Dusty Nelson, and Pat Buba, Tony Buba's brother. It was an intense psychological thriller about the making of a low-budget horror movie called *Something's Wrong,* in which the cast and crew are unaware that the special-effects murders will be real, and that the unknown actors are actually being filmed secretly by another camera crew hidden in the walls of the remote house for a snuff film called *Duped.* It was a clever piece of work, genuinely horrific, in fact so much so, with none of these films officially rated by the Motion Picture Association of America, we noted: "Explicit violence, may be offensive to some." We might have suggested that a dozen years later; when Quentin Tarantino came along; it would be reason for celebration. The national jury had an extremely hard time sitting through the parts of *Effects* where the people were supposedly killed. Obviously, when it came to special effects, this crew was very good. But the film had so many twists and turns in the narrative that viewers couldn't help but get caught up in it. It was one of those precursors to one of the most imitated scripts in Hollywood, Chris McQuarrie's *The Usual Suspects.* Just when viewers think they've figured out the plot, it veers in an unanticipated direction. Properly set up, these twists can be terribly seductive.

However, "seductive" probably doesn't best describe a film that I actually enjoyed but the jury and audience revolted against. Iconoclast Jon Jost, also from the Bay Area, made the film *Chameleon* on a $35,000 budget, which included the 35 mm blowup. It was the cautionary tale of the self-destructiveness of American opportunism, featuring a lean, mean Los Angeles hustler who sucks dry both his victims and his own humanity. With bold visual metaphors, the film portrays the changing colors of the hustler's dramatic transformations. It was a nervy, intelligent, and exciting film by one of America's leading avant-garde filmmakers. It also had about a seven-minute shot of the character driving down Sunset Boulevard, saying the words "Fuck you, gorilla" over and over again.

It was too much for the national jury from Hollywood. Later in the jurying session, they couldn't understand why I had chosen that film. I knew then Jon Jost was someone to watch. He was so committed to his way of making films, using a skeleton cast and crew, a minimum of camera movement, and lengthy takes from a static camera with no cutaways, again working with a stable of actors who all collaborated to create the film. It was another introduction to another way of working with actors and narrative and dialogue, which opened the doors for so many others to follow.

Of course, Jon Jost has created a large body of films, remaining rather obscure in this country, but wildly popular in Europe. *All the Vermeers in New York* is probably his most accessible film. Jon is one of those cranky guys who actually served jail time as a conscientious objector during the Vietnam War rather than serve in any capacity in the military. He is still marching to his own beat, having repatriated to Italy the last I heard.

I have to say that Jon is one of the few filmmakers who has actually caused me to completely change my opinion of a film by the end. I detested his *Last Chance for a Slow Dance* until those last few frames. I can't say that about many films, that the payoff in the end justified the entire experience. Despite the jury's revolt to the "Fuck you, gorilla" sequence, I became a fan of Jon Jost and his style of filmmaking. I thought he was exactly the kind of person we should be supporting.

We also programmed Mort Rosenfeld's last film, *Down in the Valley,* shot entirely with a local cast and crew in Salt Lake City—including the now-infamous scene, featuring Shelly Osterloh, local news anchor for the Mormon Church–owned KSL television as a young nubile actress in a frontal-nudity bathtub scene. *Down in the Valley* is about a filmmaker who wants to make a film about the "real life" going on around him and reveals how that process inspires, manipulates, obsesses, and fragments, separating the artist from the very people he wants most to touch. It was an irony not lost on anyone who knew Mort and how he ultimately died, bludgeoned to death in his sleep, probably in a case of mistaken identity. That is one of the remarkable things about films as a permanent record of how we lived and what we were thinking about. They endure longer than we do, and the ultimate irony may not surface until long after we have departed.

DIRECTOR JONATHAN DEMME AT THE CLOSIN NIGHT CEREMONY.

One of the honorable mentions of that year was another documentary, this one by Ross Spears, who would return in 1984 with another timely documentary, *The Electric Valley.* His 1979 film was *Agee,* the informative film on the poet, novelist, screenwriter, film critic, and journalist James Agee. It was fitting because he had written and delivered the narration to Janice Loeb Levitt and Helen Levitt's *The Quiet One,* which we had played at the inaugural festival.

Again, Sharon Swenson had put together an amazing collection of retrospective films, including one of the all-time greats, Terrence Malick's *Badlands*, starring a young Sissy Spacek and Martin Sheen. With Martin Sheen in attendance, it was a wonderful screening.

MARTIN SHEEN AT THE SECOND FILM FESTIVAL.

She also programmed Jonathan Demme's heralded *Citizen's Band;* the quintessential independent film of all time, the hugely successful *Easy Rider;* Stanley Kubrick's classic *Dr. Stranglove: Or How I Learned to Stop Worrying and Love the Bomb,* based on the Peter George novel; Bob Rafelson's *Five Easy Pieces;* Truman Capote's *In Cold Blood,* directed by Richard Brooks; John Carpenter's franchise still being produced by Moustapha Akkad, *Halloween,* with a young Jamie Leigh Curtis; Peter Bogdanavich's *The Last Picture Show;* Brian de Palma's *Obsession,* cowritten with Paul Schrader; Sam Peckinpah's *Straw Dogs;* Steven Spielberg's *Sugarland Express;* and a whole slew of Alfred Hitchcock films. A tribute to Frank Capra rounded out the program.

The real fear and daily fantasy was whether we would be able to scrounge enough money to pay off the debt. A lot of the people we owed money to thought it was wrong for us to hold another festival before we paid them off in full. Although on the surface there was a certain logic to that idea, it was times like those when my debating skills came in handy. I tried to explain that the grants and donations we received specifically couldn't be used to retire debt; it was only through the box-office proceeds generated from holding another festival that we would be able to pay off the debt.

JAMIE LEIGH CURTIS IN ATTENDANCE IN 1979.

Cirina Hampton stepped in, on loan from the Utah Film Commission office, to serve as the executive director of the event, running (everyone hoped) a tighter ship.

One of the real distinctions of the second film festival was the inclusion of the Independent Filmmakers' Seminar, a kind of precursor to Sundance. In fact, Redford's picture was used as the lead to the seminar article. At this point, Sundance was only a figment of Redford's and Sterling's imaginations. The first planning conference for the Sundance Institute was still eight weeks away.

But the first festival seminar was headed by two talented and savvy women: Cathy Main, now an independent producer and the former president of Alpha Cine Labs, based in Seattle, and Glennis Liberty, who divides her time between Los Angeles and Utah and who is the former manager of Martin Sheen and his acting

THE PARTICIPANTS AT THE 1979 PLANNING CONFERENCE FOR THE SUNDANCE INSTITUTE.

brood. They really wanted to do a nuts-and-bolts, hands-on seminar, full of key players and specific information that looked beyond the veil of war stories and anecdotes. The list of attendees was as impressive as the discussion topics were specific: Claire Townsend, the vice president of production at United Artists; Mike Medavoy, the executive vice president of production at Orion; Deborah Hill, the producer of *Halloween;* Paul Almond, vice president of business affairs at New World; Larry Casey, director of programming at Showtime; James Cavazzini, vice president of program operations for Warner Cable's Star Channel; Gordon Stulberg, an attorney and former president of 20th Century Fox; Rob Nilsson and Sandra Schulberg, director and producer of *Northern Lights;* and George Romero, director of *Martin* and *Night of the Living Dead.* It also included director Sydney Pollack on directing, actor Martin Sheen on his film experiences, and Alan Mitosky, the pipe-smoking administrator for a noble National Endowment for the Arts program, *The Short Film Showcase.* In this program, he attempted to convince local exhibitors that they should play one of his selected shorts—all in 35 mm and provided free of charge and all very fine examples of short filmmaking—before each of their features, which they resisted doing for fear of throwing off their three-screenings-a-night schedules. There was also a funny little bearded dynamo named Jivan Tabibian, who was listed in the program guide as a "Senior Marketing Consultant to Schick-Sunn Classics and a board member of the Aspen Design Conference." His presentation was the rather odd rant entitled "The Political Economy of the Independent Feature Film." He went on to consult with Redford on a contemplated high-rise hotel development for Sundance, which, to Bob's credit, he never pursued.

The topics included rudimentary problems like "Where Do I Get the Money" and "How Do I Get the Networks and Cable Interested?" But they also were right on target with seminars on "How Do I Get Theatrical Distribution?" "What Kinds of Films Are Distributors Looking For?" and "How Can I Get into Foreign Markets?"

They really were very sophisticated and specific dialogues with some key industry players. The only problem was that the audience in 1979 for these seminars mostly consisted of local residents who were not exactly on the verge of making a feature film. The supply of valuable information in the seminars really outstripped the demand and desire of the audience in attendance. But it was an admirable effort, where one of the unforeseen benefits was the realization that people in the industry really were enthusiastic for this type of a forum to share information and ideas. It started a tradition that is still going strong at the festival. Thankfully, it didn't take but a few years for audiences to finally catch up to the material being presented. In 1979, we had to worry, "What if we threw a party and nobody came?" The party did finally catch on, and it caught on because it had a real reason to exist.

In an effort to put on a scaled-down event to save money, the 1979 festival was cut from seven days to just five days. It was held October 26–30, 1979, at the now-defunct Elks Building Cinemas and the newly created Utah Media Center, still housed in the Salt Lake Art Center. Back then it was headed by the capable Chris Montague, husband of ticket coordinator Liz Welty-Montague, whose father was a well-known and beloved weatherman on the CBS affiliate. I remember Bob Welty well from the first year because I sat in front of him at Redford's panel discussion, listening to him clip his fingernails throughout the entire discussion. It was one of those funny annoying moments. We were only about six rows back from the stage, and little bits of the weatherman's fingernails were flying all over the place!

The John Ford Medallion recipient was Frank Capra with his son, Frank Capra Jr., in attendance to accept the award. Frank Capra's own words from the program and his autobiography, *The Name above the Title,* were fitting for an event celebrating American diversity:

> When I see a crowd, I see a collection of free individuals: each a king or queen; each a story that would fill a book; each an island of human dignity. Yes, let others make films about the grand sweeps of history, I'd make mine about the bloke that pushes the broom.

One of the highlights of the closing evening just after the awards ceremony came when Jimmy Stewart, who was there to support the Frank Capra award, circulated around the room and specifically came back into the Birdcage at the Alta Club, where we radical staff members had been relegated, and said with his laconic drawl, "I understand this is where the people who put this little shindig together are sitting, and I just wanted to stop by and say hello." It was a grand gesture from a grand man.

When we pushed the broom at the close of the event, we were able to pay off more than half of the $40,000 deficit in a single year, which was admirable. We also discovered again that the most widely attended films in the festival were the unknown competition films. I was convinced we were onto something significant.

If it could only be sustained.

The three-day planning conference for the Sundance Institute was held in November of 1979. Sterling, as usual, had done a masterful job of finding a model on which the Institute might be based. The model was the Eugene O'Neill Theater in Connecticut, run by George White. It was a theater retreat where new and traditional plays were performed, critiqued by visiting dramaturges, and, in the case of the new plays, revised and reworked in the hopes of improving them. George White was to attend the planning conference as were many other industry and philanthropic people, including Cathy Wyler, William Wyler's daughter, representing the National Endowment for the Arts; Howard Klein, the director of the Ford Foundation; Alan Jacobs, with the New York–based Association of Independent Video and Film (AIVF) organization; the delightful Czech instructor and filmmaker Frank Daniel, who had been at the American Film Institute and who went on, after serving as one of the Institute's early artistic directors, to teach at the University of Southern California; filmmaker Larry Littlebird, a Native American from New Mexico; my good friend filmmaker Victor Nunez from Florida; Annick Smith, writer and filmmaker from Missoula, Montana; Claire Townsend, the bright and energetic studio executive, first at United Artists, then at 20th Century Fox; and the stalwart and talented Sydney Pollack, who has directed some of the greatest films of the last thirty years, including *Tootsie, The Way We Were, They Shoot Horses, Don't They, Jeremiah Johnson, Out of Africa,* and many others. Also in attendance were filmmaker Robert Geller of Learning in Focus; Reg Gipson, one of Redford's lawyers; and former congressman and friend of Redford's Wayne Owens. A couple of other Utahns attended: Diana Lady Dougan, Stephen Rapp, and Redford's longtime assistant, the always amiable and unflappable Robbi Miller. Sterling ran the show and led most of the discussions.

ROBERT REDFORD.

Certainly Redford was deeply involved in the conference. A couple of gatherings were held at his modest mountain digs, at least by movie-star standards, high above the resort. He was very approachable, friendly, and even poured the beers from behind his bar. One was immediately struck by Redford's native intelligence, obvious passion, careful thinking, and deep insight into his chosen profession, and his ability to concentrate on the subject at hand, take in the information, assess his perspective, then condense the details into a coherent frame of reference. It was obvious he wanted to hear what everyone else in the room thought. He also has an innate skepticism, especially for anything institutional.

Robert Redford is a very smart man. He knows how to take advantage of what he's got without creating the appearance of exploiting it. His whole persona, on screen and off, is about understatement. It doesn't take much work to communicate an idea or response in a gesture, a frown, a tug on an ear, a smile. One either gets the program or not. Besides, it's hard not to love a guy who has a Porsche parked out in the garage and the most amazing Kachina-doll collection I've ever seen.

Redford has led a charmed life only enhanced by his careful choices. He felt compelled to put his stamp of approval on independent films via the film festival and the Sundance Institute, but seriously investing his resources in their future was of no small consequence. He needed to listen so that he could make the commitment to be in for the long haul. He, perhaps more than anyone in the room, sensed what the potential of all this was, and he was the perfect man to make it happen—a Hollywood insider who felt a tinge of guilt over all his success, whose heart was actually invested as an artist, and who was looking for some artistic identity for his mountain-resort development.

Of course, my agenda during the conference was also quite clear. I was hoping to find a home for the film festival. I was invited as the guy who, through the film festival, was most in touch with independent filmmakers around the country. And I saw the creation of the Sundance Institute as an opportunity to find a home for the film festival. In my mind, it was the perfect alliance. During the conference, I argued that whatever Sundance did to assist independent filmmakers to hone their skills and talents, there should also be a public event whereby audiences could be developed and exposed to these types of film experiences. Without a public component, Sundance could run the risk of becoming an elitist organization, whose impact would be limited to the handful of projects they might assist each year. The American Film Institute had long suffered from a similar reputation. As I made my point, I could see Redford's skepticism setting in. He had been quoted as saying he wasn't a big fan of film festivals. I could see this was going to be an uphill battle, but I knew logic was on my side. I would just have to be patient.

By the end of the planning conference, some sort of consensus had been reached, a convergence of ideas and insights, to form the nexus of what Sundance would be. It would emerge as a center, a resource, bringing together talented aspiring filmmakers with collaborating skilled professionals in an extraordinarily supportive environment, which would allow greater experimentation with scripts, direction, and performance and also provide access to expertise in the areas of financing, marketing, and distribution. Eight to ten scripts would be selected, and collaborative teams of writer, director, and producer would come to the Sundance resort in June 1981, live in the surrounding cabins, hold meetings outside on the picnic tables by the river, work with an ensemble of professional actors, shoot selected scenes on videotape with a professional production crew, and spend the month-long lab refining their material, so that when they left, with the imprimatur of Robert Redford and the Sundance Institute, they might have better opportunities to get the projects financed and made. That remains the fundamental model for Sundance's June Lab, so ably run from the earliest years by the remarkable and quietly influential Michelle Satter, and before her, the always generous Jenny Walz.

At the end of the planning conference, we all gathered outside in the field just below Redford's house to have a group photograph taken and to witness Redford release a golden eagle that had been injured and nursed back to health into the wilderness. It was a wonderfully symbolic moment as Redford single-handedly took the hooded eagle from the handlers, removed the hood, letting the bird stretch its wings and take flight, and a glorious occasion made doubly so by the fact that the handlers of the eagle were Jim and Stephanie Ure. Jim had been the publicist for the first film festival. No matter how reluctant Redford and Sterling were to taking on the fledgling film festival, it was going to be hard to ignore. Like the bird that soared overhead, the defining logo for the film festival was a strip of film made into the silhouette of an eagle. It was a quiet affirmation for me that Sundance and the film festival were destined to come together. Like two wings of the same bird. I just needed to be patient and assure the festival's continuation by any means possible.

SUSAN BARRELL, THIRD FESTIVAL DIRECTOR IN AS MANY YEARS.

Chapter 3

A Snowball's Chance in Hell

The third film festival heralded many landmark changes. First and foremost was the hiring of Susan Barrell, an actual arts administrator. She was brought into the organization by Maximillian Farbman, a Salt Lake City attorney who was on the board of directors. She was smart, hardworking, and ultimately became a friend. She was the person who put form and shape to the event in a way that still lives to this day.

Although, when the board of directors invited me to meet Susan for the first time, I wasn't quite sure what to think. She was wearing a kerchief on her head, which I was also likely to wear during that period of my life. This could either be a good thing or a bad thing. I was afraid she might be a roll-up-your sleeves member of the Junior League who was trying to look revolutionary for the meeting with the long-haired film programmer. But I remember she was stretched out on the floor like a dancer, not like a Junior Leaguer, and I could tell she really wanted to understand what in the hell I was selling. I explained what my role had been in starting the competition and that I had gone to New York in the fall of 1979 to attend the first Independent Feature Film Market (IFFM). I also told her I was reasonably confident I could create an entire program of new independent films, augmented with a few like-minded premieres. The few retrospective films could be devoted exclusively to the John Ford Medallion recipient. It was really just flip-flopping the emphasis of the film festival. It was a major gambit on my part, but the time was right.

PRODUCTION STILL FROM JOHN SAYLE'S THE *RETURN OF THE SECAUCUS SEVEN.*

I'd gotten the idea in New York from attending the first Independent Feature Project, as it was called in those days. It was a great experience, and I've attended every IFFM since. A lot of people think it is the last stop for a film, but as Robert Hawk and I know, a careful eye and an emphasis on works-in-progress can unearth interesting prospects. In 1979, I remember in particular, Sandra Schulberg and John Hanson, two-thirds of the team that made *Northern Lights.* I also remember a woman who—at the end of two days of collective diatribe, which was descending into a polemic of us versus them in one of the small ballrooms at the Mayflower Hotel on 57th Street—finally stood up from the audience and announced she and her filmmaking partner had just done a feature film, and if anyone wanted to know how they had done it, that person should ask now because otherwise she was going to leave. Her name was Maggie Renzi, and her filmmaking partner was John Sayles. The film was an unlikely candidate named *The Return of the Secaucus Seven.* It had been shot in 16 mm and blown up to 35 mm, was full of unknowns, and was about a weekend gathering of 1960s friends who had been arrested in Secaucus, New Jersey, on a phony charge while trying to attend a Washington, D.C., political demonstration. They later dubbed themselves "The Secaucus Seven." The story takes place eight years later as the group gathers in New Hampshire. It was destined to be one of the early breakthrough films, but in 1979, in New York, it was drawing major blanks among the IFP audience. It was almost as though they preferred to speak abstractly about the problems of making films than about the actual potential for making films.

I made a lot of contacts in New York from that first trip, where I stayed in Robbi

Miller's apartment in Greenwich Village, and my brother Colby, who was attending Columbia Law School, came over and stayed to escape his dorm. I would talk excitedly late into the night about the festival's potential. I returned convinced that the festival should reverse its emphasis, putting the independent films at the forefront and limiting the retrospective ones. It was a major move, but I felt confident I could deliver an exciting program. With the festival still nearly $20,000 in debt and with a more business-oriented local board of directors, which now included attorney Max Farbman and a Coopers and Lybrand CPA Richard Goode, the board thought my idea was a good one. Other supporting factors were the Sundance Institute's creation and the hard-boiled fact that we typically paid rental for retrospective films. Although there were hard costs associated with screening independent films and committing to bringing in the filmmakers and housing them during the festival, we didn't actually have to pay rental fees. The filmmakers recognized and received value by showing their work as long as we worked hard to invite and involve the press to cover it. The board became enthusiastic for the programming change.

Meanwhile, Susan Barrell expanded the advisory board of the festival to involve more people in Los Angeles and New York. It included producer Walter Coblenz, Universal executive Verna Fields, Jan Hagg from the AFI, *Playboy* photographer Dwight Hooker, Mike Medavoy (then with Orion), Fred Roos at Zoetrope, Mark Rosenberg at Warner Brothers, Angela Shapiro at HBO, Don Simpson at Paramount, Claire Townsend at Fox, John Veitch (then president of Columbia Pictures), and Tom Wilhite at Disney. It was an impressive alliance of industry support, helpful not only financially but also for securing some higher-profile premieres for the festival.

Still, none of it was more important than meeting with Sydney Pollack who was on the board of directors with his friend Bob Redford. It was Susan Barrell, Max Farbman, and myself, sitting in the boardroom of Van Cott, Bagley, Cornwall, and McCarthy, located in a downtown Salt Lake City skyscraper, who sought Pollack's advice as to what to do with the festival. It was spring of 1980, and he said something that forever changed the course of the event. He was wearing his traditional Levi's and cowboy boots, and he leaned back in a big leather chair, speaking in that raspy voice one gets only from years of smoking, "You know what you ought to do? You ought to move the festival to Park City and set it in the wintertime. You'd be the only film festival in the world held in a ski resort *during* ski season, and Hollywood would beat down the door to attend." I'll never forget that moment. Susan and I turned to each other and said, "That's a really good idea."

Not only was it a good idea, but it would buy us a few extra months of planning before the next festival. Had we really thought about it, we might have fainted. As it was, we were up against having enough lead time to pull off another fall festival,

DIRECTOR SYDNEY POLLACK IS CREDITED WITH THE IDEA OF MOVING THE FESTIVAL TO PARK CITY IN THE WINTER.

so the idea of skipping the 1980 festival and pushing it to winter of 1981 was immensely appealing. What the hell, why not move this marginal film festival with a continuing debt and a whole new emphasis on unknown independent films to the tiny mountain resort of Park City in the dead of winter, fully thirty miles from our original audience? It bought us a few months of planning time, and we thought it was a great idea. Little did we know how right Sydney would ultimately be. (Hollywood did beat down the door, a couple of times literally, like the time Peter Douglas, Kirk Douglas's son and Michael's brother, was involved in an altercation with Park City police outside the Memorial Hall door trying to get in out of the cold to attend a Los Lobos concert during the festival.) I will always credit Sydney Pollack for this brilliant idea, and I only wish I had invested early on in a good pair of snow boots.

The Park City of 1980 was far different from today. What is now the Egyptian Theatre was known as the Silverwheel. It put on miners' musical revues and faux western shoot-'em-ups. It was run by a couple of real old-timers, whose bib overalls were so greasy they were capable of standing alone in the corner. The projection booth wreaked of pipe tobacco and oily lubricants, but things worked reasonably well, especially after the glass in front of the projector was cleaned with Windex, probably for the first time in a couple of decades. I remember one of the guys, a tall Ichabod Crane–looking gentleman, showed me his invention—a little piece of metal that fit into the palm of his hand and made lugging heavy film cans up and down the stairs much less painful. The whole town was still very homey. There were hardly any restaurants to choose from, though the Holiday Village Cinemas in the strip mall by Albertson's grocery store did exist and were heavily utilized, much as it is to this day. In fact, we could only use the Silverwheel Theater Monday through Thursday night because the proprietors still had their musical revue on Friday and Saturday nights, which they refused to reschedule. Our offices were in the Yarrow Hotel conference rooms, and most of the filmmaker discussions were held around the fireplace in the bar.

One of my all-time favorite festival memories took place at that fireplace in the bar at the Yarrow Hotel. We premiered Jonathan Demme's wonderful film *Melvin and Howard,* shot in Utah about the true story of Melvin Dummar, a Utah gas-station attendant who one day claimed to have received a mysterious will. It was from none other than Howard Hughes and named Dummar as the recipient of $156 million. Melvin said he had once picked up an old man who looked like a bum out in the middle of the desert. The old man claimed to be Howard Hughes and asked to be driven back to Las Vegas, which Melvin did. It seemed the favor wasn't forgotten. At the premiere, when it came time for the filmmaker discussion, director Jonathan Demme and the real Melvin Dummar from Willard, Utah, were interviewed by Roger Ebert who was on the national jury.

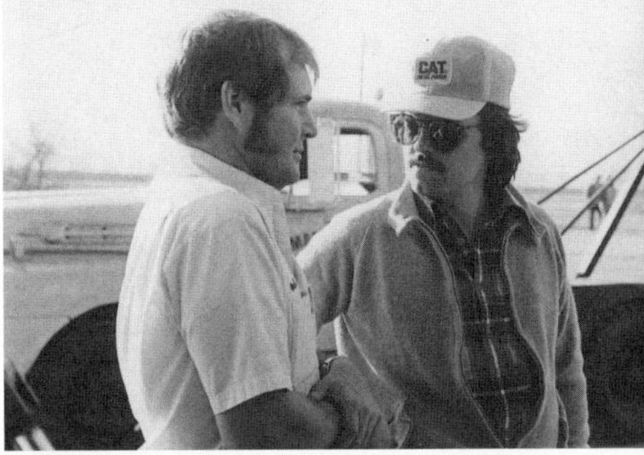
MELVIN DUMMAR, INSPIRATION OF *MELVIN AND HOWARD*, WITH DIRECTOR JONATHAN DEMME.

It was a fabulous conversation in which Jonathan Demme suggested he thought Melvin Dummar's telling of the story was accurate and that he deserved the money. Melvin took the opportunity to announce, whether he ever got any money or not, he was planning on moving to Las Vegas to become a singer and entertainer. Somehow one had the sense that there could be a sequel in Melvin's life story—he might be one of those rare guys with a second act, and probably a third. In fact, Melvin Dummar may be more of a miniseries.

Besides expanding the festival's board of directors and advisers, moving the event to Park City in the winter, and devoting the program exclusively to independent film, Susan Barrell did one other remarkable thing. She assembled a staff of unique and talented people who all remain friends and colleagues and whose influence in the arts continues to flourish, well beyond the confines of film.

Among those assembled were people like Cinda Holt who came on board to coordinate ticket sales and volunteers and ultimately became the managing director of the festival and the institute before she moved on to Missoula, Montana, to work for the Children's Theater. She was full of life, energy, and wit. She was an earth mother—unafraid to tell it like it was even if that meant Redford had to hear something that wouldn't please him. I'll never forget the image of Cinda, pulling out of Salt Lake City one summer on a tiny moped, headed out on an overland adventure through the Northwest. She never could get the moped to exceed 15 mph, and it took weeks to reach her destination. We all thought she was crazy, but that was Cinda, and we loved her for it.

Nancy Borgenicht was also a fabulous discovery of Susan's. Nancy is one of the sharpest wits I've ever encountered. A writer and actress, Nancy was brought in to coordinate promotion and advertising, and she was great fun to work with. Nancy went on to be a key member of the Salt Lake Acting Company, one of the most innovative, original, and successful regional theater companies in the country. She cowrites, directs, and continually updates the annual Salt Lake classic cultural send-up, *Saturday's Voyeur,* a musical satire on a renowned local Mormon production, *Saturday's Warrior.*

CINDA HOLT WITH THEN SUNDANCE INSTITUTE EXECUTIVE DIRECTOR TOM WILHITE.

Fran Pruyn, also brought in to coordinate advertising and promotion, is a talented individual who also went on to become an accomplished theater director, founding TheaterWorks West.

There were many talented, wonderfully fun people that third year, including Don Anderson, Kay Barrell, Vicki Mischler, June Fenn, Cathy Main, Larry Finn, Valerie Kittel, and Peggy Stuber. It was an exciting time, full of possibilities as we were determined to change the course of American cinema, to make American independent film a vital force in the cinematic landscape. We were naive enough to actually believe we could do it.

After consulting with Park City authorities, we determined that the second and third weeks of January were the slowest times of the ski season, a time when a film festival with a bit of glamour, national press in attendance, and out-of-state filmgoers might be a nice boost to the economy. Early on we had excellent community support in the form of donated housing for filmmakers, even donated airfare. Now the film festival generates over $17 million for Park City and Utah annually during the ten days in January, but back then it was a leap of faith for all concerned. In many ways, it still is.

Fortunately, it was a banner year for independent films, with features such as *Heartland,* directed by Richard Pearce and starring Rip Torn, Conchatta Ferrell, and Megan Folsom. It was about a widow and her young daughter arriving in Burnt Fork, Wyoming, in 1910 to cook and housekeep for the Scottish homesteader Mr. Stewart. The film had been funded in large part by the NEA and produced by a group of Montana women known as Wilderness Women productions, which included Annick Smith. It was line-produced by the great Michael Hausman and shot by the talented Fred Murphy. It won top honors at the 1980 Berlin Film Festival and remains one of the early success stories, at least on paper. By the end of 1981, it was listed as one of the top fifty grossing films of the year by *Variety.* For executive producer Annick Smith, the arithmetic never really did work out as is so often the case for the people who risk so much to see the production come to fruition. In the crazy world of independent film, to see a project get made, marketed, and distributed, there are often many layers of people and payments lined up in between the price of admission and the producers.

This year also marked the first appearance of Victor Nunez, one of the truly great independent filmmakers whose uncompromising sensibility should be an inspiration to a whole new generation. His film *Gal Young 'Un,* based on a short story by southern writer Marjorie Kinnan Rawlins, was a story of class and one woman's strength during prohibition when her philandering husband becomes successful as a bootlegger, arriving home one day with a blue, sleek 1929 Buick convertible and a slinky giggling "gal young 'un" in tow. The long-suffering wife balances her wrath with a kind of understanding until one determined day. It is an exquisite tale and was very well received in the Director's Fortnight in the 1980 Cannes Film Festival, and Victor has had each of his subsequent films play at Sundance, including *A Flash of Green* in 1985, *Ruby in Paradise* in 1993, and the acclaimed *Ulee's Gold* in 1997.

Anna Thomas and Gregory Nava also arrived in Park City with their richly textured period drama, *The Haunting of M.* Shot entirely in Scotland, it was an elegant and disturbing ghost story set in 1906—a most assured debut film, directed by Anna Thomas who we also learned was an accomplished cookbook author. Roger Ebert said the film was "perhaps the most audacious, ambitious and generally successful debut feature film since Orson Welles made *Citizen Kane* in 1941." Greg and Anna have continued to make some of the great independent films of the decade with *El Norte* and a film I truly loved, *Mi Familia.* They are a funny couple, who, given their culinary background, complained incessantly about the food available in Park City in 1980. Of course, this was way before the Riverhorse, Chez Betty's, Mercato Mediteranneo, Grappa, the Barking Frog, Alex's, and Cafe Terigo.

Many other notable films and filmmakers would go on to achieve significance, including John Sayles's *The Return of the Secaucus Seven,* Andrew Davis's *Stony Island,* Frederick King Keller's sweet *Tuck Everlasting,* Mark Rappaport's zany *Imposters*, Rick King's hilarious *Off the Wall,* and actor Ralph Waite (from *The Waltons* fame) in the heartfelt, but decidedly unWaltonesque *On the Nickel,* a gritty tale of alcoholics and skid row.

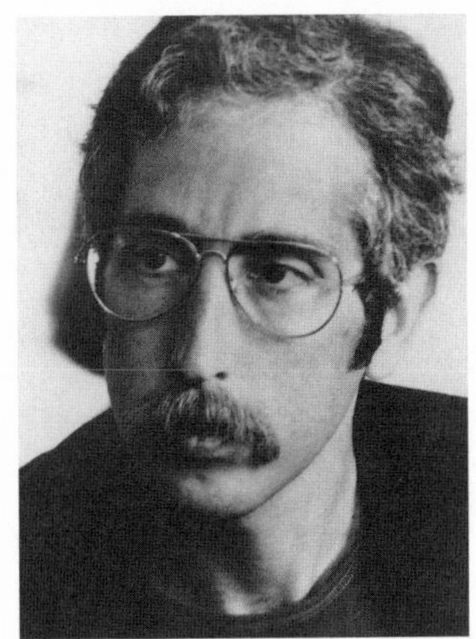

FILMMAKER MARK RAPPAPORT, A PIONEER OF LOW-BUDGET INVENTIVENESS.

Documentaries also had a strong presence with Jon Else's haunting *The Day after Trinity,* about physicist J. Robert Oppenheimer and his role in the building of the first atomic bomb; Glenn Silber and Barry Brown's Academy Award nominee, *The War at Home,* about the student protests of the 1960s; Connie Field's wondrous *The Life and Times of Rosie the Riveter,* one of the precursors to the Ken Burns style of historical documentary made of interviews blended with archival footage; Diane Orr and C. Larry Robert's *The Plan,* about a highly managed Mormon family; renowned editors Caroline and Frank Mouris with the delightful *LA, LA, Making It in L.A.*; Tom Johnson and Lance Bird's *America Lost and Found*; and Mary Benjamin's *Eight Minutes to Midnight: A Portrait of Dr. Helen Caldicott.* It was a radical bunch of films and filmmakers who descended onto the snowy streets of Park City in 1980.

PRODUCTION STILL FROM *EIGHT MINUTES TO MIDNIGHT: A PORTRAIT OF DR. HELEN CALDICOTT.*

The event was augmented by a supportive collection of premieres and special screenings, which included David Carradine's directorial debut, *Americana,* about a man returning to a town in Kansas to refurbish an abandoned merry-go-round; British filmmaker Brian Gibson's eerily violent new-wave rock drama *Breaking Glass;* David Lynch's groundbreaking *The Elephant Man;* Jonathan Demme's *Melvin and Howard;* Rob Cohen's *A Small Circle of Friends;* Lee Grant's distinguished and deeply felt *Tell Me a Riddle;* Art Linson's turn as a director, *Where the Buffalo Roam,* based on the Hunter S. Thompson book *Fade to Black,* an inventive horror film set in Hollywood, directed by Vernon Zimmerman; and last but certainly not least was the regional premiere of Robert Redford's directorial debut *Ordinary People,* for which he would win an Academy Award as best director in March.

Henry Fonda was selected as the recipient of the John Ford Medallion, having worked with John Ford on *Young Mr. Lincoln, Drums Along the Mohawk, The Grapes of Wrath, My Darling Clementine, The Fugitive, Fort Apache,* and finally, *Mr. Roberts,* the stormy production which caused the rupture of their relationship. This was in the year Ronald Reagan was elected president, and as was so succinctly pointed out by critic Andrew Sarris in the program catalog, "Fonda strikes a provocatively discordant note as a lifelong liberal. The very name of Fonda reverberates across the generational barriers through those two contemporary icons of the counterculture—Jane (politics), and Peter (lifestyle)."

PRODUCTION STILL FROM MARK RAPPAPORT'S *IMPOSTERS.*

Peter Fonda attended to accept the award for his father. He was a close friend of Jonathan Demme's, and the three of us got together in Demme's suite late one night. Demme had warned me about Fonda before he arrived. He said he had a funny way of greeting people by saying "Good-bye" instead of "Hello." And when the evening was over, he would say "Hello" instead of "Good-bye." I'm an easygoing guy, so I figured no problem. Peter Fonda arrived, and we drank a few beers while he told stories of having to carry a gun with him on many movie sets, particularly *Easy Rider* because the unions would show up and intimidate him. He said he had to fire it into the air a couple of times to get their attention. As we sat there, the three of us, I thought of myself as the Jack Nicholson character in *Easy Rider,* the naive bumpkin getting turned on to the rest of the world, at least as it pertained to Peter Fonda. Sure enough, when I decided I'd had enough, I got up to leave, and Peter Fonda stood up, shook my hand, and promptly said "Hello," like we'd just met.

PETER FONDA IN ATTENDANCE AT 1981 FESTIVAL WITH BOARD MEMBER MAX FARBMAN.

Recently, I was deeply moved to see his Academy Award nomination for his performance as the taciturn beekeeper grandfather in Victor Nunez's *Ulee's Gold.* It is a worthy acknowledgment of a fine talent.

With Roger Ebert, Julie Corman, Janet Fleming, Mark Rosenberg, and the esteemed Arthur Knight on the national jury, they were deadlocked over who should win the prize. When I suggested it could be a split prize between *Gal Young 'Un* and *Heartland,* the jury seemed relieved to have an answer since both camps were adamant for two excellent films. Victor Nunez is the only filmmaker in the history of the festival to have won the grand prize twice, and in both cases it was split, as was the case in 1993, when *Ruby in Paradise* shared top honors with Bryan Singer's never-released *Public Access.*

A few other remarkable things happened during the 1981 festival. One was that the board of advisors, as they are sometimes wont to do, decided that video was the up-and-coming thing. Remember, this was still in the infancy of VCRs. The big coming debate was Beta, VHS, or laser disc. They thought, rather belatedly, we should insert the word "video" into the name of the event. Never mind that we didn't have time to actually do a video program; we'd just stake out the territory before anyone else got there first. We'd catch up to the idea the next year. They thought we should also drop the Utah/U.S. Film connotation, so the festival went through its third name change becoming the United States Film and Video Festival. We also decided to start to compile a filmmakers' directory as part of the festival's program guide, an idea that continues to this day.

The other unforeseen circumstance that affected everything was the huge

ROGER EBERT MAKING A POINT IN PARK CITY.

accumulation of snow Park City and the Wasatch Mountains received during the week of the film festival. It shut down the freeway coming up Parley's Canyon from Salt Lake City, which severely cut into our audience base. The result—and I'll never forget this sensation—was stepping into our noon screenings on some days and being able to count silhouetted heads on two hands. The evening performances obviously drew much better crowds, but the bottom line was all the snow hurt our box office to the tune of running another $80,000 deficit. At the end of the third annual film festival, we were looking at a deficit of over $100,000. But we had an excellent base of genuine support in Los Angeles and friends who pledged to help bail us out, enough so that the board of directors again understood the only way to get out of debt was to do another film festival. Once again, in a funny way, it was that very debt that helped ensure our continued existence. Looking back on it now from the hindsight of success, I think it is an important lesson to heed, namely, not being afraid to go into debt for something one really believes in, but I had to be prepared to call on friends and family to help see me through. Without this kind of commitment from everyone involved, the festival would have had about a snowball's chance in hell to survive.

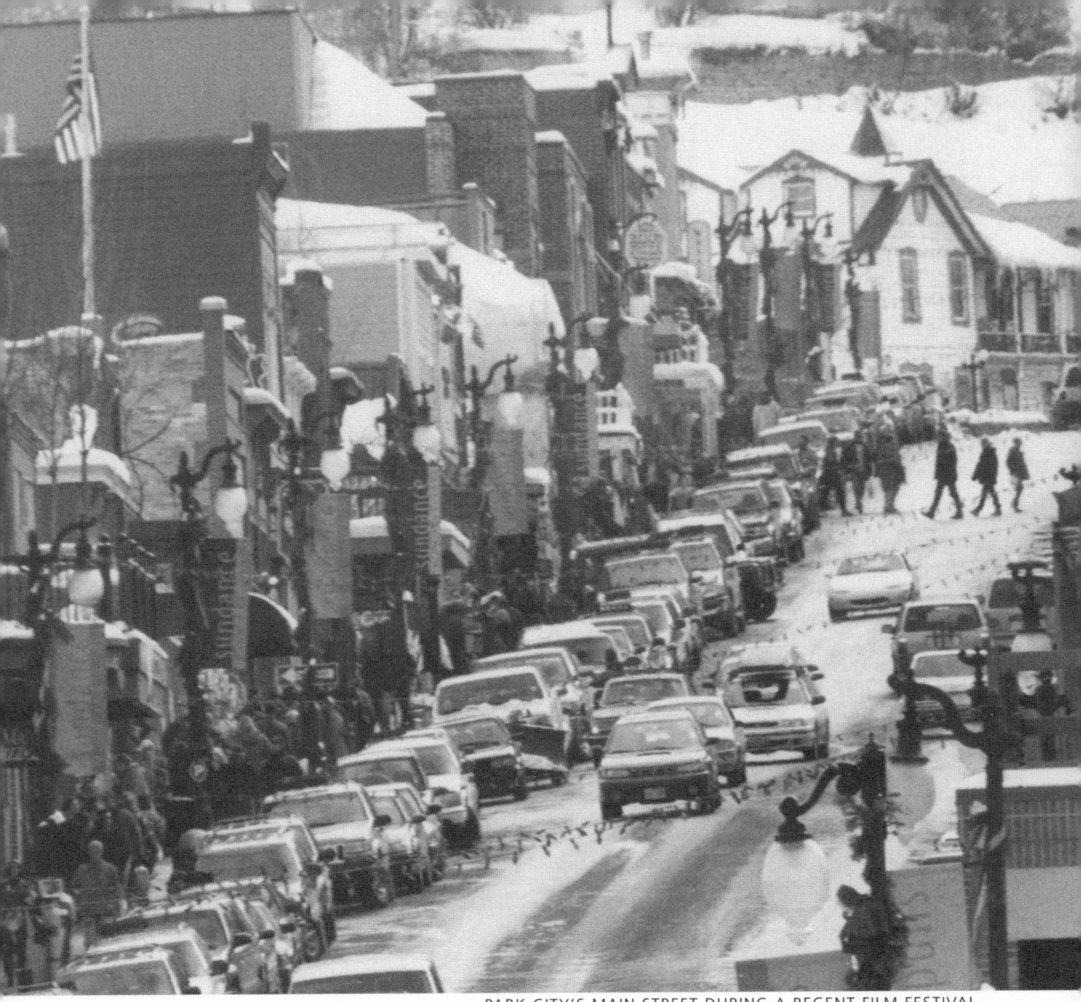

PARK CITY'S MAIN STREET DURING A RECENT FILM FESTIVAL.

CHAPTER 4

Bare Bones and Knuckles

When the festival wrap-up was completed, the board of directors and key staff met to go over the results. It was a fairly ominous sign, when, three hours after the meeting, we discovered we'd all been food poisoned by the sandwiches ordered for lunch. We were literally sick to death over what had happened.

It turned out that moving the festival to Park City had caused a major budgetary rupture. As a result of moving the offices and box office, bringing in all the filmmakers and speakers, paying the high cost of the facilities and a burgeoning staff, and lower-than-expected attendance because of the blinding snowstorms, we were over budget again. The festival quickly disintegrated into a regime whereby whoever had the most clout got his or her bills paid first. There was even some discussion about whether we really had to honor the prize money awarded. I argued that, indeed, we did, though I know in some cases it took a long time for winners to receive the money.

By now my CETA grant was well past concluded, and I was cut loose by the festival, as was the rest of the staff. I was assured I'd be called back, but maybe not for a few months that stretched into six. I was convinced I shouldn't do anything else but wait it out, perhaps do odd jobs, and support myself by having garage sales of all my weird stuff on the front lawn of my apartment building. I used to set up a full-size female mannequin I'd dubbed Una Vulgare on the lawn of the garage sale, which almost caused accidents as people drove by and did a double take.

Needless to say, my wife got tired of this pecuniary attitude and insisted I try to find an actual job. When I balked, we ended up separating for a time, and I went to Los Angeles to hole up with my father and try to write a screenplay. These were the best of times and the worst of times. I was penniless, finally getting work with Sterling, basing out of Redford's Wildwood office on the Burbank lot, and securing the prints for the first Sundance Lab in June, which I came back to Utah to attend.

However, before I came back to Utah, I screened many films in Los Angeles, including once going with my father to a private screening that had been arranged for me at Laird Studios by Frank Capra Jr. As I recall, the film was called *Vice Squad,* a far cry from the films associated with his father, but it was funny because when my father—who always dresses as if he's going to church or to get a loan—came with me, the long-haired slouching kid, they assumed my father was the one looking at the film for the festival. They dismissed me but were very solicitous of my father, getting him coffee and refreshments. After he got comfortable, I had to speak up and explain I was actually the one there to screen the film, and I'd just brought my father along for the ride. The film wasn't anything the festival would be interested in, but I think my father enjoyed it.

I also had the occasion to attend a few screenings at Melnitz Hall put on by the UCLA Film Archives. There my path crossed with one of the programmers, who would ultimately become my successor—though at the time obviously neither of us could know that. Geoff Gilmore, in his rumpled and rather gruff intellectual way, even as a young man was introducing the films. Although I consider Geoff a terribly talented programmer, even then he demonstrated a tendency toward long-winded pontification. During the question-and-answer session after screening one of Jon Jost's films, which as I recall was *Last Chance for a Slow Dance,* someone asked Jon, given his radical background and his antithetical cinematic leanings—extremely long takes, sometimes full magazine loads of eleven minutes of film with a static camera and not much going on in front of it—if he had ever considered writing essays instead of filmmaking. Though the question was rhetorical and a bit unfair, it was one of the few times I have ever seen Geoff Gilmore and Jon Jost simultaneously at a loss for words.

When I arrived back in Utah for the June Lab, plans were under way for another film festival. Some progress had been made in Los Angeles to raise some financial commitments. The Utah Film Commission again was willing to step up to the line. Sunn Classics and Chuck Sellier still believed in the event and would help financially. Most of the creditors were willing to be patient about the money we owed them, including Ira Sachs, a local Park City character with business interests in the Far East. He happened to own the Yarrow Hotel, where most of the festival events had taken place, including the closing-night dinner.

The board of directors, however, was split as to how to manage our rather substantial financial shortfall. Richard Goode, the certified public accountant, and Max Farbman, the local attorney, both wanted to send out letters offering to settle for a fraction of the debt. They explained this was a standard business procedure and that creditors would be happy to receive even a small percentage of the debt rather than no payment at all. Norm Chesler, who ran the Theater Candy Distribution Company, tended to agree. John Earle from the Utah Film Commission and a continuing source of money and influence really didn't like the idea of not fully honoring our commitments. The staff wasn't exactly fond of the idea, either.

This was the beginning of the development of two camps within the board of directors, which frequently were at odds over its direction and management. Other members of the local festival board included Diana Lady Dougan, a presidential appointee as a director of the Corporation for Public Broadcasting; wealthy industrialist Blaine Huntsman; Park City Councilwoman Tina Lewis; interior designer Marilyn Nelson; socialite Nancy Shanaman who the last I heard was living in a trailer on the Navajo reservation working on a project about trading posts; and stockbroker and radio talk-show host John Prince. They were all a dedicated, hard-working collection of talented people whose expertise and commitment really did see us through some difficult times. But there was a great deal of infighting, with Max Farbman and Dick Goode usually winning the day.

As with any struggling event, there was always a certain amount of pressure to make the thing a bit more glamorous for the local Salt Lake City and Park City crowds. People didn't mind spending money for fund-raisers if they could get dressed up, see, and be seen, and rub shoulders with the rich and famous. The only problem was there weren't that many rich or famous independent filmmakers. I was always being prodded to find more glamorous premieres. In fact, it was suggested that perhaps we should abandon the emphasis on these misfit filmmakers and instead simply make this a celebration of all things Hollywood. I told those factions within the board that if this was a direction they wanted to go, it was fine, but they'd have to do it without my services. This always stumped them because they really were clueless how I came up with these films each year, independents and premieres alike. They needed me, but I also needed them. It was a threat I had to employ sometimes, but it became a dance we all got used to.

In an effort to shore up our financial house, the board of directors in a lifesaving move of sheer gallantry each agreed to personally sign on a line of credit at the bank—for $10,000 extended to the film festival. It was a magnanimous gesture on everyone's part, but one that would ultimately bring the dissension to a head.

At the time, it was the thing that allowed us to set in motion plans for the fourth annual United States Film and Video Festival. My friend Jeff Dowd—a producer's representative and marketing consultant, one of the founders of the Seattle Film Festival, a holdover from the political culture of the 1960s in Washington state and someone I'd met at the first June Lab—first suggested the festival should span two weekends. "Those are your biggest box-office days," he said.

PRODUCER JEFF DOWD AND FRIENDS.

So the fourth festival was expanded to nine days, and for the first time documentaries were placed in their own competition category. That decision effectively doubled the competition while it highlighted one of my favorite cinematic experiences—watching well-made documentaries or nonfiction films. Documentaries, political and personal alike, have all the elements inherent in fiction films: high drama, interesting characters with choices to make, humor, irony, tragedy, and heroism, but they include the added knowledge that these people, events, and circumstances are real. Documentaries aren't constructed the same way fiction is—as compelling as that can be—and every year they have played an important part of the buzz at Sundance. In 1982, I knew creating the documentary section was the right thing to do, but not everyone on the board of directors agreed. They wanted more stars, and I was proposing a competition for documentaries! As it turned out, it was a groundbreaking year for documentaries, with Errol Morris's amazing *Gates of Heaven*—one of my all-time favorite films—leading the way.

Another major competition launched in 1982 highlighted video art, video documentaries, and invitational screenings that included movies made for television. I must confess, I was never a huge fan of this whole idea because it had been foisted on the festival by certain members of the advisory board who were involved in television. Go figure. I thought it was a nice idea in theory, but in reality I thought it diluted what we were doing with independent film. In my mind, it was just win-

PRODUCTION STILL FROM ERROL MORRIS'S *GATES OF HEAVEN*, A FILM ABOUT PET CEMETERIES AND MUCH MORE.

dow dressing to access television money in Hollywood. Although there was some very interesting work going on in video, a competition was just going to clutter the landscape. But then, I'm probably one of those old-fashioned guys. I don't care what a person shoots on, if one doesn't have a print, one doesn't have a film, as was pointed out by a film critic who questioned the value of playing made-for-television movies in a video program when they were all shot on film. Touché.

It was also determined that there should be some kind of video award equivalent to the John Ford Medallion. Given all the trials and tribulations associated with the medallion each year, we should have seen it coming and turned the other way, running. Francis Ford Coppola, who was getting all this media attention for his innovative use of video technology in the making of *One from the Heart,* was to be the first and last recipient of the video award. The fact that no one could come up with a name for the bloody award should have told us something. It was also determined that in order to celebrate the immediacy of the technology at the awards-night ceremony, we would do a live feed with Francis sitting in his living room in San Francisco, broadcast to the audience at the Yarrow Hotel conference-center ballroom. Does this sound like a scenario fraught with disaster or what?

The film festival of 1982 was fortunate for several other reasons, however. The first thing was that it didn't snow. In fact, the skiing conditions were so poor, half the town's service industry had been laid off because of lack of visitors. It was the first time the town of Park City seemed palpably to appreciate the festival's presence. I remember picking up a hitchhiker who was a waiter just hired back because of the film festival. I always liked hearing stories like that. Even though there was little snow, it was bitter cold. I remember because the ticket box office that year was an old, double-decker English bus parked out in the lot in front of Albertson's.

FRANCIS FORD COPPOLA BEAMED LIVE TO PARK CITY.

It was so cold inside the bus that volunteers had to wear coats, hats, and gloves the entire time they were working. If nothing else, it was memorable in the annals of the film festival and temporary space. I saw that bus not too long ago, broken down, faded, peeling, and sitting in the middle of the desert on the way to Wendover, Nevada. Somehow it is a fitting resting place, where it is warm and dry and metal is slow to rust.

The big news of 1982 was the new documentary competition. It included Errol Morris's quintessential warped worldview, demonstrated in one of the greatest documentaries ever made because it teetered on the edge of reality in a perfect mind meld of subject and object—style and substance. It was a groundbreaking style and the signature of a unique voice who has continued to make extraordinarily complex films, using the absurdities of reality as mirrors on the world. To say *Gates of Heaven* is a film just about pet cemeteries is to miss it altogether. As David Ansen said in *Newsweek:*

FRIGID FESTIVAL BOX OFFICE SET UP IN GROCERY-STORE PARKING LOT.

> It brings us vital news from the heart of the country. Few films have revealed so much about the way Americans speak, how they justify themselves, how they spin jargon to hold themselves at arm's length from despair. It is a film about middle-class dreams, metaphysical illusions and the artificial interiors we cradle ourselves in. The accumulated pathos of bereaved pet lovers gives us a wacky setting for a meditation on American disappointment. A slice of American life crumbling around the edges. It is appallingly funny.

Still, there were so many great documentaries in 1982. Nicholas Broomfield (whose special screening of *Kurt and Courtney* was pulled from the 1998 Sundance Film Festival in a major controversy, especially with Nick serving on the jury) first surfaced in 1982 with *Soldier Girls,* a film he made with Joan Churchill about a group of three female recruits going through basic training. As a sergeant says in the film, "You can't teach people to kill nicely." The camera unobtrusively captures the reality of the grind-them-down school of military training and the pain inflicted upon women who find themselves unable to cope with the pressure, as they are forced to march and chant "Pillage, plunder, burn, and rape." Two of the women quickly become disenchanted with military life, but the third one embraces it. It is a bracing look at women and the military.

Another strong film with women at the focal point was Mary Beth Yarrow and Lee Grant's *The Willmar 8* about a group of eight female bank tellers who go on strike outside the Citizen's National Bank of Willmar, Minnesota, over equal pay and opportunity. These women, who find themselves locked into a two-year battle that shakes their community to its very foundation, picket through two bitter-cold Minnesota winters. They also find themselves at the center of a nationwide controversy about feminists, without having much of an idea what that really means. The film is a stirring chronicle of adversity and hardship. Bittersweet and moving, it is a revealing portrait of women's struggle in America.

A truly memorable film about two women's struggle of a different kind is the incredible film by Martha Sandlin, *A Lady Named Baybie,* about two indomitable friends, Baybie and Ginger—both in their sixties and blind since birth—who hitchhike from Kansas to New York by singing religious songs on street corners with a tin cup. As Baybie says in the film, "When a person is far out in New York, a lot of people enjoy them. In Kansas, we were just a hunk of junk." Their spirited lives and utter lack of self-pity are an inspiration. It is one of those films that still haunts me.

Frederick Wiseman, one of the true originals working in the unfettered documentary field, arrived with *Model,* a look behind the scenes at Zoli's modeling agency in New York. Another standout documentary that year was Jim Brown's *The Weavers: Wasn't That a Time,* the reunion film of the famous folk-singing troupe with political overtones. The group was comprised of Pete Seeger, Lee Hayes, Ronnie Gilbert, and Fred Hellerman. It was a fitting political connection communicated through the magic of film and audio preservation because several of the other documentaries were clearly political in nature, including Glenn Silber's and Tete Vasconcellos's *El Salvador: Another Vietnam,* an indictment of United States policy in Central America; *We Are the Guinea Pigs,* a film by Joan Harvey about the disturbing effects of the Three Mile Island nuclear accident; and *In Our Water,* a film by Meg Switzgable and shot by Barry Sonnenfeld, which focuses on Frank Kaler, a housepainter, and his South Brunswick, New Jersey, family. They begin to fear their water has been contaminated by hazardous waste from a nearby landfill. Frank Kaler's desire to protect his family by obtaining safe drinking water turns him into a political activist. His six-year struggle is a call to action for anyone who has

FRANK KALEN, HOUSEPAINTER TURNED POLITICAL ACTIVIST FROM *IN OUR WATER*.

determined to stop relying on bureaucrats for answers and take matters into his or her own hands.

The other documentaries were filled with a sense of place, with Ken Fink's beautiful coal-mining film *Between Rock and a Hard Place*, Dennis Lanson's *Booming,* Carol Stein and Susan Wittenberg's *Brighton Beach,* Alan and Susan Raymond's *The Third Coast,* and James Szalapski's unvarnished country-western homage, *Heartworn Highways,* confirming the fact that America's best whiskey and music come from the same part of the country. It was an impressive collection of documentaries spanning the spectrum of styles and subjects. But they were a uniformly strong program that made a statement about the validity of showcasing documentary films in a competitive event. The timing was just right.

The dramatic competition was also strong. As any programmer would say, festivals live and die by the kind of films available in any given year. In the earliest years, I lived in constant dread that one year there would be a drought of independent films, and I wouldn't have enough to play. I'm happy to report that in nearly twenty years, that circumstance never presented itself. But that never stopped me from worrying about the possibility. One of the techniques I developed, which I ultimately passed on to Tony Safford, was to be in touch with the various film labs around the country to discover what they were processing, then to contact the filmmakers from there.

FROM JOAN HARVEY'S THREE MILE ISLAND DOCUMENTARY *WE ARE T GUINEA PIGS.*

In 1982, we had some memorable dramatic finalists in Mark Berger's ahead-of-its-time, completely whacked-out, musical comedy *The Curse of Fred Astaire;* J. Terrance Mitchell's roller-disco docudrama *Get Rollin'*, which was executive-produced by the head of DuArt Film Lab in New York, Irwin Young, and which did get some limited theatrical release; a film by Eli Hollander called *Out,* which introduced a young actor named Peter Coyote, mentioned as an affable true-life hippie; and Bobby Roth's second feature film *Mystique,* a clever dramatic takeoff on one of several self-development weekend seminars popular at the time, starring Yvette Mimieux. It was executive-produced by Anthony Quinn. Bobby's first film, *The Boss's Son,* was a highly regarded autobiography of a young son deciding not to follow in his father's successful footsteps into the family business. True to form, Bobby was probably the only independent filmmaker I knew who drove around Los Angeles in a Rolls Royce. But he turned out to be a talented director as we also played his film *Heartbreakers* in the 1985 competition, and he has gone on to a successful directing career in Los Angeles.

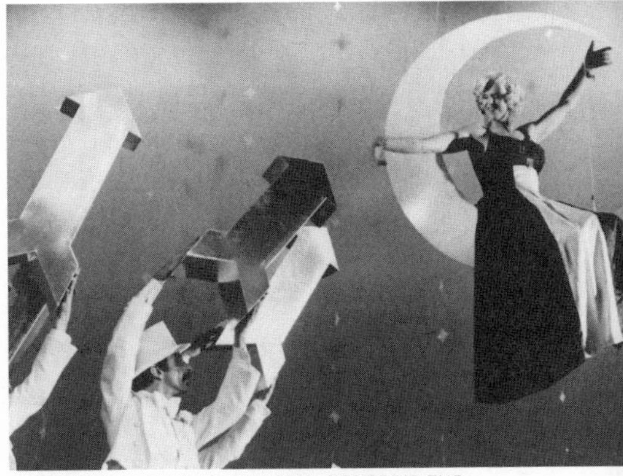
PRODUCTION STILL FROM MARK BERGER'S THE *CURSE OF FRED ASTAIRE.*

Other standout films included the return of Penny Allen from Portland, Oregon, with another film shot by Eric Edwards: *Paydirt*, a film about the start of a winery that is being financed by a marijuana cultivation operation and how the community prefers to look the other way. It is a prescient film in its anticipation of a continuing cultural issue about which drugs are legal and which are not. It confirmed Eric Edward's growing reputation as a very fine cinematographer.

PRODUCTION STILL FROM PENNY ALLEN'S *PAYDIRT*, ABOUT WINE AND POT GROWERS.

Boston filmmakers Christine Dahl and Randall Conrad scored big with their gritty film *The Dozens,* a fictional portrait of a woman, realistically played by Debra Margolies, who is just being released after two years in prison for check forgery. Trying to navigate her course through personal, professional, and emotional entanglements, she finally emerges a fully realized character, capable of bravery and determination.

The other truly memorable film in competition that year was Charles Burnett's *Killer of Sheep,* the eloquent story of a black man who lives in South Central Los Angeles and works in a slaughterhouse to support his family, but is in search of moral order and personal dignity to the point where he loses touch with his family and himself. The film won the 1981 Critics' Prize in Berlin, and as juror Lee Grant said, "It is a film which takes you to places inside yourself you never knew existed." Even in the face of Charles Burnett's subsequent work, the underrated *My Brother's Wedding* and the more visible *To Sleep with Anger,* starring Danny Glover, *Killer of Sheep* stands out as a uniquely powerful film. He is one of those filmmakers who deserves a great deal more support. He is a talented writer and director, devoted to showing the human side of his culture as opposed to the flash and spectacle. If Spike Lee really wants to support other black filmmakers, might I suggest he be in touch with Charles Burnett, the most talented and heartfelt of the bunch.

Two of the other prominent films in the 1982 competition were Mark Reichert's *Union City,* shot by Ed Lachman and starring Deborah Harry of Blondie fame, Irina Maleeva, Pat Benatar, and Everett McGill. The film is a highly stylized, deadpan, absurdist fantasy full of stifled sexuality and potent moodiness about an accountant and his pallidly attractive and very bored wife. The accountant becomes obsessed with finding out who is stealing sips from his morning milk bottles.

PRODUCTION STILL FROM CHRISTINE DAHL AND RANDALL CONRAD'S *THE DOZENS.*

The other film, perhaps the most successful of the year, was Jenny Bowen's *Street Music.* Shot by Richard Bowen, the film is a glorious tribute to love among the ruins. Set in the Tenderloin District of San Francisco, it is about a street performer, her funny, live-in boyfriend who drives a tour bus, and their odd assortment of elderly neighbors in an old Victorian hotel set for demolition. What each discovers about the important things in life and when one needs to make a stand is the essence of the story. One young woman learns to grow up as one old building comes down. It was an oddly old-fashioned tale that seemed to split the difference between the spirit of the independent world and the look of a Hollywood feature—what many independents thought they should be striving toward—making a film that looked as though it cost a lot more than it did.

Although it worked in the case of *Street Music,* I don't necessarily concur with that kind of thinking. In fact, often I find that slick-looking films work against the spirit of independence, if not against the actual material. I'm much more forgiving of a film with limited production values, providing the story and characters are there. It has always been a contradiction in terms to have an independent film that looks like it cost $10 million. But Dick and Jenny Bowen are terrific people, and Dick shoots lots of major commercials, so the polished look shouldn't have surprised anyone. They shot the film nonunion in their hometown of San Francisco, made difficult by the teamsters and unionized firemen driving by their exterior location and blasting car horns and sirens.

We also had one slight problem during the premiere of *Street Music* at the Egyptian Theater. The projector we were using was called a "double-mutt," whereby the entire film is built up on one giant reel that weighs about seventy-five pounds. In the middle of the screening, there was suddenly a loud crash from the booth, and the screen went white. As it turned out, the mechanism that holds the reel in place on the projector had a design flaw, and as the film played, it was unthreading itself until the reel finally came off with enough tension to send it rocketing across the booth. The projectionist, Aysha Quinn (who also happened to be one of the videomakers in competition, receiving honorable mention for *Spine/Time in 1983*) was very lucky she wasn't seriously injured when the hundred-pound reel shot across the booth. Our brilliant technical consultant Clayton Stauffer, who continues to manage the challenges of the film festival, finally figured out what had happened. Fortunately, Jenny and Dick Bowen were understanding despite the loss of the torn frame and a new splice in their print. The reel was put back on and had to be handheld in place during the rest of the screening. The film was enthusiastically received even with the near miss in the booth.

As I mentioned in the accompanying article in the program catalog, entitled *A Hollywood in Every Town,* the point of the competition was:

> . . . to help them [the films] gain wider distribution by building popular and critical reviews, by gaining notoriety in the national press. The more successful the films, the easier it will become for other films to follow in their path. These kinds of events are helping to create an informal network of interested people, all hoping to advance this kind of filmmaking. This is a movement that is gaining momentum throughout the country.

But I added a cautionary note:

> And it is here that the challenge to American independent filmmakers becomes most critical. Will these films and filmmakers emulate Hollywood or will they continue to strive for their own unique visions of the world? In their search for commercial appeal, will they lose their very value, through compromise or caprice? . . . Will success spoil them, or lull them into a more passive kind of filmmaking? . . . The cultural responsibility that has been passed along to this new breed of filmmakers is both intimidating and immense. To help manufacture the symbols and images with which we as a people are to live with, support and imagine, is no small task.

The 1982 festival also had some interesting premieres and special screenings, including Mark Rydell's *On Golden Pond,* and a screening Verna Fields helped to arrange, Costa-Gavras important political thriller *Missing*, starring Jack Lemmon, Sissy Spacek, and John Shea. Michael Mann showed up with his film *Thief,* starring

James Caan, Tuesday Weld, Willie Nelson, and James Belushi. We also played Ivan Passer's excellent *Cutter's Way*, starring Jeff Bridges, John Heard, and Lisa Eichhorn and Luis Valdez's stagey *Zoot Suit*, starring Edward James Olmos and based loosely on the famed Sleepy Lagoon murder that took place at a reservoir on the outskirts of Los Angeles in 1942 and resulted in the much-publicized Zoot Suit riots one year later in an effort to right a judicial wrong.

The other exciting program established in 1982 that is still going strong is screening short films, many taken from university programs or other festivals, such as my friend at the Aspen Film Festival, Ellen Kohner Hunt, who has always loved short films. In fact, to this day with the guidance of Laura Thielen, formerly from the San Francisco Film Festival, they run the excellent Aspen Shorts Fest, dedicated entirely to short films from around the world (in addition to their main festival). Who can forget *The Wizard of Speed and Time*, a short film years in the making.

When it was all over, once again we were delighted to find that audiences flocked to these independent films and our box office was much better than in previous years, though the video program was underwhelming in its presentation and attendance. At the awards dinner, the video people were in a tizzy over their perception that they were playing second fiddle to the films. They wanted to make a stink about it, so they sat off by themselves, got drunk, and pouted for the rest of the evening. This was really okay because director Tony Bill had been coaxed into being the master of ceremonies for the closing-night gala, and to say he was underprepared would be kind. In fact, once we got the live feed of Francis Ford Coppola up on the jumbo screen behind the stage and he had accepted the still unnamed video award graciously, Tony Bill turned the floor over to questions from the audience; whereupon, an extremely drunk man stood up and went on for several minutes incoherently trying to pose a question. Francis tried gamely to find the thread of it but finally gave up, and the guy went back to his drink. Francis did congratulate his Bay Area friends Jenny and Dick Bowen for winning the grand prize with *Street Music*, and the beacon of new technology broke into hundreds of pixels and static and was gone.

PRODUCTION STILL FROM THE SHORT FILM *THE WIZARD OF SPEED AND TIME.*

The good news was that the costs had been held down, and we were able to pay down about $40,000 on the $100,000 deficit. It was a major accomplishment and word was getting out about this little film festival being held in the mountains of Utah.

It was the fifth festival, however, held in 1983 that was both a challenge to get off the ground, led to a major fight among the board of directors, and, at the same time, marked the maturation of the event and the focus of our efforts, particularly in regard to courting the national press.

By this point, the festival staff had made friends with Mike Spencer, an executive at Walt Disney and a former editor with the *Los Angeles Times.* Mike was one of those wizened bearded guys who, not unlike the rest of us, always had a kind word, a funny joke, an expense account, and a willingness to help this little film festival even at the risk of jeopardizing his own future. Only, he had more to risk. He was able to secure some in-kind support from Disney and promised to handle the physical production of the program book from Burbank, utilizing Disney's substantial printing operation. This pulled a big item out of the budget. It was a nice gesture that ultimately became something of a boondoggle.

Nevertheless, our money was extremely tight, even with the fund-raising that continued in Los Angeles and in Utah. There were now nineteen board members and forty-two members of the national advisory council. The thinking was the more the merrier and the better the chances of accumulating donations and or services. This isn't to say all was handled on such a quid-pro-quo basis. Many of the people had great ideas, lots of energy, and the opportunity to talk up the event with countless associates. Some had lovely homes for having meetings and parties, but, at a certain point, Susan Barrell and the management staff began to reach a point of diminishing returns on having to service so many people in so many advisory capacities. Still, raising money required constant attention, especially for a small film festival that was carrying a sizeable deficit, that was held each winter in the Utah mountains, and that was out to change the course of American cultural life. Yet, somehow, the idea of what we were doing was contagious. What we discovered was that many people wanted to give something back to an industry that had been very good to them, who saw the potential in what we were talking about, who got behind the idea of somehow opening the gates of our cinematic culture to more diverse voices and points of view. It had the effect of reinvigorating people, reminding them of why they got into this business in the first place. When they could see what others were doing, it emboldened them to believe in what they could do, causing this remarkable cultural synergy. Filmmakers, whether they're working on a project at the time or not, consistently comment that to attend the festival and see what everybody else is doing is inspiring. So many talented, brave, committed, and singular people are out there trying to bring these stories to fruition on film and tape to share with others. By 1983, the festival had clearly tapped into a wellspring of energy and ideas, a network of like-minded people, and it was well on its way to articulating a vision for the future of American independent film.

As is still the case, the view from the inside sometimes feels surreal. Insiders know full well all the smoke and mirrors that are used to help create the illusion for the press and the public. It is almost an amorphous experience, whereby a person cobbles a program together film by film—inviting interesting people to discuss technique, finding sponsors to help pay for all of it, throwing a few parties—presto! whammo! a film festival is created. But the thing that always set our film festival apart from all the others was our dedication to showcasing American independent film, just at a critical time when it needed someone who had an overview to articulate the vision in a way that made it real, definable, and universal. We had a message to get out. We had a cause we could all believe in. We had a genuine purpose to exist. That, in my mind, is the principle reason for the unqualified success of the film festival. We had an ambition that far exceeded our infrastructure. I remember sitting some of the staff down from time to time to make sure they understood just how important our mission was to so many people—filmmakers around the country. Without our support and opportunity to present their films in a friendly supportive setting, intermixing many of their peers with average filmgoers, and without the national press in attendance, these filmmakers would have a much more difficult time getting their work out. What we were doing was extremely important, it was going to change the course of American filmmaking! I'm sure some of them thought I was a bit off my rocker, and perhaps I was, but I really believed it. And I enjoyed getting other people to believe it, too. One of my secret pleasures was to stand at the back of the darkened theater and watch the audience watching the film. It gave me immense satisfaction to see an audience enjoy a different kind of film experience, one that respected their intelligence rather than playing down to it, one that made them think and feel and see the world maybe a little bit differently. Then, to be able to meet with the people who made the film and get a sense for who they were as individuals was all tremendously exciting to me. It was empowering on many levels.

One of the key reasons for this kind of synergy was the film festival's recognition of the need for the national press to be in attendance—a vital component in the mix. Roger Ebert became a significant supporter of the festival as a critic and as a member of the board of directors. Duane Byrge at the *Hollywood Reporter* also became an early advocate of the festival and an early attendee, as did Deborah Caulfield with the *Los Angeles Times.* Todd McCarthy, one of the key reviewers at *Variety*, eventually became a supporter of the festival, but it took him a little longer. I think he had a tendency, as did others, to only start paying attention to the festival from the time Sundance took over the management of the event.

The film festival was fortunate to bring in a talent from the Utah Film

Commission. Saundra Saperstein ran the press office and, more specifically, courted the press to attend. She just retired from directing the Sundance Film Festival Press office in 1998, having done a remarkable job overseeing worldwide press attendance since 1983. That journey saw the press attendance increase from a few dozen in the early years to over 700 journalists from around the world this past year. It was a savvy strategy to have in place—a sophisticated, intelligent, funny, irreverent, and strong personality in Saundra to form long-lasting relationships with members of the press who were critical to getting the word out about these films and about our film festival. Her efforts and those of her always-cool staff, aided lately by R. J. Millard, resulted in massive coverage of the event and really introduced the general public to the idea of American independent films. It was through decades of her efforts that the term "independent film" finally seeped into the consciousness of the country and found a way into the cultural lexicon. This was one of the things that also set our festival apart from other festivals. We wanted key members of the press in attendance, and she did a masterful job of seeing to it that they did attend and write about what they saw. Saundra Saperstein, my dear friend and colleague, deserves enormous praise for doing a difficult and increasingly demanding job with such aplomb and style. My prediction is that Sundance will miss her presence more than they know.

FESTIVAL MEDIA DIRECTOR SAUNDRA SAPERSTEIN ASSISTING FILM CRITIC PAUL SWENSON.

Another thing we did early on was to attempt to do group sales to interested organizations who might have a specific connection to one of the films in the program. We brought in an enthusiastic actress named Rebecca Hunt who could've sold orange juice to orange farmers. This was clever because we were able to help fill seats during nonpeak screening times with people who otherwise might not have thought to attend a film festival had we not contacted them, alerting them to the opportunity and the group discount. We had busloads of senior citizens, disabled people, and, just this year I'm happy to say, school children. It really was an effort to do some outreach, to take the whole idea deeper into the culture, and it is something I think distributors and filmmakers looking for audiences for their films need to consider more often. Not enough attention is paid to finding creative ways to reach an audience and motivate them to attend.

In 1983, we were fortunate because it proved again to be a very strong year for independent films. Robert Young arrived with Edward James Olmos's remarkable performance in *The Ballad of Gregorio Cortez.* Produced by Moctesuma Esparza and Michael Hausman, it is the authentic 1901 story of a Mexican cowhand who shot and killed a Texas sheriff in self-defense over a mistaken translation from Spanish to English by an inept interpreter. For the next eleven days Gregorio Cortez eluded hundreds of mounted Texas Rangers by outriding, outsmarting, and outguessing them. Texans feared him, but Mexicans saw him as a border hero. It was a memorable performance by Eddie Olmos, and a beautifully directed film, full of nuance and a range of emotions. It still stands out as one of the great independent films.

Also in competition that year was Paul Bartel's breakthrough film *Eating Raoul,* which was cleverly distributed by Jane Alsobrook and 20th Century Fox Classics. It is the kinky but hilarious story of Paul and Mary Bland who live next door to a pair of swinging neighbors. The Blands' lives get more interesting when they are mistaken for the swinging couple by a misguided Raoul who is summarily conked on the head by Paul with a frying pan after he starts making passes at Mary. And that is only the beginning. Suffice it to say this black comedy didn't strike a chord in culinary circles, but it did blend high-concept satire with low-concept camp to become a bit of a cult hit around the country.

Another bonafide hit from 1983 was Wayne Wang's funny and mysterious *Chan Is Missing,* the story of two Chinese American taxi drivers in San Francisco who are looking for a businessman named Chan who has disappeared with some of their money. The more they find out about Chan, the less they know. It is one of the early black-and-white, grainy, personal films that broke through into the marketplace, having been distributed by New Yorker Films. It was a marvelously crafted story of identity, assimilation, and meaning. Vincent Canby, the influential critic with the *New York Times* proclaimed the film "a matchless delight," especially for the astonishingly low $20,000 budget. It was the launching of the talented Wayne Wang's directing career who went on to direct *Dim Sum, Slamdance, Smoke,* and the big-budgeted *Joy Luck Club.*

Another Bay Area filmmaker, William Farley, directed the lyrical film *Citizen,* a nontraditional narrative about a marginal group of people wandering around that attempted to counter the cynicism and neurotic apathy prevalent in contemporary society. This puts it in a class with so many other independent films about groups of people sitting around talking, but in this case they were moving. William Farley is one of those wonderfully eccentric and individual filmmakers whose point of view drives everything. In this case, he attempted to redefine the global role of being a citizen, realizing optimistically that in the end each person chooses to live life however he or she wants. *Citizen* also featured the unknown talents of a Bay Area actress and comedienne Whoopi Goldberg—so unknown at the time, we misspelled her name in the program guide, calling her Whoopi Goldbert.

Another film debuting an actor who would become a significant Hollywood player was Ed Harker's film *Dream On,* starring an unknown but even then very intense Ed Harris. The film was a sophisticated piece of material about a group of actors hopeful of finding a theater to stage a play and, in the process, coming to terms with their commitments and relationships. It was successful in the end because the visual style of the film supported the story, and we had come to genuinely care about what happened to the characters. I've run into Ed Harker over the years, but to my knowledge, he was a talent who was never able to mount another film.

On the other hand, Frederick King Keller, who had attended in 1981 with *Tuck Everlasting,* returned with *The Eyes of the Amaryllis,* a turn-of-the-century ghost story about a young girl and the mysteries of long-lost love and the sea. Fred Keller, who lived and worked in Buffalo, New York, with his lovely wife Elizabeth, who was also the costumer on his rather elaborate period films, was one of the more prolific of the bunch in part because he had tried to develop a niche. Just as George Romero was known for horror, Fred was tilting toward a youth market. I haven't spoken to Fred in some time, but the last I did, he was prospering thanks to a Nickelodeon series called *Dude,* which he created and directed. Fred was one of those salt-of-the-earth guys who always had a sense of playfulness balanced with a seriousness of purpose, or maybe it was just the accumulation of all those Buffalo winters. I remember his father appeared in *Tuck Everlasting* and in a subsequent film. Evidently, his dad was an actor in Buffalo, who also ran the local movie house as Fred was growing up. Fred and I became friends, although I did have to pass reluctantly on a film he made about Santa Claus with his dad in the role. I just didn't think it worked as a festival film. That Santa thing is a tough one to pull off in an independent film except for in the case of Trey Parker, creator of the popular animated *South Park* who also made the short animated film *The Spirit of Christmas.*

DIRECTOR FREDERICK KING KELLER.

Two films in the competition with unique points of view included Yan

Nascimbene's relationship film *The Mediterranean,* about a couple and their young daughter moving out to a secluded California ranch to serve as caretakers. Through flashbacks, they remember a time in the Mediterranean when their relationship was new and fresh. The second film was by documentary filmmaker Robert Jones who moved into fiction with the gritty east-coast urban drama *Mission Hill.*

As a counterpoint, the rather broad but funny, ahead-of-its-time comedy was one of the more difficult things to pull off in an independent film during the early years. It was one thing to be funny and hip, but it was altogether something else to just come flat out as a comedy. It was a genre that independents had a difficult time mastering, but Peter Markle's *The Personals* was an amusing, if predictable, observation on the single life.

One film that emerged out of all the splendid contenders of 1983 was David Burton Morris's 1968-set *Purple Haze,* which was fueled by the turmoil of the not-so-distant past and set on fire by music that included Jimi Hendrix, The Animals, Buffalo Springfield, The Byrds, Cream, and others. It was an electrifying coming-of-age story, accurately evoking the period in a way that wasn't repeated again until Oliver Stone's *The Doors.* David and his wife, screenwriter Victoria Wozniak, were a presence all through the festival with many late-night parties held in their condo, attended by almost everyone who was in town for the festival. David went on to direct the controversial *Patti Rocks* and has been nominated for several Cable Ace Awards for his continuing work as a director for HBO.

DIRECTOR DAVID BURTON MORRIS.

Again this year, the big news was to be found in the documentary category. Who could forget Kevin Rafferty, Jayne Loader, and Pierce Rafferty's *Atomic Cafe,* made entirely from American propaganda films from the 1940s and 1950s. Like a nuclear *Reefer Madness,* it was a film that as Vincent Canby said, "Has one howling with laughter, horror, and disbelief, coupled with the contemporary nuclear film *Dark Circle* by Judy Irving, Chris Beaver, and Ruth Landy, which chronicled the complex human costs of a nuclear economy even in the absence of nuclear war.

Diane Orr and Larry Robert's bizarre love triangle set in a military reactor in Idaho Falls, *SL-1,* was the true story of the first United States nuclear accident that occurred on January 3, 1961, and may have been caused by a jilted husband. He purposefully raised the fuel rod out of the water, knowing full well it would contaminate two others and himself in the reactor that day. Amazingly, the filmmakers built the story out of actual footage shot by the military to reassure the public that this kind of nuclear accident was manageable. In a classic turning of the tables, the filmmakers were able to use the government's own footage to expose the hazards of nuclear radiation and the extreme vulnerability to an unstable individual.

PRODUCTION STILLS FROM DAVID BURTON MORRIS'S *PURPLE HAZE.*

There were three other politically charged films that year, including Robert Hillman's excellent *Fire on the Water,* the story of Vietnamese refugees in a confrontation with Texas Gulf Coast shrimpers who feel like they've been invaded. The two others were Ken Levine's touching film on Hmong refugees coming to America after six long years in a northern Thailand refugee camp, *Becoming American,* and Josh Hanig and Dennis Hick's *Coming of Age,* about a group of racially and sexually mixed teenagers who gather at a summer camp to confront issues in their lives.

One other political program was in that year's package of documentary films—*Conversations with Willard Van Dyke,* by Amalie Rothschild—an interview with the documentary filmmaker who was then in his eighties and who had set out in the 1930s to make documentaries that change the world. He eventually became the director of the film department at the Museum of Modern Art, and he was one of those grand old gentlemen with sweet, sincere eyes, moist around the edges, as he spoke with such conviction and nostalgia. We screened his landmark 1940 film *Valley Town,* a stark examination of the consequences of unemployment.

However, not all the films were political documentaries. We also had Errol Morris's return with his very odd *Vernon, Florida,* in many ways the precursor of his 1997 entry *Fast, Cheap, and Out of Control. Vernon, Florida,* is the portrait of three regular residents of this backwater town: a man whose obsession is hunting the elusive wild turkey, the town cop who discusses the places he likes to sit and wait for crimes that never happen, and a preacher giving a sermon on the word "there-

DOCUMENTARY FILMMAKER ROBERT HILLMAN.

fore," which Paul used 119 times in his Epistles.

Errol is the master of philosophical juxtaposition in which the camera acts as father confessor for the subjects. He then takes all this rough footage and makes the actual film—alone in the editing room. That sense of the camera placement in regard to the subject is one of the ways Errol is able to achieve the almost surreal results. In the beginning, he would get as close to the camera as possible so that the subject would have the effect of looking directly into the camera, engaging the audience in an altered way. Later on, Errol perfected the technique by creating something he calls the Intertron, whereby he creates a mirror image of himself at the camera and the subject engages him through the mirror projection, a kind of visual teleprompter, making Errol's life, if not the audience's, a bit more comfortable.

We also had George Nierenberg's rousing *Say Amen, Somebody*, a superb documentary on gospel music featuring performances by "Mother" Willie Mae Ford Smith, Thomas A. Dorsey, the Barrett Sisters, and the O'Neal Twins of St. Louis. The film was a marvelous fusion of gospel music and gospel life with real insight into the fervor that this kind of music inspires in people.

Another memorable performance-oriented documentary from 1983 was *Moses Pendleton Presents Moses Pendleton.* Directed by Robert Elfstrom, it was the extraordinary dance performances choreographed by Moses Pendleton, one of the founding members of Pilobolus Dance Theater who Robert Joffrey called the Charlie Chaplin of the dance world. His offbeat sculptural tableaux made him an internationally acclaimed choreographer. The film follows him on his thirty-third birthday around his twenty-two-room mansion in Connecticut where we get a glimpse of how his past informs his imagination and creativity. We were especially privileged to have Moses perform what he had created while in town for the film festival. On very short notice, we were able to fill the house at the conclusion of his screening at the Egyptian for what turned out to be an astonishing dance, performed entirely in downhill skis and boots. Moses was a great personality, full of energy and ideas, and he proved it on stage that evening. The crowd was electric

DANCER MOSES PENDLETON PERFORMS AN ORIGINAL DANCE ON SKIS AT THE EGYPTIAN THEATER.

after the film and the performance.

The other interesting documentary was the first film we screened made by the taciturn ethnographer, filmmaker, and garlic expert Les Blank. We played *Burden of Dreams,* the chronicle of Werner Herzog's struggle in the jungles of the Peruvian Amazon to make his operatic *Fitzcarraldo* with Klaus Kinski and the Indians of the Campa, Aguaruna, and Michiguena tribes and their haunting, red-painted faces. It was about a man obsessed with getting a ship up a river, over a mountain, and through the jungles of the Amazon in a case of life imitating art to the extreme.

Outstanding premieres and special screenings included Caleb Deschanel's directorial debut *The Escape Artist*, Susan Seidelman's *Smithereens*, Graeme Clifford's *Frances*, Alan J. Pakula's powerful *Sophie's Choice*, and the film that won the hearts and minds of the audience with the winning performance from old-time wrangler Richard Farnsworth, *The Grey Fox.* It was about the turn-of-the-century true story of Bill Miner, an old stagecoach robber, who is released from prison into the twentieth century. Finding no more stagecoaches to rob, he turns to the next best thing—trains. Directed by Philip Borsos, the film was still not quite completed for its screenings, with the print hand delivered by the coproducer who drove down from British Columbia in his Porsche. This required him to read the still unincorporated title card at the end of the film, updating us as to what happened to each of the characters. The audience gave the film a standing ovation, and it was the beginning of Richard Farnsworth's resurgent career as an actor who just reeks with character and emanates an honest empathy.

One additional program in the 1983 festival was probably a bit ahead of its time, even though its films were made in the late 1950s and 1960s. In fact, it would probably be more popular now than ever. Organized by Media Study in Buffalo and The Walker Art Center in Minneapolis, it was a retrospective program of 1950s and 1960s New Wave films—the precursors of independent films—if not even a bit more avante-garde and underground, especially given the historical context. Films such as *The Savage Eye* (1959), shot by Haskell Wexler; edited by Verna Fields; and directed by Ben Maddow, Sidney Meyers, and Joseph Strick was one of the early examples of the direct-cinema movement. It combined brazen social realism with a coldly expressionistic style that fell into obscurity after receiving major prizes at the Edinburgh, Mannheim, and Venice film festivals.

Pull My Daisy (1959), written and narrated by Jack Kerouac and directed by Robert Frank, featured Allen Ginsberg, Gregory Corso, Peter Orlofsky, Alice Neel, and Larry Rivers. Praised for its fluidity, the film is often mistaken for a spontaneous document of beat life, but the camera work and action were meticulously conceived. As stated in *Film Culture, Pull My Daisy* ". . . breathes an immediacy that the cinema of today vitally needs if it is to be a living and contemporary art."

Another film on this program was the first feature film by John Cassavetes, *Shadows*, also made in 1959 on a $15,000 budget. It became the rallying point for the "New American Cinema" because of its innovative use of improvisation and its realism as portrayed by the incredible range of acting, particularly Ben Carruther's performance. Cassavetes's signature was his sympathy with the actor's need to inhabit the characters and work improvisationally in a visually freewheeling style along with his commitment to finding the emotional truth of a scene through the character's reactions.

Shirley Clarke's groundbreaking film *The Cool World* (1963) was the first feature film shot in Harlem. It was all handheld 35 mm shot by Baird Bryant, focusing in on the world of gangs and the hard life with many of the gang members playing themselves in the picture.

PRODUCTION STILL FROM SHIRLEY CLARKE'S *THE COOL WORLD*.

Also included was Clarke's 1967 film, *Portrait of Jason,* a self-funded project in which she allowed the camera and subject Jason Holliday, a gay black man, to use the camera to confess to his many discoveries.

Robert Downey's first film *Babo 73* (1964) was an improvised tableaux that featured Taylor Mead as president of the

United States in an endless pursuit of the absurd—a kind of hipster's *Duck Soup*.

Adolfas Mekas's 1963 *Hallelujah the Hills* was ostensibly about two young men in love with and deceived by the same woman. Filled with many cinema references, this film combines lyrical images with high comedy. Brother Jonas Mekas also screened his 1964 *The Brig*, a depiction of the horrors of authoritarianism that won

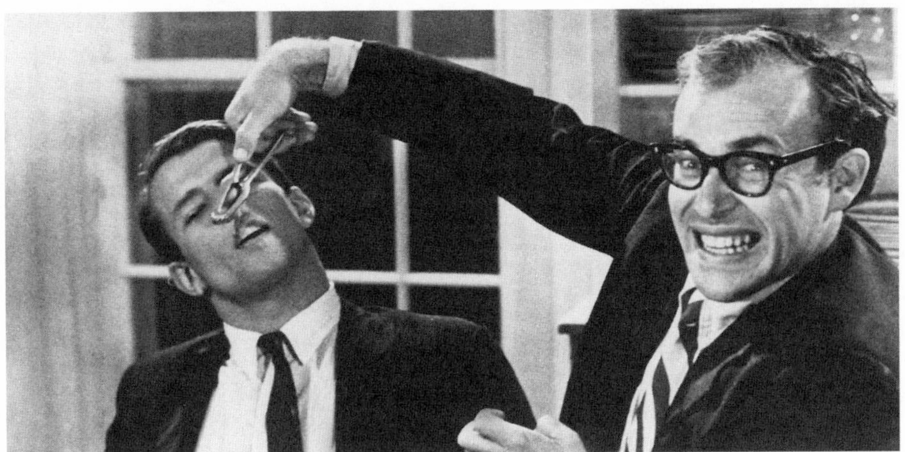

PRODUCTION STILL FROM ADOLFUS MEKAS'S *HALLELUJAH THE HILLS*.

the grand prize for documentaries at the 1964 Venice Film Festival.

Finally, Jim McBride's *David Holzman's Diary*, featured L. M. Kit Carson, in a cinema verité experiment about a young man who turns his life into a film in which the fictional world of the diary and the real world surrounding the film merge.

It had been a program that came to the festival under peculiar, though not unwanted, circumstances. In a board meeting while we were still in the planning stages of mounting the 1983 festival, I had proposed Sterling and Sundance help us mount the filmmaker seminars. Sterling had indicated earlier that the institute would be able to commit to these seminars. It was only later, and rather late in the game, that he privately bowed out of the commitment but instead offered this program from the Walker Art Center in Minneapolis and Media Study in Buffalo. I was delighted to have the program of films, but it really left me in the lurch for a seminar program.

As it turned out, Sundance's Michelle Satter was able to coordinate and moderate the most effective of the daylong seminars, called "Survival Techniques," devoted to financing, deal making, marketing, and distribution. But the rest of the seminars were cobbled together out of the American New Wave program and filmmaker's in attendance, which, all in all, wasn't a bad mix of people. It included the irascible George Kuchar, Adolfas Mekas, and the amazing Haskell Wexler. Jeff Dowd and Sterling Van Wagenen moderated a panel of filmmakers in attendance. Martin Sheen conducted an actors workshop, and Shirley Clarke, Kit Carson, Taylor Mead, and Robert Young did a panel on acting and directing the actor. We were able to pull it off, but just barely. With the help of Johann Jacobs, a terrific fellow with a South African accent and a sense of humor, and Michelle Satter, we were able to make it work.

The same couldn't be said for our video competition. Try as we might, even with exquisite work from Bill Viola in *Hatsu-Yume (First Dream);* Max Almy's *Leaving the Twentieth Century*; Shirley Clarke's (a collaboration with Sam Shepard and Joseph Chaikin) *Tongues*; Robert Wilson's *Deafman's Glance;* and a host of excellent video documentaries, including *How Much is Enough? Decision Making in the Nuclear Age; Art and the Prison Crisis; In Our Own Backyard: The First Love Canal;* and *Jeannette Rankin—The Woman Who Voted No,* we just couldn't find the critical mass necessary to bring the work to the public and have them respond. Despite Chris Montague at the Utah Media Center and his staff, which included Susan Doi, it continued to be an underattended event. Perhaps all those obscure or hyphenated titles had something to do with it. But it happened despite James Hindman (on the video jury and director of television at the American Film Institute) and his assertion in the program guide: "It is refreshing to know that, as a unique American form, the video documentary is not only alive and well in the perilous '80s, but genuinely thriving."

It may have been thriving but certainly not with audiences. The reality was that we had taken on more than we could reasonably do. It is one thing to get people to come to see feature-length narratives and documentaries made independently. It is a whole other thing to see the same thing in a less-expensive-to-produce format that couldn't escape the made-for-television connotation. There was little doubt these formats offered extremely low-budget alternatives to film. At the same time they provided a conversational intimacy and style, a present-time impact, hard-edged reality and a surreptitious cultural camouflage. What was missing was in the presentation of the material. The event needed to feel like something more than just a video screening, but it could never generate, except in broadcast, the quality of an event that people were willing to spend money to attend. Michael Moore was able to exploit the advantages of the technology in his *Roger and Me,* and still, through a blowup to 35 mm, provide the sense of scale and drama to the presentation, making an impression in the marketplace. But in a little screening room in Park City, using only a video monitor, video just wasn't going to connect with an audience much beyond the diehards. This was further evidenced during the awards dinner when the video people all clustered together and acted like a bunch of separatists at a union convention.

The Disney printers were acting in a similar manner when it came time to print the program guide. Despite Mike Spencer's best efforts, even risking getting fired to make good on the commitment, the production schedule at Disney's printing operation was hectic; they weren't sure they could get us the guide by the opening of the festival. It is next to impossible to hold a film festival without a program guide to the movies being screened and a schedule of events. Disney printers did finally print the guide but just barely and thanks only to Mike Spencer's prodding, shepherding, and threatening.

The only tribute really hit home that year. It was to Verna Fields who had passed away shortly before the event. She had been so helpful to us, really taking the festival on as a personal crusade. As was noted in the program guide:

> Verna made a difference for these reasons and many more. She was honored and respected by her peers for her creativity, technical expertise, common sense, and caring. The difference Verna made was that she transcended her profession—and whomever she touched transcended it too. . . . Through it all she raised a family. After her husband, editor Sam Fields, died Verna brought her editing equipment home to Van Nuys and set up a cutting room. In addition to bringing up her two sons, Kenn and Ric, while continuing to work, she also raised a second family—a generation of young directors and editors who camped out at her house and learned their profession. Verna was more than a teacher here; she stood behind these promising filmmakers and gave them support at a time when they needed it. The group included Steven Spielberg, George Lucas, and Peter Bogdanovich, as well as a continual stream of many others. To them all, she was the Mother Cutter.
>
> Verna always continued her interest in young filmmakers. Experienced filmmakers sought her out as well, even those with whom she wasn't immediately involved. Her voice was direct, and she spoke her mind. It was a voice of insight and expertise.
>
> Numerous movies were allowed to develop because she placed her reputation with them. Many others were improved through her advice. Everyone with whom she worked was enriched. All who knew her were too.
>
> Verna Fields made movies a wonderful place to visit. She made her world an even better place to live.

I'm proud to say she was a friend. By the conclusion of the festival, besides a handful of filmmakers, friends were hard to come by, especially for Susan Barrell. Although the festival had continued to reduce the deficit, part of which she inherited, the board was looking for ways to cut back, and thought eliminating the staff was a good way to go about it.

After three years of mounting successful film festivals under difficult financial circumstances, Susan Barrell felt burned out, underappreciated, and betrayed by a contentious board of directors.

She had helped to refine the concept and format, the duration, and the marketing of the event. Her only failure was remaining involved with the event she'd helped to create.

By fall 1983, with the sixth festival looming uncomfortably on the horizon, the board again contracted with me for the programming elements of the festival and brought in a hired gun to manage the festival in the person of Karin (pronounced Cairn) Brockbank. It was a difficult circumstance for all concerned to say the least, and the 1984 festival showed the strain.

Given the board of director's treatment of Susan, I didn't feel as though I could trust them, and in Karin's instance, I knew I couldn't trust her. Her allegiance was clearly with the board of directors. I just wanted to be left alone to put together a program, and, as a result, our contact was kept to an absolute minimum. She was the sort of person who, in the midst of some important meeting, would suddenly come up with some important connection or claim to have some specific expertise, often from Harvard or Stanford, to solve the problem. At the time she was big on some guy who was supposed to be the guru of market research. By that time in my experience with the festival's management, I didn't believe much of what I heard or saw, and I certainly didn't cash their checks without making certain there was money in the account to cover them. I do remember going for about three months with only promises of a paycheck. It was a tough way to live, but by then I was too committed to help myself, let alone listen to anyone else's advice. I did know that as the festival drew closer, the only way they were going to get a program was to pay me, so I had some credit cards and I wasn't afraid to use them.

I used to joke that the way I knew the festival was imminent was when I would go grocery shopping and buy dairy products with expiration dates after the festival would be over. Like the festival would be over before the cottage cheese would go bad. It was my own absurd yardstick, but it had symbolic significance, particularly with the 1984 festival.

Although we were still known as the United States Film and Video Festival in 1984, we just about gave up on the video program. Only through the valiant efforts of Guilo Scalinger, then head of the Utah Film and Video Center, and formerly of the Athens (Ohio) Film Festival, were we able to mount a video program at all.

Karin and the board decided once again the festival should only play for seven days—Monday through Sunday. I thought Monday was an awfully tough day to open a film festival. It was ironic when the program guide was produced. It had a fabulous cover design from Peter Pigot and Gilberto Schaefer of a photograph depicting the rear end of someone wearing Levi's, a pair of festival tickets in their back pocket. This person is walking up the snowy Main Street of Park City with four other people to the Egyptian Theater as dawn is breaking on the horizon. There's not a single car on the street—parked or moving—just these five moviegoers. One moviegoer was Donnette Davis, our administrative assistant, who showed up at five in the morning to be in the shot. David Quinney was the photographer. It was a strong graphic, if a bit sexist, and it was as though these were the only five people who were going to show up. The tag line was "Follow Closely . . . The Show's Not to Be Missed." I guess this was how Karin's market research was supposed to pay off.

The idea of the poster/graphic/guide cover art has always been important to the event. From the very first year, the image the festival created through its graphics was a very important way to communicate with the public. In fact, it is one of the key ways we communicated with the public and the participants. The festival is about first impressions. A clunky graphic indicates a clunky organization and a clunky event. An innovative graphic indicates an innovative event. There has always been careful consideration of the graphics. It continues to be an important consideration. In fact, it is one of the many details in which Redford becomes personally involved.

The problem was inside the program guide. When it came out, I was amazed and perplexed by the large number of advertisements and filler articles. Of the sixty-eight-page guide, thirty pages were festival related and thirty-eight pages were not. My film notes notwithstanding, there was a four-page article on skiing, a three-page article on things to do in Park City, a four-page dining-out guide, a four-page events calender for Salt Lake City, and, finally, the topper of the guide, a three-page spread on industry in Utah with a large photograph of the Kennecott Copper Mine—better known locally as "The Pit." I remember I was terribly disappointed when the guide came out—so much for market research and striking graphics.

The films, however, were far from disappointing. Among the principal reasons for this year's success was the down-home Robert Duvall. He came to town with not one, not two, but three quality films. *The Apostle* wasn't his directorial debut; *Angelo My Love* was. Made in 1983, it was the result of a chance meeting with a five-year-old tough gypsy on the corner of New York's 71st and Columbia Avenues. Duvall happened to overhear him telling an adult woman, "Patricia, if you don't love me more, I'm going to move to Cincinnati." This was the beginning of a beautiful relationship. Although *Angelo My Love* is the fictionalized account of the young gypsy and his family, it does star Angelo Evans himself. His street smarts and wide liquid eyes were mesmerizing—like a pint-size Al Pacino.

In a classic Duvallism, the director stated, "The trick was to show all sides of gypsy life without exploiting them. If I didn't show them stealing, that would be dishonest." This is a guy who cares enormously about honesty, certainly in his performances and professionally, but one has the distinct sense in his personal life as well. That is ultimately the power of Robert Duvall, the actor.

One has the sense he has lived the life of his characters. He seems less an actor than an actual person who is going through the drama. It is a testament to his skills as a performer that it is so seamless.

From Boo Radley in *To Kill a Mockingbird* to his characters in *The Godfather, Apocalypse Now, The Great Santini,* and *The Apostle,* Duvall has built a career out of nuanced performance. He lives inside the skin of the character and his own persona never gets in the way. It leaves the appearance that one can never get to know him beyond his performances. Perhaps that is a sacrifice other actors, particularly younger ones, should be willing to make in the face of celebrity. Duvall didn't come to Park City with a publicist.

What Robert Duvall did bring with him was his personal favorite film appearance, the rarely screened *Tomorrow.* Made in 1973 and based on a William Faulkner story with a script written by Horton Foote, it was the story of Jackson Fentry (Robert Duvall), a Mississippi cotton farmer who leaves his father's barren farm to become a watchman at a sawmill in a nearby county. While patrolling the grounds of the mill on a cold December day, Fentry discovers the collapsed Sarah Eubanks (Olga Bellin) lying unconscious on the ground and obviously in the advanced stages of pregnancy. Fentry takes her back to his shack and nurses her back to wavering health, discovering that she has been abandoned by her husband and her family. The innocent and muted love that grows slowly between these two lowly and inarticulate people of the earth, carrying them through the ordeals of a harrowing pregnancy and birth and culminating in a baffling murder trial is one of the most tender and touching cinematic experiences imaginable. Duvall's performance is so intense, yet quiet, so guttural, yet beautiful and exquisite. It strikes a deep human chord.

ROBERT DUVALL DOING A TELEVISION INTERVIEW AT THE 1984 FESTIVAL.

It is a sparse and aching portrayal of two people who come together in their mutual isolation and compassion. The tenderness that results is so delicately earned and so profoundly affecting that one realizes he or she is watching less a performance than some kind of actor's channeling of a more well-rounded and less-threatening, previous incarnation in the form of Boo Radley.

As if that weren't enough, Duvall also brought along a terrific documentary he directed in 1983, produced by his wife Barbara Duvall about the B. A. and Eunice Peterson family of Ogallala, Nebraska. *We Are Not the Jet Set* chronicled the behind-the-scenes glimpses of a family of rodeo performers and trick riders, living on their twelve-thousand-acre Nebraska ranch and performing in rough-tough Wild West shows. The film is both funny and scary, exposing a patriarchal family in all its fury, bravado, and tenderness. In a tribute to the filmmakers, the film ends up showing a much more complex relationship than one might imagine from a family living the "simple" rural life. When it comes down to it, there is no such thing as a simple life, and Robert Duvall fundamentally understands this concept. It runs like a direct current through all his work. *We Are Not the Jet Set* was no exception.

We were fortunate to have one of the truly strong years for documentary films, which helped to set the stage for what was to follow. The winning film was Tony Silver's *Style Wars*, the first feature-length film to document in depth New York City's world of graffiti artists, rap, and hip-hop cultures. It was an energetic, potent, kaleidoscope of music, art, street poetry, and dance. In the words of graffiti artist and rapper J. Walter Negro, "They are the art forms of the new urban tribes." *Style Wars* packed an energetic wallop that predated the hip-hop's slide into gangsta rap. It captured the innocence and vibrancy of this inner-city cultural movement before it spread into the suburbs and beyond.

It was also interesting that in 1984 we played Robert Mugge's excellent documentary on fabled bluesologist Gil Scott-Heron, who calls himself "the most dangerous musician alive." Lacing his music with political commentary and a scathing analysis of socioeconomic reality makes him so potent. It is a blending of musicianship with political agitprop that forms the basis of Gil Scott-Heron's impressive ouevre. He, too, anticipated the direction of this potent new form of music, and Bob Mugge, living in Pennsylvania, has made a name for himself over the past decade or so for making excellent music documentaries in which he lets the characters and their music speak for themselves. I think over the years, some members of the festival selection process felt Bob's work was too passe, too traditional in its approach, but that is precisely why I admired it. Instead of being stylistically influenced by a whole MTV generation of approaches, Bob stuck to his own portrayals, consistently and lovingly produced. When it comes down to it, these treasures are the ones that will stand the test of time.

Two other performance-related documentaries in 1984 were played in the film festival. The first was Nick Broomfield and Sandi Sissel's remarkable *Chicken Ranch,* the look behind the closed doors of a legalized brothel fifty miles from Las Vegas. This veritable sex stockade set amidst the desert sands and sweltering heat is one of thirty-eight legalized brothels in Nevada. As the girls practice the world's oldest profession, earning up to $2,000 per week, they are like slaves to the laconic owner of the brothel and his hard-driving wife, a kind of warped mother and father figure for the girls. Once a couple of the women start to warm to the camera, through the eyes of the documentary they begin to question their own involvement, status, and conditions of employment. This brings about a confrontation, and the owner is last seen and heard threatening to sue the filmmakers for the disruption they have caused to his business. He promises the film will never see the light of day. Given Nick Broomfield's 1998 run-in with Courtney Love, over his *Kurt and Courtney* and having Sundance pull the film at the last minute from the program over a threatened lawsuit, it is apparently a threat that often comes Mr. Broomfield's way—a legal testament to his skills as a filmmaker to not just scratch the surface of his subjects but to honestly get under their skin.

The other performance documentary was Katherine Matheson's delightful *Comedienne* about two very different women who set out for New York to accomplish their dreams of doing stand-up. Cheryl is seeking anonymity, and Zora is seeking fame. Both utilize their dreams, ambitions, and journeys to plumb the depths of comedy for their stage acts. What is revealed about the human condition in general and women's struggles in particular is that we are all alone on stage and the comedy of life always has the best punch line.

All the other films in the documentary competition were decidedly political, as is usually the case in the best of the documentary field. The rich tradition of documentaries was almost always about the revelation of some social problem, some new perspective on lives we would otherwise never come to know. That is the magic of the documentary—to reveal a world of nonfiction in which the audience understands the human plight of the characters in empathetic ways that fictionalized drama can seldom achieve. These are real events happening to real people with real consequences for all.

Seeing Red: Stories of American Communists, made by James Klein and Julia Reichert, was the splendid chronicle of a much misunderstood collection of ordinary people, who in their youthful exuberance wanted nothing more than to close the gap between poverty and wealth. Instead they were reviled and spat upon, despised as villainous radicals.

The filmmakers interviewed over 400 party members—some active, most no longer—over a five-year period, and what results is an affectionate portrait of thinking men and women who are articulate, funny, warm, and charming. *Seeing Red* was provocative and insightful, utilizing a great deal of archival footage that highlights some of the most noteworthy commie haters, including Ronald Reagan and J. Edgar Hoover, and exposing how far off some of the stereotyping actually was. *Seeing Red* showed us the real faces of people who knew what it was like to have been young, gifted, and red. It was a fascinating historical document.

As fate would have it, *The Good Fight: The Abraham Lincoln Brigade in the Spanish Civil War,* by Noel Buchner, Mary Dore, and Sam Sills, also screened. In one of history's most dramatic expressions of international solidarity, 40,000 volunteers from around the world went to fight against the fascist armies of Franco, Hitler, and Mussolini in the Spanish Civil War, a full five years before the United States was to enter World War II. Americans—3,200 of them—went to Spain to fight, and to a generation of Americans, these volunteers in the Abraham Lincoln Brigade were considered "the conscience of the thirties." As Lillian Hellman put it, "When you saw steel-workers and teachers and cab drivers and seaman and college boys fighting as these men fought in Spain, you felt fine about being an American."That wasn't necessarily the case with Jacki Ochs and Daniel Keller's *The Secret Agent,* a devastating film about the use of Agent Orange during the Vietnam War and the long-term lingering effects of this deadly chemical agent. More than eleven million gallons of the defoliant were sprayed over the jungles and villages of South Vietnam, and the tragic legacy continues to this day, mostly in the form of the deformed children born in its midst. It was a gruesome demonstration of the collusion between the military and industry with apologists on both sides of the table. The fact that the dioxin was one of mankind's most deadly toxins but that we dumped it on our enemies as well as ourselves and our allies only underscores the insanity of our strategy to eradicate the enemy by decimating the landscape of jungle foliation where they might be hiding. The crime of this sorry saga is that no matter the redress sought in the courts, for most of the veterans and survivors of the war the damage has already been done.

Three other historical documents rounded out the competition. The first was the portrait of former Congressman Allen K. Lowenstein who played a key role in the civil-rights and antiwar movements until his untimely shooting death at the hands of a former campaign worker who was deemed to be insane. *Citizen* was made by Julie Thompson, executive-produced by the actor Mike Farrell and the producer Michael Jaffe, and shot by Frederic Elms. It was a moving illustration of how one person could truly make a difference.

Ross Spears's excellent documentary on the history of one of the grand social/environmental experiments of all time, the Tennessee Valley Authority, was the second. The TVA was begun in the 1930s in an effort to harness the rivers, control the annual flooding, and reinforce the area's unstable economy. By the 1950s, it was being heralded as "the greatest peacetime achievement in twentieth-century America." But by the 1970s, the TVA was accused of being the nation's number one air polluter—responsible for land-grabbing for future pork-barrel water projects and for irresponsibly strip-mining vast sections of Kentucky for coal. It operated unsafe nuclear power plants, all under the protective funding of powerful lobbyists and politicians in Washington. *The Electric Valley* not only looks at the fifty-year history of the TVA and what went wrong with the experiment, but it also looks at the people. In trying to tame the rivers and forests, TVA also tried to tame the people and with about the same results.

Finally, *When the Mountains Tremble,* directed by Pamela Yates and Thomas Sigel and produced by Peter Kinoy, was the story of a Guatemalan Indian woman, Rigoberta Menchu, as history transforms her from being a poor migratory peasant to a leading voice in shaping the destiny of her people.

From the limbo of exile, she weaves together the exquisite fabric of Guatemalan history, the beauty and richness of the culture, the strength and courage of the people, and the tragedy of human greed and corruption. In fleeing her native country as the only surviving member of her family, her story was so compelling that she was asked to speak about her experiences before the United Nations. It is a harrowing eyewitness account, filled in with moody re-creations, but all told through the eyes, ears, and mouth of a remarkable woman.

Remarkable would also describe the films in dramatic competition. Eagle Pennell was to return with a feature utilizing his regular cast of characters, Sonny Davis and Lou Perry. *Last Night at the Alamo* is the bittersweet tale of a night at the almost down-and-out bar known as The Alamo. It is a sneakily funny tribute to the great American hangout that, in this case, may be the last night for this establishment before it is to be bulldozed to make way for a development. The local rednecks' last hope hangs on the shoulders of a character named Cowboy who they wait for most of the night to come and save the bar from its demise. In the end, the characters realize that The Alamo's last stand is as inevitable as the sunrise and that this part of their rambunctious existence has come to an end. Like a buzz saw at full tilt, this rips through the heart as a poignant yet funny take on one of the great national pastimes—a place where the patronage is more like family, where people can find solace and comfort, and where dreams go to die.

I had seen the film in New York in September at the New York Film Festival. In classic Eagle Pennell style, when he was introduced at Alice Tully Hall, he was so drunk I thought he wasn't going to make it across the stage to the microphone. He bashfully thanked the audience for coming and then did a kind of cowboy yelp into the night. The film had been shot by Eric Edwards from Portland and Brian Huberman. It was very well received and yet another clear example of Eagle Pennell's talents as a filmmaker capable of creating memorable characters. The film had been written by Kim Henckel who also wrote *The Texas Chainsaw Massacre.*

Eagle Pennell arrived in Park City with his girlfriend of the time, the actress Ronee Blakely, who had once been linked with Wim Wenders, and had delivered such a fine performance in Robert Altman's *Nashville*. She was a stunningly beautiful woman who was also a helluva lot of fun to be around. I remember a whole contingent of us getting drunk and dancing at Park City's own Alamo Bar. In a funny way, we kind of acted out our own version of the film at a bar that shared more than just a name. By the end of the night and back at the condo, Eagle was running around the hot tub totally naked, chasing a giggling Ronee Blakely. It was really Eagle Pennell's last good picture. He went on to make *Ice House*, written and performed by Bo Hopkins and his wife at the time, Melissa Gilbert. It was a film I turned down for the festival the year it was made, which was difficult to do because I admired Eagle's work so much, and I liked him as a friend. But when I told him the film had been too shrill and claustrophobic for me, and that I really didn't think it worked, he put his big old Texas arm around my shoulder and said, "That's all right, Lory. I don't mind. It really wasn't my film. I was just a hired gun." But it was, to my knowledge, the last film Eagle was able to make. I've seen him in a couple of small acting roles, still in Houston, ironically clean and sober and playing a local sheriff.

This was also the year that Eagle called me from his condo and said I needed to come right over and deal with four Brigham Young University coeds who had moved uninvited into his condominium—pink suitcases, curlers, pantyhose, and all. I told him to put one of them on the line. She sounded like she was probably a member of the Valkyrie volleyball squad, and she tried to convince me that she and her friends had been invited to stay at this condo and that they didn't have any other place to go. She wondered who in the heck I was to be telling her what she had to do. I finally had to insist that she and her friends remove their pantyhose from the bathroom and vacate the premises. I told her I would give her ten minutes to clear out of the place, and if I received one more phone call, my next call would be to my good friends at the Park City police department. And this would go down on her permanent record.

Last Night at the Alamo was to take the special jury prize behind Marissa Silver's fine female coming-of-age story *Old Enough,* which won the grand prize. Eagle made the comment at the after-hours awards party that he'd again taken second place behind a woman's coming-of-age tale, first with *Girlfriends*, now with *Old Enough.* But both of those films were excellent films, extremely well made, with strong performances, urban settings, fresh perspectives and a bigger movie look. In fact, Marissa Silver and her producer sister Dena, daughters of Joan Micklin and Raphael Silver of *Hester Street* fame, were the first filmmakers to be besieged by interested distributors in the lobby of the Egyptian Theater, following their Park City screening. Their film was the first to create a frenzy among distributors—a full five years before *sex, lies, and videotape,* often referred to as the film that created the first buying frenzy among distributors at Sundance. Obviously, they did more business with a sexploitation title that entered the lexicon of

PRODUCTION STILL FROM EAGLE PENNELL'S *LAST NIGHT AT THE ALAMO.*

DIRECTORS EAGLE PENNELL, ROB NILSSON, AND JOHN HANSON SPEAK ON A PANEL IN 1984.

American references, full of sexual repression and revelation, and a great cast of dynamic actors, than did the coming-of-age story of a twelve-year-old girl who flirts with a friend's streetwise brother and in the process finds her own voice and confidence. It doesn't take much to figure which one might have more potential in the marketplace. Simply put—sex sells—always has and always will. The trick is in the execution and presentation. The presentation and marketing of a movie about sex must cause us to be curious enough to want to go spend seven dollars and two hours of our time to see it.

Rob Nilsson's *Signal 7* dealt with two San Francisco cabbies, Marty and Speed, played with believable diligence by Bill Ackridge and Dee Leegant, who also moonlight as occasional actors. Dedicated to John Cassavetes, it is a fluid performance-driven piece, a kind of long night's journey into daylight and self-discovery. *Signal 7* is a cabbie's term for a driver who is not responding and may be in trouble. This distinctive film was originally shot on three-quarter-inch videotape and blown up to 35 mm—one of the first films to do so. The consequence was a unique, grainy, almost liquid nighttime look that truly served the picture. Rob Nilsson has continued to work with new technologies, shooting *Heat and Sunlight* (1987) on tape and blowing up and shooting a Sci-Fi Channel film in 1997, based on a Rod Serling story *A Town Turns to Dust* with a digital video camera.

Another filmmaker with an excellent follow-up to his previous work *Killer of Sheep,* Charles Burnett returned with *My Brother's Wedding*—a much more accessible film shot in color and made entirely from short ends (film that has been opened and maybe even loaded in a camera from another movie but unused and sold back at discounted rates. Of varying lengths, it can be tough to use, if scenes are longer than the raw stock). *My Brother's Wedding* is the well-observed story of Pierce Monday, a thirty-year-old unmarried man who works in his family's Watts dry cleaners, struggling in a love-hate relationship with his tightly knit community and within himself. He's highly critical of his brother—a lawyer—and contemptuous of his future sister-in-law who was raised in an affluent household. He thinks they sold out and still wants to affect some change without taking on the status and qualities of upwardly mobile blacks. In his family's mind, Pierce hasn't made much of his life, but when an old neighborhood friend named Soldier is released from prison, Soldier's mother asks him to keep an eye on her son. With Soldier's arrival, Pierce's dilemmas are complicated. It is a handsomely crafted drama about responsibility and commitment. As was the case with *To Sleep with Anger*, Charles Burnett is a serious independent filmmaker who deserves more support so that his films can continue to reach a wider audience.

Two other standout films were antithetical to traditional narrative and subject. Penelope Spheeris arrived with her groundbreaking alien-nation tribute in the fictional *Suburbia*, a tale of a dozen or so runaways who live under one roof in a condemned suburban development, near a Los Angeles freeway. Informed by her experiences in the much-acclaimed documentary *The Decline of Western Civilization,* Penelope Spheeris actually took punk kids and turned them into actors, which created a vibrancy to the performances that mere actors may not have been able to authentically pull off.

The other remarkable film in the 1984 competition was Alexandre Rockwell's debut film *Hero*, a wonderfully quixotic and surrealistic journey of a disabled child who loves to take Polaroids as a way of communicating with his adopted sisters, Kim and Mika, a Mexican cab driver and a silent Japanese girl who leave New York to drive in a classic Marathon Yellow Cab to Truth or Consequences, New Mexico. The story really kicks in when the unlikely trio encounters Cody, a western hitchhiker who runs at the mouth and has a suitcase full of "valuable information about America." When they have to tow his oversized plastic restaurant cow behind the Yellow Cab, the film starts to take on mythical images compounded by a mysterious, ephemeral Native American who keeps appearing out of nowhere. The film is a breathtaking metaphor—an imaginative road picture, with no real destination in mind—a kind of travelogue for the soul. Music was provided by the Rolling Stones and David Bowie. And of course, Alexandre Rockwell was to return and win the grand prize in 1992 with his superbly funny take on making a low-budget film, *In the Soup* with the incomparable Seymour Cassell and the great Steve Buscemi.

Beyond the films in competition, the premiere was also an interesting collection of provocative films. It included Henry Jaglom's *Can She Bake a Cherry Pie*, starring the fabulous Karen Black; Louis Malle's caper film, *Crackers*; Peter Greenaway's baroque masterpiece *The Draughtsman's Contract*; and Mirra Banks and Ellen Hovde's *Enormous Changes at the Last Minute* with a script from John Sayles and Susan Rice, and starring the largely unknown Ellen Barkin, Kevin Bacon, and David

Strathairn. We also played Robert Altman's *Streamers*, Martin Rosen's wonderfully moving animation classic *Plaque Dogs,* and were scheduled to play Ron Howard's *Splash,* which was pulled from our list the day of the scheduled premiere because Disney was unsure what to do with the film and didn't want to generate a bad review. It was unfortunate because the film would have been very popular at the festival—as it later proved to be elsewhere. Out of courtesy to Disney who had been so helpful in the past, I was left in the position of having to stand up before the audience and make up the fiction that there had been some problem with the print arriving. I thought it was a boneheaded move by someone in marketing and distribution, leaving no time to rectify the situation. It was ironic that the first person to congratulate me on my little white lie was none other than David Begelman, the former studio executive who was diagnosed as a compulsive liar and who had forged Cliff Robertson's signature on a check in an effort to embezzle money from the actor. I guess he, of all people, could really appreciate a well-concocted lie.

The lie was a fitting conclusion to the 1984 film festival because there was so much distrust among the management that I couldn't imagine going through another year of the insecurities associated with it. Although we were able to hold down costs and deliver a good portion of the box-office profit to further reduce the debt to approximately $20,000, something big was going to have to give for us to mount another festival under the same set of circumstances and with the same individuals involved.

The board of directors had become increasingly divided over the way income was dispersed, particularly when it came time to address the lines of credit that had been extended by each member of the board and that had been drawn on to mount the effort. As we got in much-needed donations, mostly from the studios and other sponsors, there was a contingent within the board of directors who wanted to apply the money immediately to the lines of credit, in effect getting them individually off the hook but exposing the festival to the severe cash-flow deficiencies at a critical time that might result in our going further into debt. It was a tough call, but it drove a deep wedge between members of the board and added to the sense of isolation and mistrust, as some of the money was ultimately diverted to the lines of credit. We needed someone to ride in on his white horse and save us from our predicament, and John Earle and I knew exactly who that should be. It was time to put the squeeze on our old friend Sterling Van Wagenen, the director of the Sundance Institute and the guy who helped to start the whole thing, later moving on to the greener pastures just down the road. It was now or never for Sundance and the film festival.

PRODUCTION STILL FROM JOEL AND ETHAN COHEN'S GROUNDBREAKING *BLOOD SIMPLE*.

CHAPTER 5

Cavalry to the Rescue

John Earle and I went to work on Sterling Van Wagenen, now the executive director of the Sundance Institute. We pleaded, cajoled, and implored, establishing a solid foundation for why the institute should take on the film festival—deficit and all.

Sterling seemed most sympathetic to the idea. The institute was attempting to provide a new forum for experimentation in the realm of independent films created out of a passion for story and character. The idea was that by being selected and going through the institute's June Lab, the scripts would emerge with the imprimatur of Sundance and therefore be in a stronger position to get financing and be made. But, if no one was paying attention to the marketing, distribution, and exhibition of these specialized films and helping to develop an audience for them, then the entire exercise would be moot and would not be able to sustain itself creatively or financially. It was incumbent on the institute to take on this part of the equation because without it, staff would be operating in a vacuum that disregarded the reality of the marketplace. It was a persuasive argument.

The other influential idea was that joining forces would create a synergy (long before that word came into corporate vogue), providing a more public forum through which the institute could articulate its vision, goals, and philosophy. It is ironic to me, given the hindsight of twenty years, just how prophetic this idea was. Without a doubt, it was the film festival that provided the focus for the world's entertainment press, which truly put Sundance on the map, and Sundance coming on board put the festival on the map. One without the other would not have created the same sense of success and notoriety or penetrated as deeply into the culture.

In fact, the film festival has proven to be a greater asset than the institute ever hoped. By taking over the film festival, Sundance has been able to complete the circle and create a brand-name identity synonymous with independent film. It was more than a marriage of convenience; it proved to be a stroke of genius. John and I eventually convinced Sterling that an alliance would be a healthy move for both organizations. Then it was up to Sterling to convince Redford.

The only problem John and I had now was convincing the film festival's board of directors that they should turn over the management of the festival to Sundance. Given the difficult financial history, one would have thought the idea of getting rid of this tar baby would be a slam dunk, especially because of the severe schism that existed between board members who would all have to come together if there was another festival. We were a bit surprised by the resistance we encountered, not that we didn't understand and truly appreciate the incredible amount of work that had been accomplished by the board. We also recognized that they, too, had a vested interest in the event. They had bonded on an emotional level with the opportunities the festival provided—

WAITING FILM REELS CAPABLE OF HOLDING AN ENTIRE FILM.

the recognition that came from the community, and perhaps even more profoundly, they had bonded on a human level through the wonderful and mysterious emotional and intellectual experiences that film offers. This bonding all happens in the dark, almost reverentially, and it does have the ability to change people's lives. It shouldn't have surprised us that with six film festivals under their belts, all their investment of time and influence and their cherished cinematic experiences, they would balk at turning over the event to another organization. I do think there also was some lingering resentment toward Sundance for not being more forthcoming with support and assistance during the previous two years.

John Earle did a masterful job in laying out this proposal so that it didn't look like a takeover. In one crucial board meeting, John and I explained that this was the way to finally give the film festival a permanent home. In six years, the festival had moved offices five times. We were living off the kindness of strangers. It was time to cede control for the benefit of the event itself. The festival needed to rise above ego and move into the realm of sacrifice for the good of the event or organization. The board had all done a splendid job of keeping the event viable, focused, and reasonably well run while another organization just down the road had come into existence on the coattails of the event. It was able to expand on the idea and through even better industry contacts, become financially solvent. Now this organization was knocking on our door and asking to come in and talk. We should listen. In reality, I argued, this was what we had always wanted in the first place. We were upset the institute hadn't been more involved in the past. Finally, the directors of Sundance were willing to take on the management of the whole thing, and we were balking? The other point we made was that if we rejected their invitation now, we could guarantee they wouldn't participate with us again in the future. We really needed to seize the opportunity, or it would be looked upon as a colossal blunder in the management of the event. By the end of the meeting, the board began to see the merit of our arguments, and they finally agreed to formally sign over the management of the event to the Sundance Institute.

Having grown tired of the hit-and-miss method of reimbursement from the film festival, just after the sixth film festival, I had taken a full-time position with the Utah Film Commission to promote film production in Utah with John Earle and Saundra Saperstein. I had always wanted to get more directly into film production instead of just marketing, distribution, and exhibition. I wanted to become intimately familiar with the techniques and strategies of film production, in part because I thought it would help to inform my own writing projects. I also just wanted to settle down for a bit and work in a more steady gig than the film festival provided. I was thinking ahead enough however to insert into my job description a section on continuing to program the film festival and attend other film-related events, festivals, and panels. I wasn't in any way turning my back on

ROBERT REDFORD AND SAUNDRA SAPERSTEIN.

the festival, but I was trying to secure a better future for myself and my wife. But in truth, I wasn't quite sure what Sterling was thinking about programming the festival. In February, it was too early to tell what my relationship would be to the soon-to-be newly managed festival, and I really didn't have the luxury to wait to find out. I needed a job, the best job at the Film Commission opened up, and I jumped on it. The essence of my new job was to read scripts, find locations, take lots of photographs, and generally make things happen with projects hoping to shoot in Utah. Over the years, I've proven to be adept at this job—in part because of my background as an artist, my ability to speak the language of cinema, and, after years of therapy, my realization that I have a real problem with authority. This last trait may be fortunate because I was a part of the bureaucracy that is there to do battle with other bureaucracies on behalf of film production in my state.

However, I did make it clear to my new boss and director of the Utah Film Commission, John Earle, and to my old boss and executive director of the Sundance Institute, Sterling Van Wagenen, that I did obviously hope to stay involved with the programming of the event.

One day Sterling showed up at the Film Commission office. He announced to me in John's office that the festival had hired a very bright guy with a programming background and from the National Endowment for the Arts out of Washington, D.C., to be the managing director of the film festival. Tony Safford would be moving to Utah with his wife, Carol, to take charge. Sterling asked me, in fact, begged me—with John Earle's encouragement—to remain the competition director of the documentary and dramatic competitions. I agreed to take it on with their assurances I would have the time, support, and autonomy to get the job done. Then I met Tony.

I called Tony Safford the Prince of Darkness. Napoleonic, dark, brooding—he was very closed off as a person although I must confess he had a certain sense of showmanship, was smart, and had an eye for more-difficult films that were emerging as signatures of independent filmmaking. My first meeting with Tony was held in the old Sundance Institute offices on Exchange Place in Salt Lake City. It was in the old warehouse they once used as offices that are now torn down. In attendance at the meeting was Saundra Saperstein, my new colleague at the Film Commission office and the media director for the film festival. Tony and I swapped stories of independent filmmakers, noting some of our agreed-upon benchmarks. I felt as if Tony seemed a bit guarded, but at first I thought I could work with him. I really tried to extend myself to him, and I'm sure he tried to do the same. I went over to his house a couple of times for beers in the backyard, but we just never really seemed to connect. We were just going through the motions, as if it were more of a truce than an alliance. He seemed to have a disdain for what he and others called "granola movies." These were feel-good, socially responsible films such as, *Heartland, Northern Lights, Spirit of the Wind, Old Enough,* and *Gal Young 'Un.* Instead he preferred darker, more-difficult subject matter with a bleaker vision of the human experience—films such as *Mother's Meat* and *Freud's Flesh.*

Our sense of competitiveness all came home when, after working largely independently of one another, it came time to meet and set the schedule in place. I'll never forget sitting in Tony's Sundance office, facing a blank grid on the wall representing all the films and all the screening times. I had imagined a scenario in which we would discuss the merits of the various possibilities, when, all of a sudden, Tony just started frantically slapping yellow Post-its all over the best slots on the grid. I caught on in very short order and started slapping my best bets for the competition in the best time slots, too. Before I knew it, we were racing through the schedule like game-show contestants. I did have the advantage of having competition entries needing to play two or three times during the festival; whereas, many of his more-eclectic international collection would get but a single screening.

It was a fortunate year in 1985 to be a film programmer because there were so many great films from which to choose. In many ways, it was the beginning of the Golden Decade for independent filmmaking. Two goofy-looking, chain-smoking brothers, named Joel and Ethan Coen, showed up with a film that marked their debut as a prolific cinematic partnership in the form of *Blood Simple*. After a sold-out screening at the Egyptian, the buzz coming out of the theater was palpable. As people poured out into the cold night air of Park City, somehow I knew the world had just witnessed two filmmakers of immense talent and sophistication who would forever change the course of cinematic history—no small task for two guys in T-shirts and Levi's, who appeared to be shy and introverted and have difficulties forming complete sentences. But Joel and Ethan Coen planted the flag on the mountain of independent filmmaking, and they haven't been knocked off the heap yet. Even though their filmography reads more like a tour de force through the genre-driven neighborhoods of Hollywood, their cinematic flair and acute visual style can not be denied. In *Blood Simple* was the portent of greatness. One could see it in the dolly shot running down the bar, when they bounced over a man passed out on the counter or when the audience is squealing regrettably with laughter when the body is getting dragged into the field. There can be no doubt that the Coen brothers—no matter how one slices their financing arrangements—retain massive autonomy and control over the projects they want to make. They are truly two of the most original voices working in or out of Hollywood. In many ways, their case histories are illustrative of the change of mood in Hollywood—the embracing of the most audacious of talents, the co-opting of ideas and the packaging of the counterculture. But who can really blame them? The Coens should have free rein to make any movie, any way they ever want to, and the maximum number of people should see their work. That is where Hollywood excels—getting warm bodies into theater seats all around the world. Where's the harm in that?

However, the Coen brothers weren't the only ones arriving in Park City with a groundbreaking film. A tall, lanky, white-haired, post-punk vision in the form of Jim Jarmusch had also made a film that is still referred to in the lexicon of independent

PRODUCTION STILL FROM JIM JARMUSCH'S *STRANGER THAN PARADISE*.

film as one that heralded hope for the truly grainy picture: the black-and-white classic *Stranger Than Paradise*. Winner of the Camera d' Or for the best first feature at the director's fortnight at Cannes, *Stranger Than Paradise* was a bracingly original, avant-garde comedy that was destined to become the most-imitated film in the history of independent cinema. With the perfect trio of John Lurie, Esther Balint, and Richard Edson, the film showcased the quirky sensibility of its writer and director, and the bleak landscape of the here and now—full of blank stares, broken promises, and failed connections. The sense of alienation and strained communication permeates the landscape of the picture almost as much as the barren winter in Cleveland provides the psychological counterpoint to the character's sense of isolation. But still, these characters and the inevitability of their failure makes for winning portraits in a classic narrative form. They are all really just "Little Tramps" all dressed up in groovy cardigan sweaters with no place really left to go. Just replace the bowlers with pork pies, and the avant-garde suddenly doesn't seem so avant anymore. But that is always the way of cultural change, and *Stranger Than Paradise* really did stake out new territory. Inevitably, others were soon to follow.

John Sayles returned with *The Brother from Another Planet,* an unforgettable grafting of Sayles's work-for-hire projects as a writer and his more personal directorial projects. The film is about a black extraterrestrial: The Brother, played by Joe Morton, who crash-lands his spaceship in New York Harbor, swims fittingly to Ellis Island, and makes his way to 125th Street in Harlem, where his bizarre and hilarious adventures begin. It was an allegorical premise, as many science-fiction films have been, and Sayles pulled it off beautifully, even playing one of the extraterrestrial bounty hunters.

PRODUCTION STILL FROM JOHN SAYLE'S *BROTHER FROM ANOTHER PLANET.*

Victor Nunez also returned with his ahead-of-its-time *A Flash of Green*, based on the John McDonald novel. Starring Ed Harris, Blair Brown, and Richard Jordan, it was a tale of political intrigue and personal compromise, set in the environmentally sensitive back bay of small-town Florida, prime for development and speculation. Ed Harris plays the newspaperman who begins to dig a little deeper into the rocky shoreline of both the developers and the enviros, with each group thinking he is on their side. He places himself in the ultimate dilemma and finally has to make his stand, though not in the way he thinks. *A Flash of Green* was an intelligent thought-provoking film but one that did not receive a strong response at its Park City screening. I think it hurt Victor very much that his film didn't come away with a stronger response. It would be eight more years before Victor got the chance to make another film. *Ruby in Paradise,* one of my favorite independent films, was a film I championed to the festival and his redemption, but it was a long wandering in the wilderness in between. A talented filmmaker such as Victor Nunez shouldn't have to wait eight years between films. His recent *Ulee's Gold* was Victor's way of saying none of it was a fluke. He is an original voice and a very talented storyteller with deep insights and concerns.

Griffin Dunne appeared in two films in the 1985 film festival. Adam Brook's *Almost You* and Bruce van Dusen's *Cold Feet* are both relationship films featuring Griffin Dunne as the male lead. Both films begin with breakups and end with love—just like in life, right? These films were to be admired because comedy, especially romantic comedy, was (and still is) a difficult hat trick for edgy independents to pull off.

FILMMAKER VICTOR NUNEZ AND ASHLEY JUDD FROM *RUBY IN PARADISE.*

Bobby Roth returned with his male friendship film *Heartbreakers*, starring Peter Coyote and Nick Marcuso. The film is about two childhood friends, one who is a Los Angeles abstract-expressionist painter and one who is a successful businessman after inheriting the family business. Each one sees in the other the very thing he thinks he lacks in himself. This begins a competition that comes full circle and ends in abiding friendship.

PRODUCTION STILL FROM RICK KING'S *HARD CHOICES.*

Rick King also returned with his excellent, if underseen, film *Hard Choices,* about a small-town robbery gone wrong. The underage offender is eventually sprung from jail by the female social worker who is aided by the local drug dealer, played by none other than John Sayles. It is a trippy little story that is well acted, honest, and it anticipated the moral dilemmas at the heart of any good narrative.

Bill Duke's exquisite *The Killing Floor* was based on actual characters and events set in the 1917 Chicago stockyards just before racial tensions culminated in the Chicago Race Riots of 1919. Frank Custer, played by Damien Leake, was an illiterate black sharecropper who moved to Chicago to take advantage of the twenty-one-cents-an-hour jobs left behind from men entering World War I. Custer attempted to bring together blacks, Poles, Lithuanians, Germans, and Irish workers in an interracial union despite the growing racial tensions that ended in the riot. It was an honorable well-acted drama that drew on the rich historical record in a unique and telling way.

The Roommate was Nell Cox's film—produced and written by Neal Miller and based on a John Updike story—about two unlikely college roomies, played to perfection by Lance Guest and Barry Miller. Shot by Jeff Jur and produced in associa-

PRODUCTION STILL FROM NELL COX'S *THE ROOMMATE.*

tion with PBS's *American Playhouse*, it was an audience-winning film, whether one had been in the dorms or not. It was a much more intelligent take on the subject than most of the other college films of the time, with the two characters polar opposites—one valedictorian, class president, medicine major, the other yoga-practicing, unorthodox, mystical seeker of truths. The mix was genuinely funny and the film was an eventual winner, though I don't recall it making much of an impression in the marketplace after the festival.

Another returning filmmaker to the 1985 festival was Frederick King Keller with his contemporary thriller *Vamping*. It starred Patrick Duffy who was riding high on television's wildly popular television series *Dallas* as Bobby Ewing. The film was actually listed in the 1984 catalog, but Fred Keller had called at the last minute and informed me he was not going to have his movie *Vamping* there. I knew who he was and that *Dallas* was a big deal, but I'd never actually seen an episode and failed to grasp the cultural significance of the Ewing family on the consciousness of America, and even the world. I discovered quickly that this man was a very popular actor of the time. Although in *Vamping* he did a credible job playing the down-on-his-luck saxophone player, Harry Baranski, who returns to his hometown of Buffalo and reluctantly meets with the Fatman (played with relish by Fred Keller's father). Harry agrees to a one-time break-in and robbery, which gets complicated when he is nearly discovered by the beautiful woman who is returning home from her husband's funeral. What follows is a gripping mystery, a play on the genre in which meeting the widow under better circumstances may prove to be Harry's last gig.

There is an odd story that goes along with the release of *Vamping*. Even with Patrick Duffy's intense popularity, the film didn't perform that well for its distributor Atlantic Releasing. Fred Keller was to discover one of the possible reasons. When the film opened in Los Angeles, it did not generate terribly kind reviews and after speaking with a friend who saw it in the theater, Fred began to question the distributor. As his friend critiqued the film, pointing out holes in the story big enough to drive a catering truck through, Fred kept insisting that, no, that point was covered in such and such scene. The friend would tell Fred that scene wasn't in the film, and he would say, "Of course that scene is in the film." After all, it was his film. Then his friend would insist that, in fact, the described scene was not in the film. In checking with the distributor, it was discovered that the lab work had been done in Europe and that it was customary to label reels 1 and 1A, 2 and 2A, and so forth. When it came time to print the film, somehow one of the "A" reels was left out of the film. In fact, the film was released and reviewed with substantial parts of the mystery missing from the picture. It was no wonder the film underperformed. One can imagine how that might affect a plot-thick mystery. Although there certainly could have been a lawsuit, Fred Keller was a gentleman about it, and the film had been profitable, even with sections of it missing. Obviously the problem was corrected in the broadcast and video versions, but there was a good lesson learned: always review the print.

The 1985 documentary competition was no less groundbreaking in the scope and quality of the assembled films, but this was still in a time when documentary films weren't perceived as having much box-office potential. In 1985, this perception began to change substantially. First and foremost was the emergence of a gay, independent, cinema subculture, as represented by the breakthrough film by Robert Schmiechen and Robert Epstein, *The Times of Harvey Milk.* The film was about the 1970s rise to power of the gay camera-store owner from the Castro District of San Francisco who became one of the most colorful and influential elected officials. He was also one of the decade's most prominent leaders of the lesbian and gay rights movements—that is, until he was murdered in his city-hall office by fellow supervisor and former police officer Dan White. The film brilliantly recounts Harvey Milk's journey up to that fateful day, combining real emotional urgency with an emerging political voice. Finally, it exposes a stranger-than-fiction confrontation and senseless murder, compounded by an incredible miscarriage of justice when Dan White pleads the infamous Twinkie defense. The film is a riveting, volatile, dynamic, and impassioned revelation, which was one of the early breakthroughs into the marketplace—in part because of its specialized audience. It is an excellent film about an important and controversial subject, and it won the Academy Award for Best Documentary in March 1985. Robert Epstein and Bill Couturie would win again for their film *Common Threads: Stories from the Quilt* in 1989, but *The Times of Harvey Milk* is one of the early success stories of nonfiction films reaching the marketplace and having some level of success—other than perhaps *From Mao to Mozart* and *Woodstock*.

To further delineate the gay subculture was Greta Schiller and Robert Rosenberg's *Before Stonewall: The Making of a Gay and Lesbian Community.* The film used a wealth of archival resources both from the mass media's portrayal of homosexuality and the gay subculture's own documentation. It included everything from Ronald Reagan in a cross-dressing musical during the war, to the Lavender

STILL FROM *THE TIMES OF HARVEY MILK.*

Cowboy prancing around the Wild West, to the experimentation of the Roaring Twenties and the scapegoating of homosexuals in the McCarthy Era, finally culminating in the 1969 confrontation between gays and the authorities at the Stonewall Inn in Greenwich Village, considered by many to be the key turning point in the gay rights movement.

Two other films utilized archival footage that in many ways were the precursors of Ken Burn's style of storytelling, relying heavily on filmed interviews mixed with carefully researched dramatic and telling footage, strong narration, and musical accompaniment. The first was the talented Nina Rosenblum and Dan Allentuck's *America and Lewis Hines* about the preeminent social photographer best known for his evocative photographs of immigrants landing on Ellis Island and for documenting the construction of the Empire State Building. Hines died in obscurity and impoverished, unrecognized for the artist he was. The second documentary was Tom Johnson and Lance Bird's *The World of Tomorrow*, a look back into the future, at least as it was imagined by Americans at the New York Great World's Fair of 1939–40. For just a glittering moment between the Great Depression and the war, one could glimpse a future of wonderful progress. The film gently and intelligently encourages speculation about the past that transcends mere nostalgia. It asks the question, "Are you better off today than you were nearly sixty years ago?"

One of the truly great things that documentaries can do for us as viewers is to introduce worlds and cultures we otherwise probably wouldn't ever encounter. They inform us as to others' experiences and cause us to reflect on their lives as well as our own. The 1985 festival was full of such cultural gems.

Hopi: Songs of the Fourth World may be one of the most beautiful and reflective films ever done by, for, and about Native Americans. Directed by Pat Ferraro, the film's narrator states from the outset that it won't be focusing on any of the problems of Native Americans, though there are many, but instead will try to show the positive, holistic side to their lifestyle. The rich visual and spiritual information gives viewers a sense of the harmony of their worldview. It is powerful medicine, faithfully administered with a seasoned knowledge like neat rows of corn, watered by rain and the river and used for ceremonies, food, and planting. It becomes a gentle and revealing affirmation of an often-misunderstood culture, especially in the media portrayal, and this film provides an opportunity to slow down and get in sync with the mind's eye that reminds us we are all, after all, sharing the planet together.

Les Blank's marvelous documentary *In Heaven There Is No Beer?* is the perfect counterpoint to *Hopi: Songs of the Fourth World.* In Blank's film, a person learns more about the polka than he or she will ever need to know. Les Blank is one of the most remarkable ethnographic filmmakers, with a particular fondness for cooking, musical life, and culture—peppered to taste with a combination of rare individuals who have an enthusiasm for life and an uncondescending manner of letting the authentic American characters speak for themselves.

Robert Mugge was back with *The Gospel According to Al Green*, a knockout film about the performer turned Pentecostal preacher that illustrates the powerful connection between black secular and gospel music. In a sweat-drenched sermon at his Memphis church, one of the sexiest soul-wailers of the 1970s lets it all hang out in his inimitable style. It is a riveting performance built on top of the personal challenges he encountered along the pop-world way, having nearly been killed in a relationship gone bad before he found his calling.

Steve Brand's *Kaddish* also introduced us to the world of religion in the portrait of a father and son, both trying to come to terms with their shared legacy. The period of mourning in Orthodox Jewish tradition requires that the dutiful son recite Kaddish, the Jewish prayer for the dead, three times a day for a year following the parent's death. Although said in a time of mourning, death is never mentioned. It is instead an affirmation of life, a commitment to carry on.

The theme from *Kaddish* was echoed in Ken Fink's *The Work I've Done*, a portrait of a retirement community in Florida. With the labor movement's victory summed up in the phrase, "thirty years and out," the film explores with candor and humor the challenges and joys of coping with retirement as Fink follows one Pennsylvania man on the verge of retirement along with a handful of retirees from the Budd Company assembly plant. These retirees in their first years of inactivity include a wonderful widow and widower who talk about their newly invigorated sex life, a man who said he had painted his house three times in the first year of retirement, and a welder who said he could weld together everything except the break of day and a broken heart.

James Heddle brought the excellent and troubling film *Strategic Trust: The*

Making of a Nuclear-Free Palau. Palau is the Micronesian republic that decided it wanted to become a nuclear-free zone—to which the United States objected—despite a thirteen-year history of conducting sixty-six nuclear tests in the nearby Marshall Islands. These tests left a legacy of genetic, environmental, and social damage that the people of the region are still living with.

Two films of tremendous importance were not sufficiently seen by the public in 1985. First was Martin Bell's *Streetwise*, a kind of *Kids* before there was *Kids*. Inspired by a *Life* magazine article, the film documents the bleak world of young runaways. Well versed in street vernacular, these kids speak for themselves in gritty and compelling ways, so much so that one is challenged in one's perception of myth versus reality. Viewers are perplexed and impassioned by their plight and wonder what could be done to retrieve them.

PRODUCTION STILL FROM MARTIN BELL'S *STREETWISE.*

Similar in some ways was Joel DeMott and Jeff Kreines's disturbing story of a group of "typical" teens, produced as part of a six-part series for PBS, by Peter Davis, "Middletown." Entitled *Seventeen*, the film follows the teens from their home-economics class, where their boredom and antagonism is barely hidden beneath the surface as they chide and taunt the teacher—a woman who seems oblivious to their routines. Viewers see them at home—the products of middle-class families, in which parental guidance seems strained, ineffective, or nonexistent—and socializing at a beer bash, smoking dope on the sly, and acting out all their adolescent fantasies. It is almost a rite of passage that is disturbingly rendered as one can almost see the inevitability of their futures: an unenlightened dreary succession of lousy jobs, lost dreams, lost love, divorce, and disintegration. What is particularly disturbing is the feeling that on some kind of profound level, perhaps part of their resentment, lack of commitment, and general anger toward the system comes from their understanding of their predicament, yet they never really confront it. It is a hopeless precursor to the world of slackers in which ambition, drive, and learning take a backseat to the pleasures of the moment and peer pressure results in a catapulting of values over the wall of self-discipline. It was a controversial film, dedicatedly crafted and ultimately pulled from the PBS series in a swarm of accusations and counteraccusations. The filmmakers refused to make cuts in the film to downplay the conflict they felt was a vital part of the story they encountered. Although the film played a full two hours and could have used some trimming, it didn't seem overly long.

Unfortunately, when the film won the documentary award at the film festival, the controversy continued spilling over into my already strained relationship with Tony Safford. With a $5,000 prize due the filmmakers, Tony stepped in to suggest that Peter Davis, the producer who commissioned the work for the PBS series should be given the prize instead of the filmmakers who had lived for more than a year with these students and their families, carefully making the film. It seemed obvious to me who was most deserving of the prize money, but Tony and I had a falling out over the dispersement. I finally had to go to Gary Beer, the vice president and general manager of the Sundance Institute, trapping him on the creaky stairs going up into the Elks Building. I suggested that something was amiss in this situation. For the filmmakers, it was insult heaped on top of injury, and they were incredulous that the festival could even contemplate such a scenario. They were the ones who had risked everything to make the film, had suffered the indignity of having it pulled from PBS's schedule, and obviously had strong feelings about their relationship with Peter Davis. In my conversations with Joel and Jeff, it was apparent they were not necessarily the easiest guys to work with, but I thought that was what our festival was all about, supporting filmmakers, not playing politics. Independent filmmakers can sometimes be, well, independent. This for me, and in some small way for the festival, was the first step down a long road. A compromise was reached whereby the prize money was split between the producer and the filmmakers—a compromise that still makes me uncomfortable.

SUNDANCE INSTITUTE VICE PRESIDENT GARY BEER.

In addition to the competition films, the premieres of note in 1985 included John Schlesinger's *The Falcon and the Snowman*; Wim Wender's *Paris; Texas*, which remains one of my favorite films; Gillian Armstrong's *Mrs. Soffel*; Woody Allen's *The Purple Rose of Cairo* and D. W. Griffith's 1920 restored print of *Way Down East*, accompanied by Ricklen Nobis and the Salt Lake Chamber Ensemble.

In an effort to put his own stamp on the festival, something I implicitly understood, Tony created an international program that included twenty-eight films from around the world, including seven from Australia, three from Japan, and Werner Herzog's *Where the Green Ants Dream,* Stephen Frear's *The Hit,* Robert Altman's *Secret Honor,* Paul Bartel's *Not for Publication,* Sally Potter's *The Gold Diggers,* Andrzej Wajda's *A Love in Germany,* Roland Joffe's *The Killing Fields,* Lina Wertmuller's *A Joke of Destiny,* and Leo Hurwitz's *Dialogue with a Woman Departed.* It was an eclectic program augmented by tributes to Francois Truffaut, who had died in 1984, Ivan Passar, Christopher Petit, and Roger Corman. Corman was the king of the "B" movies who had spawned so many important film careers, including Francis Ford Coppola, Jonathan Demme, Jack Nicholson, Joe Dante, Martin Scorcese, Peter Bogdanovich, and Allan Arkush.

The jury for dramatic features in the independent competition were Peter Biskind, editor of *American Film* and author of the 1998 book on filmmaking in the 1970s, *Easy Riders, Raging Bulls;* filmmakers Robert Young *(The Ballad of Gregorio Cortez, Dominick and Eugene, Caught,* and many others) and Mirra Bank, director of *Enormous Changes at the Last Minute* that had played in the 1984 festival.

The documentary jury consisted of a triumvirate of experienced documentary filmmakers, really some of the giants of their generation, Frederick Wiseman *(Titticut Follies, High School, Model)*; D. A. Pennbaker, *(Don't Look Back, Monterey Pop)*; Barbara Kopple *(Harlan County, U.S.A., American Dream,* and *Wild Man Blues)*; and Leo Hurwitz, blacklisted filmmaker and committed lefty whose epic four-hour *Dialogue with a Woman Departed* documented conversations of the turbulent life and career of his now-deceased wife, Peggy Lawson.

Tony Safford also did a splendid job of putting together the seminars. The speakers really were many of the leading lights of their respective fields, and the discussion and panels were focused and direct, giving savvy audiences very specific information from the worlds of financing. They included Lindsay Law, executive producer of *American Playhouse*, a significant player in the early years of successful independent production; Roland Betts, president of Silver Screen Management; Eric Weissmann, partner in a major Los Angeles law firm; and Sam Grogg, who headed up FilmDallas and who had been quite successful in the early years—from putting up P & A (prints and advertising) monies to producing what turned out to be too many films in too short a period. They eventually went bust, but not before being involved with some of the more successful independent films and distribution. Another speaker, Tom Bernard, was then vice president of marketing and distribution at Orion Classics and one of the original people in all of this, putting independent and foreign films in front of audiences. Having first been involved with United Artists Classics, the forerunner of all the classics divisions, after he booked such films as *Reefer Madness* on college campuses. He is currently one of the troika

DISTRIBUTORS AND MARKETERS TOM BERNARD, IRA DEUTCHMAN, AND JEFF DOWD.

at Sony Pictures Classics and one of the saviest, hardest-working, all-time characters in the business. Speaker Ira Deutchman was the vice president at Cinecom, another very successful company that eventually went belly up. He had a long and distinguished career at the start of Fine Line, and is now a producer at his own Redeemable features, who, unbeknownst to me at the time, also had a long and largely antagonistic relationship with Tom Bernard. Other participants in the seminars included Jeff Dowd, the Dude—a very smart marketing consultant and also one of the all-time characters in this part of the business; Cary Brokaw, president of Island Alive; and Randy Finley from Seven Gables Theater in Seattle, a longtime supporter of specialized films. Stars that year included Nick Mancuso, the actor with his director from *Heartbreakers,* Bobby Roth; and Patrick Duffy with Frederick Keller from the film *Vamping*, moderated by *Los Angeles Times* staff writer Deborah Caulfield. It was a knockout documentary panel with Frederick Wiseman, D. A. Pennebaker, and the infamous Roger Corman—a producer and director so cheap he was well known for creating low-budget films, utilizing some other films' sets, and for yelling at a producer who was about to messenger over something (before fax machines). He said, "You messenger over a dozen contracts, and that's a week's worth of flatbed rental. You want to cut the picture for an extra week? I'll take it over myself." And he did. Roger Corman did a panel with some of his prodigies, Joe Dante, Paul Bartel, and Jonathan Demme. The panel was moderated by Jane Alsobrook.

These were heady times with things coming together. As Tony said in the program guide introduction, "I realize that it's impossible for any one filmgoer to see all the films presented at the 1985 festival. But this is part of the excitement—the urgency of selection and the excellence of the product. The Festival aspires toward a 'critical mass' of people, movement, energy . . . and fun. Enjoy it."

As Deborah Caulfield from the *Los Angeles Times* noted in her article from the guide, "The independent filmmaking movement has gained momentum, stature and, most importantly, increasing power in the domestic and international marketplaces."

With the security and contacts the Sundance Institute provided, it was a whole new ballgame. It was still the same film festival in structure and tone, in commitment and heart, but it was taking on a new mantle, slowly at first, almost imperceptibly, but it was the beginning of what the Sundance Film Festival would become.

I have to admit, I was always a bit nervous with Tony Safford's and even now Geoffrey Gilmore's predilection for foreign films. I was always concerned that the primary focus of our festival remain devoted to American independent filmmakers. It may have been cinematic jingoism, but as a filmmaker and someone who has been at the center of this country's sea change of filmmaking activity, knowing just how difficult it is to compete with many foreign countries who subsidize and give tax incentives to their filmmakers, I knew how utterly independent this kind of low-budget, by-the-seat-of-your-pants, risk-taking to make a personal film actually is. I felt it was critical that American independent filmmakers always be the backbone of the event.

I've been fortunate because I had a powerful ally in the form of Robert Redford. On the back cover of the 1985 program guide, the first name at the top of the page was Robert Redford, as president and founder of the Sundance Institute and at the bottom of the page, the last name mentioned in a long list of more than fifty names, including Senator Christopher Dodd, Michael Ovitz, and Frank Mancuso, was my name. Still, between Robert Redford and me, there was an unspoken commitment to this kind of uniquely American filmmaking.

PRODUCTION STILL FROM JOEL DEMOTT AND JEFF DREINES'S CONTROVERSIAL DOCUMENTARY *SEVENTEEN*.

Chapter 6

Different Strokes for Different Folks

I think there exists in every person a kind of spiritual energy that radiates on the outside what is on the inside. It manifests itself in various ways, but it does reveal itself. In Tony Safford's case, our little tiff over prize money to the filmmakers for *Seventeen* was just the beginning of a rift that grew to be the size of the Grand Canyon. It wasn't completely Tony's fault. Some of it was a natural response to taking over a fledgling festival and having to work with the person and structure already in place.

The 1985 festival under the tutelage of Sundance doubled the attendance. The question was whether the growth was because Sundance had become involved or just a natural evolution. In my mind, we were on the cusp of success whether Sundance had become involved or not, and I felt that Sundance was actually an outgrowth of the film festival, not the other way around. Yet Sundance seemed determined from the outset to rewrite the festival's history as well as its own—to make it seem as if they had rescued a small-time festival from obscurity. It is a debate that can never be resolved. Still, I'm happy for Sundance's involvement because it catapulted the festival into the stratosphere of press and public attention. That has boded well for independent film and filmmakers, and it certainly has proven to be a boon for the ubiquitous organization known as Sundance. As Robert Redford stated in an interview with Duane Byrge at the *Hollywood Reporter* in January of 1986:

> We've created a symbiotic relationship that did not exist before. We have a place of development at Sundance and a place of exhibition with the festival. The reason for forming Sundance is to develop new product and other voices speaking. We've tried to develop the concept of regional filmmaking. We've created the equivalent of a theater workshop without the risks of money and financial success tied to the projects. A lot of people in film today, in contrast to the old days, have as their frame of reference other films, rather than life. Regional filmmakers know life, what we're trying to do is help them develop their skills, tell their story. That's what this festival is all about.

What Redford said next worried me at first, mostly out of concern that he might not stick with this commitment, which, after all, was only made on a yearly basis. He stated the following emphatically:

> I'm not interested in film festivals. When we were approached to take over this festival, I had no interest in becoming involved unless it would take a course that was unique. We said yes but only if we could concentrate on independent films. The film industry has a lot of fear. There is competition and people get tense—it's easy for them to lose their perspective. We pride ourselves on our perspective. What we have tried to do is to eliminate the tension that can exist between independents and the studios. We're not anti-Hollywood at all. Many industry people participate, and it's a great place for independent filmmakers to make contacts.

I couldn't have said it better myself.

In the early years, I was always concerned that Redford, like many actors such as Ronald Reagan while president, didn't actually connect with the words he was uttering except on a superficial level. But as time passed, I did come to trust Bob's heartfelt commitment. He has a deep insight into the business strategies and position of alternative films. But I have always been perplexed by Sundance's refusal to acknowledge the festival's early history as though, by recognizing these humble beginnings, Sundance would be diminished. Part of my motivation for writing this book is to celebrate all the marvelous people who helped to make the film festival and Sundance what they are and tell the accurate and unexpurgated story of how it all started and developed.

With me programming the independent film competition—both dramatic and documentary—and Tony programming the international sidebars, tributes, premieres, and seminars, the 1986 film festival was quickly becoming a behemoth undertaking. People used to ask me if my job was full-time. At this point, mounting the film festival was a full-time gig for half-a-dozen people, a part-time job for another fifteen or twenty, and a temporary job for hundreds, including volunteers who started early on showing up from film schools to participate as best they could. It was a strategy that paid off for many people, including Steven Soderbergh, who volunteered for the festival as a driver the year before he made *sex, lies, and videotape*.

Still, 1986 started out a little rocky. Tony informed me that he didn't want me to sit in on the national jury's final deliberations, something I had always done in the past. I was obviously not a voting member but was present as the staff person most responsible and knowledgeable about the competition. I simply detailed the process, got jury members started, helped with stalemates, and answered any questions I could about the entries. But Tony was concerned I was somehow influencing the outcome of their decisions. I found it preposterous to believe I was influencing Roger Ebert or Frederick Wiseman. To deflect the personal affront, I said it was important to have a festival representative at the final jurying session to make any necessary clarifications. I also remarked that I was flattered to know he had such high regard for my powers of persuasion.

ROGER EBERT AND CINDA HOLT.

On some level, I knew I was hanging on by my teeth. Diminishing my responsibilities would be a slow and drawn-out process, and this was just the first step down a long road. A former Sundance staff member has described the process as being "Sundanced"—a shuffling off laterally while new blood, usually better credentialed comes along without much acknowledgment of past personal contributions or appreciation of a former individual's role in the organization's current success. This was the beginning of my being Sundanced.

Fortunately, we were in the midst of a strong year for independent films, both documentary and dramatic. The 1986 festival really paved the way for the big breakthrough year of 1988 because it was filled with a remarkable number of powerful dramatic films. In sheer numbers, 1986 had the highest percentage of dramatic films in competition that ultimately got theatrical distribution, eleven out of the fourteen.

It was to be a benchmark year for gay-themed dramatic films, with Donna Deitch's quite excellent and deftly handled *Desert Hearts* and Bill Sherwood's humorous and touching *Parting Glances*, which marked one of Steve Buscemi's early appearances as a cynical and HIV-infected rock musician. *Desert Hearts* was distributed by Samuel Goldwyn Company, and *Parting Glances* was sold to Cinecom by producers rep John Pierson.

Ethnic identity was also a big theme for dramatic films in 1986. Glen Pitre's *Belizaire: The Cajun*, made in Lafayette, Louisiana, and set in the bayou of the 1850s, was about an herbal doctor's love for another man's woman. It starred Armand Assante and Gail Youngs. Wayne Wang returned with *Dim Sum,* an extension of his first film *Chan Is Missing*, which had played in the 1983 festival. Peter Wang's (no relation to Wayne) *The Great Wall Is a Great Wall* covered similar terrain, although it was the first film to actually travel to China to confront the issues of cultural identity from the point of view of successful and Americanized Chinese Americans returning to their ancestral homeland to pay long-lost relatives a visit. The tone and point of view were light, but the film made its point with humor instead of irony and detail instead of mystery.

The other significant ethnic film hailed from Scotland. *Restless Natives* was Michael Hoffman's first feature film. Hoffman is from Idaho. He was a Rhodes scholar and met producer Rick Stevenson in London, a fellow Rhodes scholar from the Northwest. Along with British native Mark Bentley, who served as executive producer, they put together a little production, set in the majestic city of Edinburgh, about two working-class lads who tire of their impecunious existence and, tempted by the untapped wealth of international tourists who swarm through the Scottish highlands in tour buses, hatch a plan to relieve them of their pocketbooks. This scheme propels the lads into the national spotlight. The film is a wildly funny, fresh, and inventive comedy, distributed by Michael Barker and Tom Bernard at Orion Classics. Michael Hoffman has gone on to direct *Promised Land,* shot in Utah in 1987 with a young Meg Ryan and Keifer Sutherland; the very under-seen but quite excellent *Some Girls*; the highly successful comedy *Soap Dish*; and the Academy Award nominee (for costuming) *Restoration*, starring Robert Downey Jr. and Meg Ryan. *Restless Natives* showed off Michael's potential for a fresh way of telling strong stories by making memorable characters. He isn't mentioned much in the pantheon of inde-

DIRECTOR MICHAEL HOFFMAN, ACTOR PETER HORTON, AND PRODUCER RICK STEVENSON.

pendent filmmakers who went on to make successful films in or outside of Hollywood, but he should be.

LONGTIME FESTIVAL PARTICIPANT TOM BERNARD, CO-PRESIDENT OF SONY PICTURES CLASSICS.

Another class act in the dramatic competition was director Joyce Chopra's and producer Martin Rosen's *Smooth Talk*, based on the Joyce Carol Oates short story "Where Are You Going, Where Have You Been?" It stars a fabulous cast of Laura Dern as a fifteen-year-old woman/child, just coming to terms with her own sensuality, who encounters the dark introduction to the dangers of adulthood in the shape of Treat Williams, who literally resides on the other side of the tracks. With Mary Kay Place, Elizabeth Berridge, and Levon Helm rounding out the cast, the film won the competition and ultimately was one of the most widely distributed films of the 1986 festival. New York–based Spectra Films distributed it to very positive reviews.

Linda Feferman's *Seven Minutes in Heaven*, a peek through the door of an average teenager—admittedly not the normal perspective on most independent films—was distributed by Warner Brothers and produced by sometime American Zoetrope producer Fred Roos.

Mark Romanek's *Static*, cowritten with star Keith Gordon, produced by Amy Ness, and shot by Jeff Jur, is the off-the-wall comedy of two childhood friends from Page, Arizona. Amanda Plummer plays a member of a successful rock band returning to her small-town roots, and Keith Gordon's character, Ernie, is rumored to have created an invention, which he claims will change mankind, while living in his motel room and working at the religious-artifacts factory. Some say the inspiration for the invention was the death of Ernie's parents in an automobile accident several years before. Judging from the number of misshapen crucifixes, factory rejects all, adorning the walls of Ernie's motel room, something's got to give in a big way.

Static, was one of those films that was probably a little ahead of its time. It could have done more business than I'm sure it did. So much of the success of any particular film is in the timing of the style, subject, and release. Sometimes the stars are lined up right, and sometimes they aren't. My feeling is that nobody really knows much about the mysterious process by which audiences are sufficiently intrigued with a film's story, style, subject, performances, and critical reception to actually plop down the seven bucks and dedicate two hours of their time to go see a particular film. On any given evening in America, perhaps throughout the world, there are only two or three films that qualify as intelligent adult fare. I'm convinced not enough effort is spent by marketers in differentiating the choices. Instead there is a tendency to homogenize films, most often to compete with Hollywood, where the huge advertising budgets almost always doom the competition to almost-ran status. My suggestion to marketers of specialized films is to stand out from the crowd rather than joining in. It is the only sensible way for much smaller films to compete.

The dramatic competition was rounded out by two period films. One was directed by Texan Ken Harrison from a script by Academy Award–winner Horton Foote. *On Valentine's Day* is about a small Texas town in 1917, really a prequel to the film *1918*, also scripted by Foote. *On Valentine's Day* involves the elopement of Horace Robedaux (William Converse Roberts), a self-made man from an emotionally and financially bankrupt family, to Elizabeth Vaughn (Hallie Foote), daughter of the town's leading citizen—a rigid, wealthy curmudgeon. Though the elder Vaughns reject the young couple for a year, they eventually reconcile themselves to the marriage. They, too, come to feel the power of love in the young Robedauxs. Distributed by Ira Deutchman while at Cinecom, the film is perhaps one of Horton Foote's more accessible dramas with a universal, almost Shakespearean, theme.

Dan Bessie's *Hard Traveling* was nearly forty years in the making, having been originally authored by his "Hollywood Ten" blacklisted father, Alvah Bessie, from his novel of the depression, *Bread and Stone*. The film is a love story set in the 1930s and based on an actual incident in Bessie's early life about a handyman's romance of the town's well-educated schoolteacher. When this repairer of roofs is arrested for the murder of one of the town's most prominent citizens, the crisis of the heart blossoms against the social injustice and desperation of the times.

Finally, given the weight of films with distribution potential, I thought it was important to include some no-budget films to offer encouragement to filmmakers seeking their own, often self-financed, paths. I have always been loyal to this sort of filmmaking effort, even when the end results do not necessarily make for exquisite cinematic experiences. In 1986, Mark Rappaport returned with the enigmatic *Chain Letters* about nine disparate characters who all receive a chain letter. One of them, a paranoid Vietnam veteran, thinks he has cracked the letter's code. He discovers an unauthorized plot to inoculate random victims with a cancer-producing virus as part of a government experiment. Sounds simple enough, but this is not a normal political thriller. The plot is really coincidental to the connections and communication, or lack thereof, among the various characters. The film reveals Mark Rappaport's distinctive style at work again with a group of deadpan people all operating without a clue.

Dan Lewk and Gary Levy's *Raw Tunes* probably received the most scathing criticism of any of the films in competition, but their story of a band of minor musicians on the Ramada Inn circuit struck me as funny and inventive. Apparently I was the only person in the country, besides Dan and Gary and their families, who thought the film had some funny moments.

Last but not least was Faith Hubley's masterwork of animation, *The Cosmic Eye*, about a trio of space musicians making their way home in their space boat. Narrated by Dizzy Gillespie and Maureen Stapleton, the film is a delight for the eyes and the ears as though modern art comes to life in the hands of a master of animation.

The national jury consisted of Brazilian filmmaker Hector Babenco, in attendance to receive a tribute and conduct a seminar on directing; Molly Haskell, critic and author; Krzysztof Zanussi, Polish director of *A Year of the Quiet Sun;* Martha Coolidge, a filmmaker whose *Not a Pretty Picture* had played in the first film festival in 1978 and the subsequent maker of one of my favorite films *Rambling Rose*, with Robert Duvall and Laura Dern; and Bobby Roth, whose film *Heartbreakers* had played in competition the previous year and was being used in a seminar as a case study.

The documentary competition was no less prestigious, heralding many outstanding leaders in the field. Ken Burns returned to the festival with his excellent new film about the charismatic demagogue, Huey P. Long, whom Franklin Roosevelt once described as "one of the two most dangerous men in the country." As the governor of Louisiana, the "Kingfish," as he was known, first transformed Louisiana politics with his brand of populist politics mixed with corruption and tyranny, and then took on the ruling establishment in Washington. When Huey Long was assassinated in the corridors of the massive state capitol he had built only three years earlier, it ended the career of one of the nation's most colorful and controversial politicians. In typical Ken Burns and Geoffrey Ward (screenwriter) style, the film illuminates the complexity of the man and the contrasts between the times in which he lived and that he influenced.

Academy Award–winner Lynne Littman brought her moving film *In Her Own Time* about Dr. Barbara Myerhoff, a cultural anthropologist who began studying the Fairfax neighborhood of Los Angeles in 1981—a rich subculture of Orthodox Jews. She was fascinated by the way religion and the neighborhood worked together to form a community. In the midst of the filming, she discovers she has cancer, and the film takes on a new, unforeseen meaning and significance. The film encompasses a vivid philosophy of life and a challenging approach to illness and death.

Susan Munoz and Lourdes Portillo's *Las Madres: The Mothers of the Plaza de Mayo* is an equally compelling film about the Argentinean mothers who protested the "disappearance" of their children and more than 30,000 other citizens during the 1970s. In April 1977, fourteen mothers began marching around the plaza in Buenos Aires, demanding to know what had happened to their children. Wearing their missing loved-ones' photographs around their necks, the mothers created an international sensation and brought the dirty war on those labeled "leftists" and "subversives" to the world's attention.

Another film that brought attention to the plight of indigenous peoples was Lee Shapiro's *Nicaragua Was Our Home*, a report on the plight of the Miskito Indians, whose villages had been razed and who had suffered terrible human loss as a result of "mistakes" now admitted by the Sandinista government. Filmed in secrecy over a five-month period, including clandestine canoe rides by the filmmakers to get into Nicaragua from Honduras, the film documents the escape of two Catholic bishops along with 2,000 Miskito refugees, all fearing for their lives, and what became an international embarrassment for the Sandinista government.

Although Shapiro's film didn't necessarily match my own political leanings, I believed in good conscience that it was a well-made film highlighting an important topic. I decided to play the film and, in my naïveté, thought it would be revelatory to contrast it with *Las Madres* to show that no matter the political philosophy, powerful interests above all else seek out their own self-preservation. The decision to combine the two films proved very controversial and ultimately was my undoing. As a programmer, I'd often found that two contrasting films with some common thread made for a more interesting program, but in this case, it completely backfired.

Yet in the case of Connie Poten, Pamela Roberts, and Beth Ferris's *Contrary Warrior: A Story of the Crow Tribe* playing with a short film by Nancy Kelly, *Cowgirls*, what could have been construed as pitting the cowgirls against the Indians became instead a wonderful mirror held up to two contemporary cultures that shared rich historical legacies and love of the land. *Contrary Warrior* is the extraordinary story of ninety-seven-year-old Robert Yellowtail who in 1910 saved his tribal lands and heritage when he journeyed from Montana to Washington, D.C., to appear before the United States Senate. He devoted his life to fighting for his people and their land, much as in times past, when "a man might declare himself a Crazy Dog, a contrary warrior, and ride backward into battle. If he lived, this gained him great honor." The film meshed perfectly with Nancy Kelly's delightful, twenty-seven-minute film that focuses on three different, modern-day cowgirls, ranging from eight to sixty-eight years old, and showed what it really meant to be "home on the range."

Another powerful combination featured Nancy Yasecko's personal documentary *Growing Up with Rockets*, a sweet, southern, almost impressionistic vision of childhood in Cocoa Beach, Florida, in the era of rockets, missiles, space races, and men on the moon. It was paired with Robert Tranchin's *Wildcatter: A Story of Texas Oil* about wily and roaming oilmen who venture forth into the barren wasteland for the costly and hazardous crapshoot of digging deeply into the earth to tap a mother lode of Texas tea. Both were stories of stubborn dreams and calculated risks, but they couldn't have been more different from one another in style and content; yet they made for a great two-hour program in the 1986 documentary competition.

Most of the other documentaries in competition were performance oriented, but with some serious emphasis on politics and polemics. First there was the avant-garde *Einstein on the Beach: The Changing Image of Opera,* directed by Mark Obenhaus and produced by Chrissann Verges about the four-hour "opera," a collaboration or shared dream of director-designer Robert Wilson and music composer and performer Philip Glass.

Terry Zwigoff's *Louie Bluie* was an early indicator of where he would eventually go with his much-heralded *Crumb*. *Louie Bluie* presents the life, art, and music of Howard Armstrong, who led one of the last black string bands in America. At seventy-six he played a mean mandolin and was a fiddler, diarist, painter of religious and pornographic themes, linguist, and all-around rogue—a unique performer and a hardy survivor from a strong, rich, culture.

PRODUCTION STILLS FROM TERRY ZWIGOFF'S *LOUIE BLUIE*.

Robert Mugge's *The Return of Ruben Blades* served for many as the introduction to this talented musician, intelligent thinker, and sometimes actor. Ruben Blades is a proud Panamanian who graduated from Harvard Law School and even harbored ambitions to one day run for president of his homeland. By the end of this polyrhythmic pop-salsa music performance, a person begins to think it isn't entirely out of the realm of possibility.

Jerome Gary's *Stripper* is his follow-up to the highly successful *Pumping Iron*. In *Stripper*, the camera follows the lives of five women who happen to take off their clothes for a living. The odyssey culminates at a strippers' convention in Las Vegas, where the best in the world converge to compete for the First Annual Golden G-String Award.

Equally enthralling was Lucy Winer and Paula de Koenigsberg's *Rate It X*, a hair-raising ride through American male chauvinism. Viewers encounter people ranging from Ugly George—the cable-TV host who gave Howard Stern the idea to entice women to take off their clothes for him on camera—to a baker who specializes in baking cakes in the shape of a woman's torso, to a Madison Avenue corporate executive who uses women and sex to move products, to an owner of a sexual emporium, a cartoonist for *Hustler*, a funeral-parlor director, Santa Claus, and the inventors of a sexist video game. The film provides an unflinching look at the extremes of male chauvinism that provokes both laughter and despair.

Ä PRODUCTION STILL FROM ROBERT MUGGE'S *THE RETURN OF RUBEN BLADES*.

Glenn Silber and Claudia Vianello arrived in Park City with *Troupers*, their exuberant documentary on the twenty-five-year-old San Francisco Mime Troup whose focus on social protest and political commentary makes them a unique performance group—perhaps most memorable for being the starting place for Peter Coyote, who is seen in home-movie footage from the 1960s cavorting in false nose and ponytail. He is in Golden Gate Park having the time of his life playing in Molière's *The Miser*.

The most sophisticated performance-oriented documentary in 1986 was unquestionably Christian Blackwood's *Private Conversations*. This intimate, behind-the-scenes look at the making of Arthur Miller's *Death of a Salesman* was adapted from the stage and directed for television by German director Volker Schloendorff. This brilliant collaboration between author, actors Dustin Hoffman and John Malkovich, and director Schloendorff, results in an irrepressible examination of the creative process; the crafts of writing, directing, and acting; and the inherent similarities and differences between theater and cinema. Hoffman's intensity and care for performance, along with his contagious sense of humor set the tone for the end results. It is a rare piece of work to give public voice to these private conversations, one that offers tremendous insight for students interested in the dramatic arts.

Finally was Lucy Massie-Phenix and Veronica Selver's moving tribute to social change and personal and political empowerment as seen through the eyes of blacks and whites over the past fifty years in the deep South. *You Got to Move* is about personal transformation, commitment, courage, and ordinary people—often undereducated—who decide to empower themselves and make a difference. The film was one of those unknown entities that arrived in a plain-brown wrapper and proceeded to knock off everybody's emotional socks.

However, we needed little help in the emotion department in 1986. The festival was dedicated to the memory of one of its important thinkers, supporters, and founders—John Earle. He had succumbed to a heart attack at the early age of forty-three while being ousted from the Utah Film Commission by the new Republican administration the previous spring.

The other important behind-the-scenes player, Sterling Van Wagenen, had the good fortune to have been asked by director Peter Masterson and writer Horton Foote to produce the film that finally won Geraldine Page an Academy Award: *The Trip to Bountiful*. It was the opening-night film at the 1986 Sundance, and it somehow made the festival seem as if in eight short years it had already come full circle.

Eugene Corr's Sundance Lab project, *Desert Bloom*, starring Jon Voight, JoBeth Williams, Ellen Barkin, and Annabeth Gish, produced and distributed by Columbia Pictures, stood alongside Frank Capra's restored print of *Lost Horizon* and Woody Allen's popular *Hannah and Her Sisters* with Mia Farrow, Dianne Wiest, and Barbara Hershey. Woody Allen said his film was ". . . about love, lust, adultery . . . and death. It's a comedy." Other films included the Michael Peyser– and Dodi Fayed–produced *F/X,* directed by Robert Mandel and starring Bryan Brown and Brian Dennehy, and Sidney Lumet's *Power*, starring Richard Gere, Julie Christie, and Gene Hackman.

Unfortunately, *Power* suffered through the worst screening in the history of the festival. During its premiere, Lumet, executives from Twentieth Century Fox, and the screenwriter, David Himmelstein, all paced outside the Egyptian Theatre in the cold Park City night, not knowing that the reels had inadvertently been put in the wrong order as the film was being built up by the projectionist. No one in the theater caught on until elements of the story became increasingly incoherent with plot explanations taking place prior to their setup. Of course, the real giveaway came with the dates that were superimposed throughout the story. When the film finally shifted from November back to July, the lights in the theater came up, and the screen went dark. It was explained that we had seen reel five of the film in reel four's position, and because of the nature of the massive platter systems now used in most automated projection, the festival would not be able to break down the film in a timely manner and re-order the reels. Afterward, Lumet embarrassingly but generously apologized for the screwup. The audience was given the choice of a refund, a corrected screening the next morning, or just finishing out the film as it was and re-ordering the scenes in their own minds.

Most people stayed on, but it was one of the most egregious errors in the festival's history, so bad, in fact, that for a time immediately following the screening, a cover-up story was hatched, mostly to save Tony Safford's job. It was claimed that the reels had been mismarked upon their arrival at the festival. The cover art of the program guide prominently showed a man in a cowboy hat and leather jacket in motion against a brick wall with a film reel under his arm. I began to joke that the pictured reel was actually reel five of Sidney Lumet's *Power*. Apparently I was the only one among the staff who thought it was funny.

In 1986, it seemed as though independents had truly arrived at the table set by Hollywood. Independents had nibbled on the appetizers with films such as *Stranger Than Paradise, Blood Simple, The Brother from Another Planet,* and *She's Got to Have It,* but now everyone had his or her eyes on the main course: the marketplace. We were still three years away from *sex, lies, and videotape*. Nevertheless, that didn't stop the dreamers who were also part of the contingent of people now attending the festival, as illustrated by Julie Salamon's wrap-up article that appeared in the *Wall Street Journal*, February 5, 1986:

> The atmosphere, generally, was collegial. Since condos are the norm, people ended up sharing living quarters with strangers. So Martin Rosen, a movie producer whose latest film, *Smooth Talk*, won the festival's award for best picture, ended up across the hall from Bobby Panzarella, a medical doctor from Humble, Texas, who hankered to be a screenwriter. Late one evening, Dr. Panzarella wandered into Mr. Rosen's room and thumbed through the four or five bound scripts piled on the floor. He began to learn something about the movie business.
>
> "Do they have to be fixed up like this?" the young doctor asked.
>
> "It makes them easier to read," Mr. Rosen replied gently.
>
> This was Dr. Panzarella's first film festival. He has written three screenplays. "In all my scripts the hero is a young, Italian-American doctor . . . short," explained Dr. Panzarella. He paused. "So I could play the lead."
>
> He took his scripts to Hollywood last year and couldn't get an agent to look at any of his work. However, he did get onto three TV game shows and won $25,000 on *Tic Tac Dough*.
>
> He found the film festival quite useful: "The best thing I've gotten out of the whole thing is getting names and addresses of people to send scripts to."

Some amazing folks participated in the 1986 festival, including Hector Babenco; Waldo Salt who wrote the incredible film *Midnight Cowboy*; William Witliff; Tom Rickman; Frank Pierson; Frank Daniel; Mitchell Block; David Fanning; Sam Grogg; Lindsay Law from *American Playhouse*; Ruth Vitale; Steven Reuther; Richard Rubinstein; Jeff Dowd, the Dude; Larry Jackson; Tom Bernard; Janet Fleming; and Ira Deutchman from Cinecom; Jesse Beaton; and such critics as David Ansen from *Newsweek*; Kenneth Turan, then from *California Magazine*; Duane Byrge from the *Hollywood Reporter;* Dave Kehr from *Chicago Reader*; Peter Biskind from *American Film*; Carrie Rickey; Sheila Benson from the *Los Angeles Times*; Molly Haskell from *Vogue*; and Julie Salamon from the *Wall Street Journal.*

The National Advisory Board had grown to forty-six prominent Hollywood individuals, including Ron Howard, Terry Semel, Sid Ganis, Michael Douglas, and Jim Wiatt. The Festival Host Committee was created to include prominent Utahns, including Dick Bass, the Texas millionaire, mountaineer, and owner of Snowbird; Sam Battistone, then the owner of the Utah Jazz; Craig Badami, president of the Park City Ski Area, who was later tragically killed in a helicopter accident; and even Alan Osmond of the famous Utah singing family. Sundance had twenty-two people listed as members of the board of directors, including Michael Ovitz, Frank Price (also to die tragically in a helicopter accident), Frank Mancuso, Pat Newcomb, Mike Medavoy, Ted Field, Nathaniel Kwit, and three or four heavy financial hitters out of Texas and the East Coast. Sundance listed a staff of nineteen and the festival added another seventeen. A pass to the 1986 festival cost \$200—\$150 for students. All in all, 20,275 tickets were sold, a 30-percent increase over the previous year. From this point forward, the festival would never look back.

DIRECTORS HECTOR BABENCO AND BOBBY ROTH GO ONE-ON-ONE AT PARK CITY GYM.

The year 1986 also marked the last time I would program the documentary competition, the program I had created and championed. The reason was the stink made by Susan Munoz and Lourdes Portillo over playing their film, *Las Madres: The Mothers of the Plaza de Mayo*, with Lee Shapiro's *Nicaragua Was Our Home*. I remember getting into a testy argument at the closing-night reception with Marc Weiss, a man who later went on to create the highly regarded PBS documentary series *P.O.V.* and someone I didn't really know at the time. He inserted himself into the midst of the controversy by insisting that no one person should have that much authority in the selection process. Being the maverick that I am, I tried to explain that I had used committees before but hadn't found the process terribly effective or satisfying. Right or wrong, I actually preferred to have the stamp of a couple of talented people's personalities on a program. Otherwise, I had a tendency to get a mishmash that lacked any cohesion. He continued to complain to Tony after the festival, and he finally came up with a solution. Karen Cooper, an excellent programmer from New York's Film Forum Theater, would serve as the documentary programmer the next year.

However, I did feel somewhat vindicated some years later, when, sadly, filmmaker Lee Shapiro was killed in a firefight while making a similar secretive and dangerous film in Afghanistan about the Russian invasion. To this day, I feel as if I did the right thing.

FORMER FESTIVAL PROGRAM DIRECTOR TONY SAFFORD AND PETER BISKIND, THEN EDITOR OF *PREMIERE MAGAZINE.*

CHAPTER 7

Full-Court Press

*The overall program for the 1987 United States Film Festival—its focus, strengths, and challenges—should ultimately speak for itself. I do hope however, that in 1987 it is no longer necessary to reiterate the merits and vision of independent cinema. The movement, paralleled and charted throughout the history of this Festival, has come of age, ushering in what I suspect will be a Golden Age not only of films, but also for key personnel in the creative areas of screenwriting, producing, and directing. Opening the past two Festivals with independent films—*The Trip to Bountiful, *and now,* Square Dance*—signals not just our commitment to this type of cinema, but also its maturation. Clearly the movement has a message, and it's here to stay.*

Tony Safford
Program Director
1987 United States Film Festival

At least something was here to stay. I wasn't feeling so secure. I certainly had my hands full, pulling together the increasingly prestigious dramatic competition, as well as holding down a full-time position as the director of producer services for the Utah Film Commission. After reading their scripts, I would meet the filmmakers, usually the producer, director—sometimes the production designer, production manager, or director of photography—at the airport and drive around in a van for days, showing them possible ways to make their pictures in Utah. It was an increasingly active role as the business went up from $18 million to over $32 million a year. By now, I've worked on over eighty feature, documentary, or television projects and assisted with hundreds of commercials shot in Utah. The state has benefited to the tune of over three-quarters of a billion dollars. In 1987, I was increasingly feeling the pressure of effectively doing two important jobs, in part because the film commission was really beginning to take off at the same time as the film festival. I guess I've always been lucky that way.

Yet, the dramatic competition came together nicely. I was beginning to understand the differences in philosophy between Tony and myself regarding what constituted an independent film. I tended to have a more homemade approach, often overlooking production values in favor of grit and heart. Tony had a slightly more commercial take. He responded to urban pictures and slicker production values. I guess maybe that's why he's now working for Twentieth Century Fox, and I'm not.

Still, Tony and all of the Sundance staff were incredibly susceptible to press criticism. In a sense, the national press dictated the terms of engagement. No matter what clever spin was put on, if the press wasn't happy with the program, it could dramatically nudge the selection process in another direction. In many ways that started with the 1987 Festival, which was unfortunate because there were really great films in 1987. The question was whether the press and public were quite ready for them. Make no mistake about it: movies are entirely dependent on the media, now more than ever. At any given time, legions of people are plotting out marketing strategies that require a level of cultural saturation only the mass media can deliver. Little independent films are even more dependent on the press than the guys who can afford to buy advertising.

For the most part, I think the national film critics understand this unique responsibility, but in 1987, some of them weren't in a cajoling mood. Many were resistant to the idea that anything like a movement was going on. When, during one of the panel discussions, Terrence Rafferty of *The Nation* and John Powers with *L.A. Weekly* completely dismissed Martin Rosen's film *Season of Dreams*, a highly touted competition entry made originally under the title *Stacking*, it was a devastating blow to the filmmakers, and had repercussions for the commercial life of the film.

What the mouthy critics didn't know was that I'd encouraged Martin to have the film ready for us at extreme costs—both financial and emotional—and in fairness to him, probably before it was ready. Particularly because he had produced the previous year's winner *Smooth Talk*, his return had a lot riding on it. I had failed to remember the lesson from Victor Nunez's *A Flash of Green* in 1985. Rushing to meet a festival's schedule runs the risk of sinking a film completely if it is not well received by the press.

When Christine Lahti, in her actors' panel discussion, caught wind of the critic's comments, she quickly came to the aid of her movie, but based on Rafferty's and Powers's nasty comments being reported in the national press, Martin Rosen left the festival an upset man. He promised to go back into the editing room, and he was convinced the problem was the music, not the pacing, tone, or theme. But the *American Playhouse* coproduction shot by Richard Bowen never recovered from the festival's criticism, despite Duane Byrge of the *Hollywood Reporter* and his earnest appraisal: "one of the strongest contenders in the independent film competition here at the United States Film Festival, this Spectrafilm release is a spare yet radiant story of independence and self-reliance." The film, starring Megan Follows, Christine Lahti, Frederic Forrest, Jason Gedrick, Ray Baker, and Peter Coyote went absolutely nowhere. I felt terribly responsible, but it was as though the national press was pressuring the filmmakers and festival to come up with something to rival the independent successes of the past like *Stranger Than Paradise, Kiss of the Spider Woman, She's Gotta Have It, True Stories,* and *Blue Velvet.*

As John Powers said in the April 1987 issue of *Film Comment:*

> Instead of following these risk-taking examples, the films at Park City emulated mainstream commercial cinema or betrayed the influence of *American Playhouse* and the Sundance Institute, two influential bodies devoted to earnest adaptation, thematic plot, and boob-tube aesthetics. One should scarcely be surprised that indie films are still on the bunny slopes when its stylistic exemplars are the likes of *El Norte, Smooth Talk,* and *Ordinary People*.

Excuse me? *Ordinary People* an independent film? Didn't *Ordinary People* win the Academy Award for 1980? Not to take anything away from the film, which I quite admired, but Redford said in a *Variety* interview it had a budget of $6.5 million. Redford has often floated the idea that the first film he produced *Downhill Racer*, was really ". . . an independent film done through a studio setup." It cost $1.5 million and undoubtedly was difficult to make—shot mostly with handheld camera—but I'm not sure a film starring Robert Redford really qualifies as an independent—no matter how early in his career it was made or how low the budget was. No one can argue that Robert Redford is actually an independent filmmaker in disguise although he may feel that way in his heart of hearts. Although a talented filmmaker and storyteller, his films certainly don't qualify under Powers's own definition.

Powers went on to blast the festival's program in *Film Comment:*

> What was missing from almost all this year's films was a sense of passion and purpose—the personal, political and aesthetic agendas that could fire an indie movement, define it against existing cinema, and give it some sass and subversive energy.

A careful review of the films in the 1987 festival contradicts John Powers's point in the extreme. *Sherman's March* was the ultimate winner in the documentary category, but the press complained it was a film that was already out in the universe, and it had, in fact, played in Telluride. But there's the rub with the press. They want the festival to be the first opportunity to make a new discovery, but the films have to be uniformly excellent and have discernible potential in the marketplace. The critics operate as though in a cinematic vacuum. They hold up the scepter of the past to condemn the vitality of the present, all the time failing to take into account the marked differences between casts and budgets, and the never-ending tension inherent to the movies between art and commerce. Practically any lout can identify a great movie. It takes real talent to point out to an audience why an odd little film made for very little money and starring people no one knows deserves attention. But in the 1987 festival, it was as though the press expectation for this independent film movement far exceeded the filmmakers' grasp.

In the December 1986 *American Film*, just one month before the 1987 festival, Peter Biskind had said:

> . . . in a year of disappointing studio product, American independent features are in a stronger position than ever before. Hollywood's virtual abdication of the sophisticated, urban adult market has created a space for small, adventurous companies like Island and Cinecom to make more of an impact than would have been felt possible five years ago.

Just one month later, many of the press were singing a very different tune. In hindsight it appears that many films in the 1987 festival were underappreciated.

In my opinion, the film that most deserved press attention was Tim Hunter's *River's Edge*. To be certain, the film produced by Sara Pillsbury and Midge Sanford, distributed by Hemdale Releasing, and starring the emerging cast of Crispin Glover (in a controversial performance), Keanu Reeves, Ione Sky Leitch, Roxana Zal, Daniel Roebuck, and Dennis Hopper (in one of his many memorable performances), was on the high end of independent film production. But the consistency of the performances, coupled with a gripping story and a milieu that anticipated *Slackers*, could have, with some support, reached a significant international audience. All the elements were there for this film to take off in the marketplace. It is a sensational story about a group of high-school friends who notice one of their clan doesn't show up for school. One of the group—the biggest and slowest—casually admits he killed her. The others at first don't believe him, but he later proves it by taking them to the river's edge where they discover her body and freak out. The group quickly becomes conflicted about what to do with this information. Where are their loyalties?

River's Edge was definitely subversive. The characters had real arc, thanks to the excellent script by Neal Jimenez. Viewers actually cared how it was all going to turn out, and Dennis Hopper's line about his beard looking like a glazed donut is one of the all-time classics in cinema. This film could have easily been the *sex, lies, and videotape* of 1987 except that it had already played in Telluride; it was on the controversial side—given the film's ethics and sexual politics—and the press failed to rally around it.

Another film that could have crescendoed at the 1987 festival is *Seize the Day*, based on the popular Saul Bellow novel and starring the up-and-coming Robin Williams in an early dramatic performance. In fact, we were just barely able to play the film because his handlers were uncertain they wanted his comedic career tarnished by the exposure. *Seize the Day* is an uncompromising and relentless film about a forty-year-old man, Tommy Wilhelm who is struggling to find some evidence of humanity in an otherwise uncaring and materialistic world. Oddly enough, the film would probably be better received today precisely because Robin Williams has become such a big star. But in 1987, the film was largely ignored by the press, which meant it was going to be ignored by the public, too.

Because of a strange coincidence, I might have had the chance to turn the situation around had I known then what I came to learn later about the handlers' misgivings. I had been in New York earlier in the fall and saw *Seize the Day* long before the public and press. I liked the film and knew that we could make some hay with it at the festival. I thought it was an authentic—if a bit depressing—film.

I was returning to my hotel from one of the many late-night affairs, walking, as I often did, alone among the deserted streets of Manhattan. Suddenly, from around a corner came an athletic man in a hooded sweatshirt, followed by a young woman, also in sweats. As they approached me on the darkened street, I thought at first that it might be a mugger, then that it was someone I knew. As we passed, I realized it was Robin Williams, probably coming home from a workout at the gym. I turned around, and in my late-night revelry shouted back at him, "Nice job in *Seize the Day.*" His first reaction was to acknowledge some drunken fan's recognition; then he realized it was for a movie that no one had seen yet and a dramatic performance. He just kept on trucking, but I often wonder what would have happened if we had both stopped and chatted about it, if he might have shown up for the 1987 festival to support the film despite his handlers' advice. The little film ended up buried on PBS. Such is the destiny of films and people who have handlers.

Two other films should have been embraced by the press but weren't for very different reasons. They also happened to split the grand prize at the festival. One was Gary Walkow's *The Trouble with Dick*, an entertaining and inventive comedy about a science-fiction writer who moves into a house in Los Angeles seeking solitude to finish his interplanetary novel only to be seduced by his old college friend (Susan Dey), the aerobicised landlady (Elaine Giftos), and her femme-fatale daughter (Elizabeth Gorcey).

The film is wildly inventive in a genre that independents have a hard time handling well. Films that have fantasy moments in which viewers enter into either dream states, flashbacks, daydreams, or pure imagination—as is the case here—usually fall flat on their faces. They don't have the money for great design or opticals, certainly not for computer-generated imagery. As a result, the few independent films that attempt these effects fail miserably. If they succeed, say in the case of the Coen brothers, they are immediately swept into the Hollywood maelstrom.

Gary Walkow's fantasy scenes involve both the state of mind of his main character, played by Tom Villard and figures from the story within the novel, titled *The Galactic Chain Gang*. This group features a hysterical David Clennon as an escaped prisoner on an alien planet, looking for a way out. The film is clever and visually accomplished, yet, despite winning the competition, received only a lukewarm reception from the press at the festival.

According to the *Variety* review: "Sci-fi sequences could have been much more imaginative and bizarre, and thereby have added to the amount of incident in the picture, which is basically restricted to two settings and a limited number of characters." Was it *Star Wars* this reviewer wanted? Undoubtedly he had never faced the challenges of actually making a film—especially on a very restricted budget. The film could have been successful had the press gotten behind it. It had strong performances and was funny, sexy, and inventive. But the press in 1987 didn't want to jump on the bandwagon of independent film before it actually rolled into town.

The other cowinner receiving a ho-hum response from the press was Jill Godmillow's *Waiting for the Moon*, starring Linda Hunt and Linda Bassett as Alice B. Toklas and Gertrude Stein. Produced by Sandra Schulberg and also starring Andrew McCarthy and Bruce McGill, the film is a rapturous portrait of the two famous Parisians. It was a mix of fact and fiction to create an imagined, though possible, five days in which the remarkable women entertain the likes of Hemingway, Picasso, and Apollonaire while testing the depths of their relationship and the parameters of their love. The literate script—written by Mark Magill—was largely atmospheric yet solidified by a remarkable performance from the Academy Award–winning Linda Hunt, who was in attendance to honor the film. However, she confessed spontaneously at the festival awards dinner that in the making, the film ". . . got a little bit lost. It was very reassuring to see it put together, to see what we had lost come together." The film was ultimately released by Skouras Pictures to weak results and aired on *American Playhouse*.

Besides Martin Rosen's film *Season of Dreams* (reported by David Galligan in a mean-spirited review in *Dramalogue* as a film where "the grass grew faster than this slow-witted dirge"), other disappointing films for the press included Sara Driver's *Sleepwalk* (shot by Jim Jarmusch; Driver had produced *Stranger Than Paradise*); *Walking on the Moon*, directed by Raphael Silver and produced by his daughter Dina (called "a delightful festival sleeper" by *Hollywood Reporter's* Duane Byrge); and Rachid Kerdouche's 16 mm oddball psychosexual comedy *Her Name Is Lisa*, which *Variety* dismissed in its review as an "inept fish-out-of-water comedy" with lines like this: "Many successful comedies from *Beverly Hills Cop* on down have effectively made hay out of similar fish-out-of-water formats, but the approach here is both unhip and unfunny." How ludicrous to compare a $26,000 self-financed film starring an East Village guy named Rockets Redglare with *Beverly Hills Cop*. The Hollywood gatekeepers, it seemed, were working overtime.

Five films in competition did receive some critical praise, including Academy Award–nominee (for his documentary on Japanese-American internment *Unfinished Business*) Steven Okazaki's excellent fiction debut, *Living on Tokyo Time,* produced by Lynn O'Donnell and Dennis Hayashi, about a nineteen-year-old Japanese woman's first visit to America and her encounter with a shy, would-be rock and roller who is unwilling to get involved in the world until he is convinced by a friend to marry the visitor so she can get a green card. It is a bittersweet romantic comedy that had the mark of a genuine hit. Well acted and superbly directed, also shot by Steven Okazaki, the film was successful because we cared about the characters and their predicaments, and they were transformed by their decisions. *Variety* gave it a grudgingly favorable review, calling it "slight, but charming . . . another regional film by and about a minority culture not often depicted on the big screen." But the review went on to suggest "There is only so far you can go with obviously amateur performers, and a little more urgency in both the pacing and the important point-making would have helped a lot." *Living on Tokyo Time* did eventually receive limited distribution, after being picked up by new president of Skouras Pictures, Jeff Lipsky.

Phillip Hartman's *No Picnic*, starring David Brisbin as a washed-up rock musician who supplies records to New York jukeboxes, is a quirky and, at times, hilarious look at one man's life run amok. Executive-produced by Chris Sievernich, who had produced *Paris, Texas,* the film garnered an award at the festival for Peter Hutton's excellent black-and-white cinematography, but went absolutely nowhere commercially. It really did turn out to be no picnic, underscoring the adage that one should never give a film a negative-sounding title that critics can use as the closing line to slam-dunk the movie.

Connie Kaiserman's *My Little Girl,* produced by Thomas Turley and executive-produced by Ishmail Merchant, starred an illustrious cast of James Earl Jones as a shelter worker and Mary Stuart Masterson as an affluent young woman who spends her summers working at the shelter, with secondary parts played by Peter Gallagher, Geraldine Page, and Anne Meara. It's a keenly observed coming-of-age story about class, friendship, idealism, and growing up. The film received a rather unenthused response from distributors and the press alike. It seemed like a softer version of *The Dozens* that had previously played at the festival. Duane Byrge of the *Hollywood Reporter,* one of the earliest voices supporting these kinds of independent films, had kind words for *My Little Girl*, calling it ". . . a warm and vigorous tale of growing up in America. It is a tale of growing up rich, and it is a tale of growing up poor. Both hard-edged and heartwarming, it is a celebratory glimpse into the inner stuff of young kids, and an uncompromising look at class distinction in the United States." But he went on to admit that the film's best venue was probably cable, not a pleasant thought for anyone who had dreams of that elusive theatrical release.

PRODUCTION STILL FROM JOANNE AKALATIS'S *DEAD END KIDS*, PRODUCED BY MARION GODFREY AND MONTY DIAMOND.

The same can be said of Texas filmmaker Andy Anderson's *Postive I.D.* Although a complex and taut thriller with a clever twist at the end, the film gained some recognition for the professor filmmaker but ultimately failed to get to market, in part because there weren't any recognizable actors in the cast.

JoAnne Akalaitis (an Obie Award–winning theater director, who took over the Public Theater after Joseph Papp) had an avant-garde, very unconventional narrative in *Dead End Kids* that looked at the illuminating key moments in the history of nuclear power. Produced by Marian Godfrey and my good friend Monty Diamond, this inventive film included song-and-dance numbers, archival footage, re-created historical and fictional characters, and a seedy comic who plays with a dead chicken. With music supplied by David Byrne and Philip Glass, the film portrays the ever-gnawing presence of nuclear war in a compelling and caustically witty way.

Perhaps the most successful film to emerge out of the dramatic competition in 1987 was Lizzie Borden's austere *Working Girls*, about the inner workings of labor and management in an upscale Manhattan brothel. The film starred Louise Smith, Ellen McElduff (who also starred in *Dead End Kids*), Amanda Goodwin, Marusia Zach, Janne Peters, and Helen Nicholas who gave amazingly believable performances as prostitutes who have chosen this as a good alternative to the drudgery of a middle-class existence. It was ultimately an empowering film that didn't shy away from the truth of its characters.

Undoubtedly, the real sleeper of the dramatic competition was the oddball *Sullivan's Pavilion*, a very personal film about filmmaking; raising a family; drinking beer; and searching for the meaning of life, art, and bears pooping in the woods somewhere in the Adirondacks of upstate New York. The irreverent film by Fred Sullivan about his own family struggles is infused with such an original sense of humor and cinematic zest for life, one can't resist its unique voice. The film became the talk of the festival, aided by the filmmaker's willingness to identify himself in the media as "Adirondack Fred." Anyone who could drink this much Budweiser beer couldn't escape without an award for originality from the national jury and some form of limited theatrical release agreement.

FILMMAKER FRED SULLIVAN MADE THE SLEEPER HIT *SULLIVAN'S PAVILION.*

The documentary films—for the first time programmed by Karen Cooper from New York's vital Film Forum alternative theater—came in for even more press criticism than my dramatic features. As John Powers in *Film Comment* vehemently stated:

> Despite its cheery staff, egalitarian vibes, and immaculate organization (under the auspices of Robert Redford's Sundance Institute), the 1987 U.S. Film Festival was more notable for the skiing and the parties than for the American independent movies that are its raison d'être. Indeed the 31 films in competition showed the aching limitations of today's indie cinema and suggested this movement isn't moving. Rather, it has settled into a complacent mediocrity whose axiom is "Play it safe."

Everyone seemed to know it. In the documentary competition, the jury was so unimpressed by the entries that it wanted to give no prizes at all. When program director Tony Safford objected, the jury ultimately awarded top prize to Ross McElwee's *Sherman's March*, a popular choice already validated by critics across the country. But to express their genuine dismay at the level of the offerings, they gave honorable mention to David Bradbury's *Chile: When Will It End?*— an Australian film outside competition.

PRODUCTION STILL FROM ROSS MCELWEE'S PERSONAL DOCUMENTARY *SHERMAN'S MARCH.*

At first glance, the documentary selections did seem to have a certain sameness—all were either about politics or personality. The films included Keva Rosenfeld's disturbing film on high schoolers in Torrance, California, *All-American High;* Barbara Margolis's history of the cold war, *Are We Winning, Mommy?*; Robert Richter and Catherine Warnow's self-explained, *Do Not Enter: The Visa War Against Ideas*; John Junkerman, Michael Camerini, and James MacDonald's *Hellfire: A Journey from Hiroshima*, a prize-winning film about a Japanese husband and wife, muralists known throughout the world as "the artists of the atomic bomb"; and an eventual Academy Award–nominee: Oren Rudavsky's film about a bar mitzvah in Cracow, Poland, *Spark Among the Ashes*, produced with David Leitner and Rick Smigielski.

Films on the personality side of the equation included some excellent pieces by preeminent documentary filmmakers: Michael Blackwood's film on composer Philip Glass as he begins to mount an opera based on an Egyptian pharaoh, *A Composer's Notes*; Aviva Slesin (who was to win an Academy Award in 1987 for *The Ten Year Lunch*) delivering a wonderful tribute to director William Wyler, called simply *Directed by William Wyler*; Amran Nowak and Kirk Simon's *Isaac in America* about Isaac Bashevis Singer's remarkable life and work (nominated for an Academy Award in 1987 and distributed by Mitchell Block's Direct Cinema); Nicholas Broomfield and Joan Churchill's insightful *Lily Tomlin*, depicting the comedienne and her collaborator Jane Wagner as they begin from scratch to create her one-woman Broadway show *Search for Signs of Intelligent Life in the Universe;* Richard P. Rogers and Jill Janows's film on the life, work, and preoccupations of the pediatrician and poet; *William Carlos Williams*; D. A. Pennebaker and Chris Hegedus's *Jimi Plays Monterey*, culled from the outtakes of their other concert films and both a teleportation back in time and a sensual tribute to the guitar master and the summer of love, which played out of competition; and David and Albert Maysles with two films—*Ozawa* (codirected with Susan Froemke and Deborah Dickson), a portrait of Seiji Ozawa as conductor of the Boston Symphony Orchestra, and *Islands* (codirected with Charlotte Zwerin) about the environmental artist Christo's wrapping some islands in Miami's Biscayne Bay in pink plastic. Amazing in hindsight, six of the film's titles were simply the names of their subjects.

Yet it was Ross McElwee's remarkable search for love in *Sherman's March* that stole the hearts and minds of audiences. Even the press recognized the wondrous qualities of this very personal film as the filmmaker retraces the Civil War general's march through the South but gets severely sidetracked by his own obsessions, namely seeking women as the source of happiness. But the press was already onto the film prior to Sundance because of its screening at Telluride and elsewhere through distribution from First Run Features, which they were only too happy to underscore in their reviews.

The press had a generally favorable response to most of the premieres, including *Square Dance,* starring a fourteen-year-old Winona Ryder and Rob Lowe as a mentally retarded character, Jason Robards as an irascible grandfather, and Jane Alexander as a hard-boiled mother; Jim McBride's New Orleans cop drama *The Big Easy*, starring Dennis Quaid and Ellen Barkin; David Anspaugh's *Hoosiers*, starring Gene Hackman and Dennis Hopper in emotionally winning performances; Bruce Beresford's *The Fringe Dwellers* about an aboriginal family living in desperate conditions on the edge of a small outback town; and David Jones's *84 Charing Cross Road*, starring Anne Bancroft and Anthony Hopkins as star-crossed pen pals.

However, at the conclusion of the 1987 festival, there could be little doubt about the pressure being added to the event by a grumbling press, and that made everyone at Sundance a little crazy. The full-court press was on.

Before the 1988 film festival, Tony Safford and I had yet another meeting. I assumed I was going to be sent packing—some kind of final break from the past, a sacrificial lamb to the hungry press keen to see some organizational response to their criticism. Instead, Tony expressed his gratitude for all I had done for the festival—a tack that has always been easier to do in private than in public for Sundance—and then said the institute was restructuring the selection process. They wanted to create a committee for both dramatic and documentary competitions and would like me to serve on the dramatic committee. I was actually surprised I was to be included at all. Tony and I didn't see eye-to-eye on many films, and I had always felt he was just biding his time to get rid of me. I was willing to be on a committee because the alternative was not to be involved at all. Tony admitted he didn't have any idea how such a committee process would operate, but they wanted my participation. In a funny way, I felt I had to prove myself all over again.

Tony explained the new selection process in the first paragraph of his introduction to the 1988 festival program:

> American independent cinema has cycles of creativity and retreat, and our festival has become the barometer to judge these vicissitudes. After last year's program, three respected national critics, Peter Biskind in *American Film*, John Powers in *Film Comment,* and Terrence Rafferty in *The Nation*, bemoaned the lack of originality in the films presented. . . .
>
> With the notable exception of *River's Edge*, we too had this sense: that American independent cinema, while gaining momentum, had lost its earlier vigor and eccentricity. "Independent cinema," once a partisan phrase signaling difference, had become respectable, conservative, perhaps even fashionable.
>
> This assessment led us to plan the 1988 program with an aggressive and challenging strategy designed to motivate American independent cinema to greater achievements. That strategy was to "surround" the American Independent Film Competition with other cinematic models offering a strong purpose and point of view—precisely those elements that seemed lacking in our own work.

In order to save face and fire up the interest for 1988's selections, Tony went on to qualify:

> The irony is the demise—or at least conservative turn—of American independent film we greatly exaggerated. A cycle of creativity has returned to the movement. The films assembled here in both sections of the competition are rich and rigorous beyond our expectations.

I determined to have a strong voice in this new committee structure. Other members of the committee included producers rep John Pierson, Marjorie Skouras of Skouras Pictures, and Tony Safford. On the documentary committee were Mitchell Block of Direct Cinema, Karen Cooper of the Film Forum, Robert Hawk with the Film Arts Foundation, and Tony Safford. Despite the obvious conflicts of

ROBERT REDFORD AND GARY BEER AT A SUNDANCE PRESS CONFERENCE.

interest among the committee members, it was a good mix of people with wide-ranging tastes.

The year 1988 also marked the introduction of Tom Wilhite, a former Disney executive, as the newly created executive director of the Sundance Institute. He was a rather shy, angular man who was brought in to expand Sundance's circle of influence as it pertained to film and other arts disciplines and, along with the Sundance Institute's vice president, Gary Beer, on Redford's orders, create a worldwide presence for Sundance. They forged a relationship between the Tokyo International Film Festival and the Sundance Institute.

STAFF AND FILMMAKERS ENJOY LATE-NIGHT PARTY AT A PINNACLE CONDO IN PARK CITY.

The other thing that came out of Tom Wilhite's tenure at Sundance was an iron-clad edict that in the future, no one was ever to use "the" in front of Sundance Institute. It was to be referred to simply as "Sundance Institute," no matter how funny it sounded in a sentence. It was as though through sheer force of will, the organization was out to singlehandedly reformat grammatical structure. The attitude seemed to be if they could change the accepted English usage for a definite article it could change the world!

By now the Sundance Institute had an ongoing staff of twenty-one people, many of whom were holdovers from the early years, including the inimitable Cinda Holt as the managing director of the festival, Johann Jacobs as the financial manager, Maria Schaeffer as the general manager, Debbie Snider as an assistant festival manager, Mark Chambers as the box-office manager for the festival, and David Chambers as the managing director of artistic development. Michelle Satter was the director of the feature-

FESTIVAL STALWARTS JILL MILLER AND NICOLE GUILLEMET BEHIND THE BARS OF THE BOX OFFICE.

film program; David Newman, the director of the music program; David Kranes, the director of the Playwrights Lab; and, of course, Tony Safford, the program director of the film festival. The 1988 festival also marked the introduction of two staff people who would become important later: Nicole Guillemet as the registrar of the festival and Alberto Garcia as the print manager.

The institute's board now numbered twenty-five individuals, representing a wide range of industry insiders and financial heavy hitters, including Jack Crosby, chairman of the Rust Group; Irene Diamond, president of the Aaron Diamond Foundation; Garth Drabinsky, chairman, CEO, and president of Cineplex Odeon; Ted Field, president of Interscope Communications; George Gund, owner of hockey and basketball teams; Frank Mancuso, then CEO of Paramount Pictures; Daniel Melnick, president of IndieProd; Michael Ovitz, then president of Creative Artists Agency; industry giant Frank Price; producer David Puttnam, just ousted as president of Columbia Pictures; Edward Robinson with First Boston Corporation; Seiji Tsutsumi, chairman of the Seibu Saison Group; and James Wiatt, president of International Creative Management. It was an impressive collection of major players with myriad reasons and agendas to be connected to Redford and Sundance. It also marked a definite strategy on the part of Sundance to place itself at the power center of the New Hollywood as the source for developing and showcasing emerging invigorating talent to an industry whose very survival was dependent on the nurturing and ultimate exploitation of this chorus of new voices.

GARY BEER, MICHAEL OVITZ, BARRY LEVINSON, AND ROBERT REDFORD.

In many ways, the structure of independent film production—raising the necessary capital privately—was Hollywood. What better scenario for studios with substantial worldwide distribution and dwindling financial resources at a time when production and creative costs were spiraling than to palm off the financial obligations of film production. Then they could pick and choose what kind films were allowed to enter the distribution pipeline. In my mind, what was critical was opening the doors to the marketplace for a personal cinema, built not on celebrity, genre, formula, or investment, but on one person's passion and vision for a story. If Sundance was going to be about anything, it had to be about sharing this vision for a personal cinema. The question was becoming whether Sundance could bridge the historic gap between art and commerce in an industry uniquely codependent on these contradictory impulses.

Traditionally a festival trailer was produced locally each year, and 1988's trailer was the most memorable and symbolic one yet. Conceived, written, produced, and directed by Tim Nelson and Arthur Pembleton, it featured a small film can with a mind of its own—determined to show up at the theater despite everything that got in its way. It was "the little film can that could." It brought thunderous applause every time it screened because it really captured the spirit of the time. All things were possible, and not even the complaints of a resistant press could deter the little film cans from reaching the theaters.

As Randa Haines, director of *Children of a Lesser God,* said in the program guide to the 1988 festival:

> The United States Film Festival provides a home for the wonderfully obsessed people of the independent film community who have had the courage to make their movies by their own wits. Here, they come together in a beautiful setting with an enthusiastic audience hungry for the possibility of new energy and fresh vision.

Redford was even more precise in his 1988 interview with *Variety's* Todd McCarthy:

> What we encourage is to support the filmmaker's point of view being protected, so that it doesn't get contaminated or touched by too many hands. Independence to me has more to do with the feelings of the filmmaker and how you feel when you make a film.

The 1988 festival marked the tenth anniversary—something to certainly celebrate. I was delighted with the progress that had been made—individually and for the organization—but most importantly for the inroads we had all made into the marketplace of ideas. In ten short years, the festival had helped put the American independent film movement on the map for the press and public, and I thought we should mark the occasion. I proposed to Tony Safford and Tom Wilhite that I write a ten-year commemorative article for the program guide. Once the article was written and about to go to press, however, Tony and Tom were uncomfortable with my point of view, which suggested that the festival had been poised to emerge as a successful event with or without Sundance's help. The article became a contentious issue between the three of us and ended up buried in the back pages of the catalogue. The feeling I always had was that Sundance could be proud of the history of the festival and how it had played a key role in the creation of the institute. What I discovered in the controversy surrounding the ten-year article was that Sundance wanted to bury the history of the organization, even if it meant revising the actual genesis. The institute acted the same way in 1998 on the twentieth anniversary of the festival.

The competition program for the 1988 festival was truly a remarkable collection of independent films, which could have been even more so had three films not dropped out at the last minute. The first was Ramon Menendez's fabulously mov-

STORYTELLING AND SCREENWRITING GURUS FRANK DANIEL AND FRANK PIERSON ON A PANEL.

ing film starring Edward James Olmos, *Walking on Water* (subsequently retitled *Stand and Deliver*), the true story of Jaime Escalante, a math teacher at East L.A.'s Garfield High School and his inspirational mentoring of his students. If the film had not been pulled by *American Playhouse* and Warner Brothers—officially because of necessary sound rerecording and clearance issues—I think the film would have won some awards and could have been one of the real discoveries of 1988.

Ken Friedman's controversial *Made in the U.S.A.* also dropped out because of a contract dispute with executive producers Derek Gibson and John Daly of Hemdale. Friedman was so exercised over the cancellation that he rented the Egyptian Theatre with his former film-school roommate Mitchell Block's help and scheduled the first midnight screening in Park City with his cut of the film. Only sparsely attended, the film was an interesting shifting of a genre's gears, a kind of environmental road movie. To my knowledge, this was the only public screening the film ever received.

Finally, Peter Hoffman's debut film *Valentino Returns*, repped by selection committee member John Pierson, was also pulled from the program.

Still, the films in competition were again an outstanding collection of groundbreaking independents. Wildly eccentric John Waters arrived in Park City with his eleventh film, *Hairspray*, the music-filled social comedy about dance-crazed teenagers and the integration of Baltimore (the Hairdo Capital of the world) in 1962. With a cast featuring Ricki Lake, Divine, Jerry Stiller, Debbie Harry, Sonny Bono, Pia Zadora, Ric Ocasek, and Waters, himself, the film was an inspired pandemonium of a movie that really defied logic. Waters called the movie, his first in seven years, ". . . a dance movie, about child stars and their pushy parents, but in a hillbilly milieu."

Once in Park City, Waters was inextricably drawn to a real-life drama unfolding just sixteen miles away in a small Mormon community known as Marion, Utah. Inside a snowbound log farmhouse, ex-communicated Mormon polygamist Addam Swapp was barricaded with his three wives, six children, various extended-family members, and an arsenal of weapons against an armed coalition of local, state, and federal police.

Days before, under direct communication from God (according to Swapp), he had allegedly blown the roof off a Mormon chapel, on the tenth anniversary of the controversial death of John Singer, also a polygamist and the father of two of Swapp's three wives. The Swapp standoff was—at the time—the longest FBI hostage negotiation in United States history. One could actually look from the top of the chairlifts in Deer Valley and see the hostage compound.

Standing outside the Swapp cabin, surrounded by hordes of lawmen and journalists in the freezing Wasatch Mountain cold, was John Waters, clad totally in black, occasionally pulling down his terrorist-style ski mask to smoke through the nose-level slit and trade off-color jokes with stir-crazy journalists. A longtime news junkie, crime buff, and voyeur, Waters was only too happy to hang out with his festival driver at the country's hottest crime scene. After all, Waters had spent thousands of dollars crisscrossing the country in pursuit of courtroom thrills. As he said in his autobiography, *Shock Value*, "All people look better under arrest. Murder is my favorite charge, with kidnapping, terrorism and armed robbery following exactly in that order." Had Water's schedule allowed it, he could've waited around until the shooting started when a corrections officer was killed and members of the Swapp family were wounded. It was a bizarre footnote and one completely in character for both Waters and the surroundings—an unholy alliance if ever there was one.

DIRECTOR JOHN WATERS SAID, "ALL PEOPLE LOOK BETTER UNDER ARREST."

The philosophical counterpoint to *Hairspray* was the delightful animated film *The Brave Little Toaster*. Directed by Jerry Rees and produced by none other than Tom Wilhite (with Donald Kushner), it probably should have played out of competition.

Not that conflicts of interest have ever been a problem for Sundance and the festival despite Sundance's affiliation with more and more projects as time goes by. First among the examples is Michael Hoffman's excellent *Promised Land*. His first feature, *Restless Natives*, was a hit at the 1986 festival, and *Promised Land* was an assured second effort, developed at the Sundance Lab and executive-produced by Robert Redford and Andy Meyer. It featured the practically unknown Meg Ryan, Keifer Sutherland, Jason Gedrick, and Tracy Pollan. In fairness, I should say that because it was made in Utah, I worked extensively on it in my role with the Utah Film Commission, but it was eminently qualified to play in competition.

The same was true of Sandy Smolan's fine *Rachel River*, also workshopped at the Sundance Lab and adapted from the short stories of Carol Bly by Judith Guest, who

PRODUCTION STILL FROM MICHAEL HOFFMAN'S *PROMISED LAND.*

also scripted *Ordinary People.* Make no mistake about it—with fine performances by Pamela Reed, Viveca Lindfors, James Olson, and Craig T. Nelson—the film belonged in the competition on its own merit. At the conclusion of its premiere at the Egyptian Theatre, Pamela Reed announced one added bonus to the film's creation—she and director Sandy Smolan had fallen in love and were going to get married.

Along with films having Sundance connections, *American Playhouse* flexed its muscles in the 1988 competition. Besides having coproduced *Rachel River*, Lindsay Law's PBS program was also represented by Joel Oliansky's *The Silence at Bethany*, written by Joyce Keener and produced by Tom Cherones about a Mennonite community torn between liberal and conservative factions, starring Mark Moses and Susan Wilder.

Jan Egelson returned to the festival with his unforgettable interpretation of Lanford Wilson's *Lemon Sky*, starring Kevin Bacon, Lindsay Crouse, Tom Atkins, Kyra Sedgwick, and Laura White. Set in the southern California of the 1950s, it is a story of a father and a son trying to reconcile their relationship as the son is introduced to the father's new family after a decade of estrangement. Told in a very dreamlike fashion—with characters sometimes revealing their inner thoughts directly to the camera in a confessional manner—the film is a standout in writing, direction, performance, and design. During the selection process, I lobbied hard for *Lemon Sky's* inclusion in the program. Had *Walking on Water*, also screened, *American Playhouse* would have had four of the twelve films in competition. Even Isaac Artenstein's period story of a Chicano radio announcer who finally risks his own success in a confrontation with the white establishment, *Break of Dawn*, had all the sensibilities of a *Playhouse* production, even though it wasn't one.

PRODUCER RICK STEVENSON AND ROBERT REDFORD VISITING A SET.

Clearly the most interesting films in dramatic competition in 1988 were by two returning filmmakers—both former winners at the festival—David Burton Morris (*Purple Haze*) with his hilarious *Patti Rocks* and Rob Nilsson (*Northern Lights, Signal Seven*) with the remarkable experiment *Heat and Sunlight*. I lobbied hard for both films, really having to champion *Heat and Sunlight* to Tony.

Patti Rocks is David Burton Morris's follow-up to his decade-earlier film *Loose Ends*, featuring the same two actors and protagonists now twelve years later. Starring Chris Mulkey, John Jenkins, and Karen Landry, the film becomes a long-night's journey into daylight in the form of a beery road trip by two friends to visit a woman one of them has gotten pregnant—the married one, of course. As the night progresses, and the beers and the miles fly by, so, too, does the riff about fantasies, preferences, dreams, and boasts in graphic language seldom heard on the big screen at the time. Once the characters reach their destination, the braggadocio of the man-to-man scenes stands in stark contrast to the emotional directness of the male-to-female encounters. It's a very controversial film, mainly due to the misogynist subtext of much of the dialogue, but ultimately a very funny and serious one. The film should have gathered a prize in Park City but didn't.

DIRECTOR MICHAEL HOFFMAN SETS UP A SHOT IN *PROMISED LAND*.

The big winner of the 1988 dramatic competition was Rob Nilsson's amazing *Heat and Sunlight*, without a doubt the most experimental film in the festival. Tearing a page from John Cassavetes, Nilsson's black-and-white drama focuses on the final sixteen hours of a love affair between a photojournalist, played by Nilsson himself, and his dancer/choreographer girlfriend Carmen, played by Consuelo Faust. Shot on three-quarter-inch video and transferred to 35 mm film, *Heat and Sunlight* is an improvised exercise that's very believable. The result is perhaps one of the most personally risky films ever committed to celluloid—an amazingly cathartic experience.

When the film won the grand prize, I was standing next to Rob because I wanted to see his reaction to the announcement. I was so happy that his experiment had succeeded this well and the jury had recognized it. I also felt personally vindicated since I had been the strongest advocate for the film's inclusion in competition. I was continuing to serve an important role in guiding the festival in the direction I thought it needed to go. *Heat and Sunlight* winning the grand prize solidified that impression, and *Lemon Sky* picking up a Special Jury Award didn't hurt, either.

The documentary competition was no less impressive. Jennifer Fox's remarkable *Beirut: The Last Home Movie* about three sisters—scions of Lebanon's wealthiest families—who live with their mother and brother in a 200-year-old palace located in one of the city's most heavily bombed areas won the grand prize.

Other highlights included Bruce Weber's *Broken Noses*, applying his penchant for men's fashion photography to the brutish world of boxing; Marc Huestis's touching portrait of AIDS victim and actor Chuck Solomon in *Chuck Solomon: Coming of Age*; Bill Couturié's heart-wrenching film using the words written home by men in Vietnam, *Dear America*; Alan and Susan Raymond's return (*The Third Coast*) with a look at a pivotal year in the life of Elvis Presley, *Elvis '56*; Alan Berliner's eloquent experiment in family matters, *The Family Album*; Academy Award–winner Deborah Shaffer's *Fire from the Mountain*, a kind of oral history based on the autobiography of revolutionary Nicaraguan Omar Cabezas; Alan Francovich's important film on the CIA's involvement in Central America, *The Houses Are Full of Smoke*; Lilyan Sievernich's *John Huston & the Dubliners*, shot on the set of his last film, based on the James Joyce novella *The Dead*; Geoffrey Dunne and Mark Schwartz's *Miss . . . or Myth*, a documentary look at the Miss California Beauty Pageant; Frederick Wiseman's latest labor, *Missile*, as he follows the training of a squadron of men in charge of nuclear warheads; Robert Stone's *Radio Bikini*, nominated in 1987 for an Academy Award, about an American veteran who witnessed the atomic blasts on Bikini Island; Anthony Thomas's incredible indictment of the marriage between fundamentalist Christians and the political right, a film that was abruptly pulled from the PBS schedule, *Thy Kingdom Come, Thy Will be Done*; and George Paul Csicsery's amusing take inside the world of romance writers, *Where the Heart Roams*.

Other highlights of the 1988 festival included Louis Malle with his very personal film *Au Revoir, Les Enfants* as the opening-night premiere; the gracious Olympia Dukakis for her role in the popular *Moonstruck*; Isabella Rossellini and David Lynch—standing like fish out of water in the cacophony of the Riverhorse Cafe—as stars of Tina Rathbone's *Zelly and Me*; diminutive spitfire Samuel Fuller, spiritual father of the New American Gothic film, in a well-earned and received tribute—traipsing around the snowy streets of Park City in a parka that was bigger than he was; an Argentinean sidebar programmed by B Ruby Rich that had problems receiving prints due to a military action in Argentina during the festival; the first year of Jonathan Sanger and Jana Sue Memel's Discovery Program, which included the eventual Academy Award–winning short film by Bryan Gordon, *Ray's Male Heterosexual Dance Hall*; the first program of new American shorts not from the Discovery Program, called Rogue's Gallery, programmed by former driver and print manager Alberto Garcia, which contained the seldom-seen Todd Haynes's film *Superstar*, the story of Karen Carpenter as told with Barbie dolls (a film John Waters said "restored my faith in youth"); and the sight of Nobel laureate Gabriel Garcia Marquez marching through the snows of Utah, having finally successfully overcome the obstacles to getting a visa to enter the country, thanks in large part to Redford.

When the ten days were over, the festival had managed to increase attendance to 33,000 tickets sold, with about 1,500 out-of-state participants. Even then, Redford was concerned about the growth of the event, stating that "a lot of thought has been put into the scale of this thing. We're at the point now where this is it. This is the first year we've put a ceiling on the number of outside visitors."

CANDACE BERGEN AND LOUIS MALLE AT SUNDANCE RESORT.

Still, when the reviews came in, a complaining press refrain continued to drive much of the decision making. As Todd McCarthy stated in his *Variety* wrap-up:

> Since a festival can only choose from the pictures that are available, an observer can only surmise that after a period of exciting growth and achievement, the indie movement has entered the doldrums, quality-wise. Few, if any, attendees expressed great enthusiasm for the general run of films offered.
>
> Visibility of corporate sponsors was much greater this year, which is tolerable up to a point, but became disturbing to everyone when it was an executive from American Express and not a filmmaker, as in years past, who announced and distributed the awards.

Deborah Caulfield, with the *Los Angeles Times*, wrote at the close of the festival:

> In this once-quaint ski town described recently by Robert Redford as "more city than park," the 10th annual United States Film Festival concluded Sunday amid signs that it too is undergoing a not-necessarily-for-the-better transformation.
>
> The exposure that Redford's Sundance Institute–sponsored festival affords to independent filmmakers is widely regarded as beneficial, but the festival's burgeoning size and popularity are threatening to erode the intimate, informal nature that has been the hallmark of the event.
>
> In addition, the festival, which used to be populated almost entirely by filmmakers, has taken on a much more commercial atmosphere with the presence of distributors, publicists, agents, managers and studio development executives.

The pressure was on for a breakthrough film at precisely the same time the festival was bursting at the seams. The scene was set, unwittingly, for what would follow the next year, when another former festival volunteer driver would emerge with a film that would change everything.

PENN AND TELLER HAM IT UP AT THE SUNDANCE FILM FESTIVAL.

CHAPTER 8

The Beginning of the Glory Years

Members of the 1988 jury, producers Gale Ann Hurd (*The Terminator, Aliens, The Abyss*) and Ed Pressman (*Badlands, True Stories, Wall Street*) made very laudatory remarks in the 1989 program guide. Hurd said:

> The United States Film Festival is without peer as the premiere forum for American independent filmmakers. It provides a vital and necessary arena for the exchange of brash ideas and unconventional approaches to original filmmaking—filmmaking which must strike a resonant chord as an art form, while simultaneously avoiding the purgatory of economic inviability.

As one of the most financially successful producers in Hollywood, Hurd had avoided economic purgatory all right. But her kind words aside, how many independent films has she financed or produced? Pressman's producing or executive-producing credits at least reinforced the accuracy of his quote:

> The United States Film Festival is one of the foremost showcases of unique and daring quality films. It is also a meeting ground for dynamic independent filmmakers, a forum for ideas and visions—ideas and visions that ultimately shape the future of American cinema.

Anyone who produced *Badlands* is okay in my book and has every right to say or support any damn thing he pleases. But the truth is that 1989's festival marked a turning point in the genesis of the festival. Perhaps the entire future of independent film was riding on the program compiled by Tony Safford and the other programers.

As Redford stated at the festival's opening press conference, reported by Todd McCarthy in *Variety* on January 20, 1989:

> The real star of the festival is the independent filmmaker. We can't have everything that's out there, but I think we have a cross-section so that the state of the art can be assessed.
>
> I also think there has been a misconception that we are somehow responsible for the quality of the films, and that's not the case. All the stuff that's out there reflects both the strengths and weaknesses of the independent film movement, this is how it is.

The price for a Package B to attend the last part of the film festival, typically the most popular (until many hardcore filmgoers realized package A was less crowded and cheaper), was still only $350. Ticket sales went to over 33,000, and a review of the film program shows why.

The year 1989 marked former festival volunteer driver, Steven Soderbergh's *sex, lies and videotape*, the film that will go down in the annals of independent filmmaking as the first film truly to cross over from obscure and low budget ($1.2 million) into a mainstream hit. It was the first film to win what would become the most coveted prize at the festival—the newly created Audience Award. With a qualified positive buzz also coming from the press in attendance, the film ultimately struck a chord with worldwide audiences. Starring the stellar cast of Andie MacDowell, James Spader, Peter Gallagher, and Laura San Giacomo, the quiet film is a controlled examination of a quartet of people who are defined by their erotic impulses or inhibitions. It was sexy, provocative, and memorable, with an interesting script by Soderbergh—shot by Walt Lloyd on location in Baton Rouge, Louisiana.

When I saw the tape sent to me before the selections were made, I must confess I was less than enthusiastic. Goes to show what I know. I'm probably one of the three people on the planet who didn't go gaga over this film. Admittedly looking at it on tape in my busy office—a real unfairness to any film—I found it to be based on a rather small conceit, namely the sexually repressed couple of James Spader and Andie MacDowell versus the sexually liberated couple of Peter Gallagher and Laura San Giacomo. I thought on some level the dialogue seemed strained and unbelievable, though underplayed, given the characters' dynamics with each other. Certainly they were four very strong performances, but at the end of it all, I couldn't really find a sympathetic character among the bunch. They all seemed cold and distant. It wasn't a film that really wowed me. This was a big mistake, I guess, but I still stand by my original take despite the film's success. Just shows what a good title can do for a film, backed up by intelligent performances, an original script, and an against-the-current style of direction.

So when the film became the buzz of the festival and won the Audience Award, I thought I must be completely out of touch or holding onto a vestige of the past, where $1.2 million would make at least three truly independent films and include one—certainly not four—name actors. But in hindsight, the film does stand by the interior world it creates through characterization. No doubt it gains dramatic momentum as it goes along. Yet, at the time I screened the film, I knew that my opinion wasn't going to matter one whit. My role on the selection committee was to represent only one kind of film—on the heels of *Heat and Sunlight* and *Lemon Sky*—the furthest fringes of the independent world, the most personal and experimental. But they still had possibility for limited distribution. All the other bases were covered.

One of the two films I championed to the festival was Rick Schmidt's *Morgan's Cake*, a wonderfully personal portrait built out of private moments taken from the filmmaker's life, even to the point of using his son Morgan as the central character/actor. Morgan confesses he was named by his mother after the British black comedy *Morgan*, and wishes his life were as funny as the movie. But our Morgan seems to want his cake and eat it, too. Without much of a support network (his divorced artist parents are barely able to meet their own needs), Morgan is fired from his job as a Sears deliveryman, is worried about his impending draft registration (his father glorifies his own days as a draft dodger), and then discovers his girlfriend Rachel, the only bright spot in his life, is pregnant.

Morgan's Cake was made for a total cost of $15,000 by Rick Schmidt, quintessential independent Bay Area filmmaker, now living and working in Port Townsend, Washington. Rick and I have kept up a running dialogue on the state of independent filmmaking over the past twenty years. I realize not everyone gets what Rick is doing, but I do. He is one of the original independent diehards—a guy who not only talks the talk but walks the walk. I've always admired Rick's cinematic efforts, even when I knew they might be beyond our festival audience's ken.

But in 1989, stacked up against all the other entries, *Morgan's Cake* stood out as an individualistic effort employing a technique of eliciting a performance by creating story elements that paralleled the actors' lives. Though the actors were just being themselves in front of the camera, the stories were interesting. The line between fiction and nonfiction blurred, while honesty and compassion came into clear focus. One has to admire someone who has committed himself to this authentic way of working and living. Rick is currently using his collaborative method of working with story and character in a Port Townsend workshop for students. If all goes well, they may emerge with a workshopped collaborative print of a cohesive group of students' work strung together into a feature film by Rick Schmidt.

The other film I supported was William Farley's *Of Men and Angels*. It is the story of a post-Beat cabbie and sometime writer Mike O'Donahue, played by Jack Bryne, who gives a ride one night to a famous Irish author, Reilly, played with a twinkle in his eye by John Malloy. Reilly is drunk as a skunk, broke, and finally passes out in the backseat of the cab. Mike takes the famous bloke home, where he bonds with Maria, played by Theresa Saldana, the cabbie's newly pregnant wife. Together they form an alliance that leaves Mike out of the loop until he has to make some difficult choices and finally own up to his responsibilities. It is a film, not unlike its filmmaker, that radiates an inner beauty, like a slash of sunlight breaking through the clouds.

William Farley remains one of the more enigmatic independent filmmakers in the country. He had a short film he resurrected from the 1970s, *Sea Space*, in the 1998 festival. It is a dark moody piece about a late-night confession from a seaman about a man who went overboard and was left behind without any effort to retrieve him. A haunting film, it brims with authenticity and is a fitting acknowledgment of William Farley's longevity and unique vision.

Gordon Eriksen and John O'Brien's no-budget *The Big Dis* was also a hit or a miss depending on who reviewed it. It is one of the first rapping films about a young black soldier returning home to New York on a three-day pass, and he's looking to get laid in the worst way. Bad luck, bad timing, bad attitude, bad cologne, and a lemon of a car all conspire against him, and he is "dissed" or rejected by all. Shot surreptitiously by the filmmakers during their senior year at Harvard, it was a gritty black-and-white film made for less than $20,000. It was really more documentary and improvisational than dramatic or narrative, but it clearly demonstrated talent. These filmmakers were so broke when they arrived—with barely a roll of quarters between them—they literally survived on the hors d'oeuvres at the receptions during the week.

As Todd McCarthy stated in his *Variety* wrap-up, "The presence of these films in the competition was enough to give hope to even the most impoverished aspiring filmmaker." It was an important political distinction to make because many other films in competition had much higher budgets and commercial aspirations, including *sex, lies and videotape* and *Heathers*.

While the festival is to be applauded for seeking out such a wide range of films, it does become problematic for the press, public, and jury to compare these disparate efforts, but this is inherent in sponsoring such a competition. What becomes critical is that low-budget films, despite their limitations, be included in the mix of films—a problem that continues to challenge the programmers of the festival.

Still, 1989 had many other impressive independent films in competition that proved *sex, lies and videotape* wasn't just a one-time fluke. *Apartment Zero*, directed by Martin Donovan and produced by David Koepp, was considered by many to be a compelling and sexy thriller, set in the ornate world of Buenos Aires. Starring Colin Firth and Hart Bochner, the film scored points for its locale, casting, and cleverness.

Cheap Shots, codirected by Jeff Ureles and Jerry Stoeffhaas and executive-produced by William Coppard (who happened to run the highest-grossing art house per capita in the country in upstate New York) was a zany black comedy about a rural motel manager and his lone tenant concocting a get-rich-quick scheme to secretly videotape motel guests in the act, only to have everything go awry, when instead of sex, their cameras document a murder. It is a very clever low-budget film reminiscent of *Blood Simple* but with its own brand of absurdity. The film stars Louis Zorich and David Patrick Kelly and could have gone on to do more business had the pump been sufficiently primed.

Patrick Duncan arrived with his well-received, if a bit nauseating, film (because of the relentless handheld camera work) *84 Charlie Myopic*, about the Vietnam War through the eyes—and lens—of a military cameraman. Developed at Sundance's 1985 filmmakers' lab, the film is a gripping portrait of the war and warriors, told in close and intense proximity to a reconnaissance mission that starts to be pursued by the enemy. Duncan, who went on to a very successful writing career, including *Mr. Holland's Opus* and *Courage Under Fire*, knows the subject of war very thoroughly from his firsthand Vietnam experience when he served fifteen months in the infantry.

Gingerale Afternoon, written by Gina Wendkos based on her play, directed by Rafal Zielinski, and produced by Susan Shapiro, starred a very pregnant Dana Anderson along with John Jackson and Yeardly Smith. It is the funny story of birth, love, and betrayal that features one of the most pregnant actresses to ever appear in a film. In this slice-of-low-life, trailer-park love story, what emerges is a stronger affinity among the principals, despite the bickering and skid marks.

Prisoners of Inertia, directed by Jeffrey Noyes Scher and produced by Zanne Devine and Deirdre Gainor, starred the accomplished Amanda Plummer and the unknown Christopher Rich. The torpor of a relationship is at the center of this romantic comedy about a newlywed couple who decide to get out of their New York apartment and go to brunch, and that is when the misadventure begins. The comic moral of the tale is simply there is no place like home, which they come to understand twenty-four hours and several bags of groceries later.

Miracle Mile, written and directed by Steve de Jarnatt and produced by John

Daly and Derek Gibson of Hemdale, starred Anthony Edwards, when he still had hair, and Mare Winningham, when she didn't. The tag line for the film was "Boy meets girl. Boy loses girl . . . boy gets girl again . . . and they're all blown to hell." Call it love on the edge of the nuclear holocaust. When a random phone call at a corner booth from a nuclear-missile-silo operator is intercepted, and he lets it be known the missiles are flying, it sets in motion a film that feels like one of those dreams where the dreamer can't find someone but becomes increasingly panicked over the person's disappearance. It is a gripping drama—believably executed—that sticks to its guns despite the inevitable conclusion. In the end of *Miracle Mile* there simply is no miracle. But the film's lavish production design belied its independent status. It was clearly an L.A. insider's movie, but nicely accomplished nonetheless. Did it belong in the competition? I was less than certain. It represented a much higher budget range than I was comfortable with despite its clever mechanics.

Powwow Highway, directed by Jonathan Wacks, produced by Jan Wieringa, and executive-produced by ex-Beatle George Harrison's Handmade Films, is an offbeat and wise story of a likable Native American loner, played to perfection by Gary Farmer, who yearns to become a spiritual warrior but is coupled with an angry activist, played by A. Martinez, as they join forces in a 1964 Pontiac Wildcat dubbed "Protector" to travel the scenic expanse known as the "*Powwow Highway*." Though it appears both characters are traveling in different directions, they eventually discover their mutual friendship and admiration and what it really means to be a warrior in this modern age. *Powwow Highway*, distributed by Warner Brothers, is really a precursor to the fine *Smoke Signals*, written by Sherman Alexie and directed by Chris Eyre, that won the 1998 Audience Award and Filmmakers Trophy.

Heathers, directed by Michael Lehmann, produced by Denise Di Novi, and brilliantly written by Daniel Waters, starred a devastatingly tart Winona Ryder (much grown up from her debut in *Square Dance*), Shannen Doherty, and Christian Slater in the most cutting, wickedly colorful view of high school ever put on film. High school isn't about learning; it's about war, and in war there are casualties. The $3 million very black comedy was distributed by New World Entertainment and went on to become something of a cult hit.

A handful of films in the competition clearly didn't work but were included as somehow genre-breaking efforts. After seeing a couple of them, I was really quite upset that we couldn't find room for other, more low-budget, experimental efforts than these ridiculous hybrids. Harry Hurwitz's *That's Adequate* starred—of all people—Tony Randall, James Coco, Anne Meara, Jerry Stiller, Professor Irwin Corey, Susan Dey, Robert Downey Jr., Robert Townsend, Robert Vaughn, and as themselves, Marshall Brickman, Martha Coolidge, Joe Franklin, Renee Taylor, and Bruce Willis. The film is a faux documentary about the sixty-year anniversary of Adequate

Pictures, whose motto is "An idea that's appealing is worth stealing." Unfortunately, the movie, despite the stellar cast, is so broad as to be reduced to a cinematic form of adolescent behavior only surpassed by watching grown men and women perform adolescently. I was surprised Tim Conway wasn't in it. When I saw this film, I thought not over my dead body should it play in the competition. But Tony found it ". . . cutting satire . . . precise and subversive, converting film histrionics (critics beware!) into giddy laughter." I guess I wasn't in a laughing mood.

Adding insult to injury was *Lobster Man from Mars*, directed by Stanley Sheff and starring Tony Curtis, Deborah Foreman, Patrick Macnee, Billy Barty, and Anthony Hickox. It was described by the filmmaker as ". . . the only comedy that combines seafood and science fiction." Do we really need to know anything more? Tony appraised it as ". . . a polished, wacky satire, mocking all the marks of its silly genre with keen efficiency and loving wit." He was much kinder than I would have been. Again, I wondered, with all the other independent films we were attracting, why would we use up precious film slots for this kind of broad entertainment?

FILMMAKERS ANNE MAKEPEACE AND PETER WANG.

Even Peter Wang's return (his *The Great Wall Is a Great Wall*, in the 1986 festival was a film I enjoyed) with another new comedy, *The Laserman*, turned out to be disappointing. Peter played a kind of Charlie Chan character on the trail of a laser scientist in New York's Chinatown, and I thought it was a terribly confused misfire. It was entirely contrived and felt like it.

Add to the mix *Clownhouse*, directed by Victor Salva, a horror film supposedly done in the manner of Stephen King, meant to ". . . expand the existing definitions of independent filmmaking." Again it was a stretch for me in this kind of competition. These films were an attempt to graft satire and genre onto the independent tree, but none of them delivered on the promise.

Yet, with *sex, lies, and videotape* and Nancy Savoca's *True Love* as the eventual winners of the Audience Award and the grand prize, the festival set a benchmark in terms of quality and audience response. *True Love* starred Anabella Sciorra and Ron Eldard, and an authentic cast of forty non-SAG actors. Cowritten and coproduced by Richard Guay, *True Love* follows a young Bronx couple during the last few weeks before their wedding. With its gritty presentation of the humor and drama in everyday life, it represents a triumph of character over plot. Anabella Sciorra emerged as a real acting discovery, and Nancy Savoca moved on to the $6 million feature *Dogfight*. Having worked as a crew member on films by Jonathan Demme and John Sayles, Nancy Savoca had learned her craft well. She was very successful at creating a lived-in world and representing the tightly knit associations of the Italian American community where she grew up and still lives.

Sex, lies and videotape was very favorably reviewed by the press, (Todd McCarthy, the notoriously tough reviewer at *Variety* noted in his review, "It is also one of the best American independent films in quite a long while. . . . Despite the limited rights available, theatrical distribs should be competing avidly for the film due to its promising potential on the upscale baby boomer circuit." It went on to Cannes in May, where it continued to make a sensation by winning the coveted Palm D'Or. Columbia/Tristar had paid for the film under the influential aegis of Larry Estes and Rob Blattner in exchange for domestic home-video rights with Virgin owning the foreign territories. The film was executive-produced by Nancy Tenenbaum, Nick Wechsler, and Morgan Mason and eventually distributed by Miramax. It is considered by many as one of the single most successful independent films of all time from a commercial and artistic standpoint.

Documentary highlights from 1989 included Al Reinert's *For All Mankind*, the documentary grand prize winner, which is compiled entirely out of footage brought back by NASA's nine Apollo missions to the moon, blown up to 35 mm The images are accompanied by taped interviews with the twenty-four men—the first humans to have left the planet for another world. Not a traditional telling of the story of the missions, *For All Mankind* becomes a transcendent experience, a mythical journey of a group of astronauts not even identified other than by voice, accompanied by an evocative score by Brian Eno.

Barbara Trent's investigation of our country's involvement in the arms for hostages sleight of hand in the days leading up to Reagan's inauguration, and the subsequent funding of the Nicaraguan contras was an early warning sign, when she identified George Bush, then president-elect, as a principal member of the secret team. *Coverup: Behind the Iran-Contra Affair* is a riveting piece of partisanship that turned out to be prophetic and right on the mark.

Bran Ferren's *Funny* includes a riotous romp through the world of jokes, told by over a hundred people from all walks of life, which ultimately reveals more about us as an indomitable and funny people. It is particularly effective when the same joke is attempted by different people in different places.

Obie Benz's *Heavy Petting* is also a wondrous comedy about teenage passion during America's recent past. The film utilizes archival footage, interspersed with folks like David Byrne, Laurie Anderson, William Burroughs, and Allen Ginsberg talking about their first sexual experiences with a great deal of wit and candor. As Tony Safford said in his excellent program note, "Ultimately *Heavy Petting* reveals that sex in the fifties was used to sell, and teens were encouraged to buy—everything but the idea of sex itself."

Frank Martin's fine film *John Huston* was a revelation for fans of the iconoclast and familial legend, as were Daniel Geller and Dayna Goldfine's *Isadora Duncan: Movement of the Soul* and Meg Partridge's *Portrait of Imogen* about the seminal still photographer and full-time wife and mother Imogen Cunningham.

Bruce Weber's stark portrait of jazz trumpet player Chet Baker in *Let's Get Lost*, produced by Nan Bush, brings a fashion photographer's eye to the sad and lonely life of a virtuoso performer who led a self-destructive life full of women, drugs, and solitude, and finally, as a victim of a robbery that resulted in the loss of his front teeth, was robbed of his artistry. It was controversial because many people thought Chet Baker was too far gone to have been fairly and honorably photographed and that the filmmaker had not exercised enough self-restraint. The other camp, including me, felt that it was an accurate and honest portrait of an artist, devastatingly vivid and yet resonating with a jazz feeling translated to the visual. Although it was a difficult portrait of a complicated man, it was done with a loving style that lent a certain elegance to a tragic tale. It was nominated for an Academy Award.

Tony Buba's *Lightning Over Braddock: A Rust Bowl Fantasy* is a definite precursor to Michael Moore's *Roger and Me*. Instead of Flint, Michigan, however, viewers are in Tony's home town of Braddock, Pennsylvania. Amassed partially from his collection of over fifteen short documentaries about Braddock, and with $40,000 from foundations and saved up from work with George Romero, Tony made the feature documentary that still could play today for its originality and heart.

Kathryn Taverna and Alan Adelson's *Lodz Ghetto* is the terrifying story of more than a quarter of a million Jews, herded by the Germans into a slum within the Polish city of Lodz. Barely eight hundred would survive the war. As the film says, "Listen, and believe this, even though it happened here. Even though it seems so old, so distant, and so foreign."

Christian Blackwood's *Motel* is a down-and-dirty tour of wayside havens, peppered by unique individuals living off the beaten path and depending on other travelers passing by who need a room for the night.

Christine Choy and Renee Tajima's complex film *Who Killed Vincent Chin?* sets out less to solve the 1982 murder, which has already been confessed to, than to develop a story about the victim, a young Chinese American who is clubbed to death by a white man outside a topless bar. It marks the collision of two paralleling American dreams that intersect tragically in a parking lot outside Detroit on a hot summer night. It was also nominated for an Academy Award for 1988.

Premieres included the quintessential, independent-goes-to-Hollywood primer—a must see for anyone coming out of film school and moving to Los Angeles—*The Big Picture*, starring Kevin Bacon, Emily Longstreth, J. T. Walsh, Jennifer Jason

Leigh, and Martin Short, with guest appearances by a host of old-time Hollywood luminaries, including June Lockhart, Eddie Albert, and Roddy McDowell. It is the story of a student filmmaker who wins an award that launches his career in Hollywood with all the trappings to make the big picture. Then he has to rediscover himself and his passion in the process. It was a perfect Sundance premiere—billed at the time as a mystery film.

The only real mystery was how the directorial debut film of Christopher Guest—cowritten with Michael McKean and Michael Varhol under the Columbia Pictures banner during David Puttnam's short-term career running a studio—fell into the same trap as Kevin Bacon's character: a changing of the regime that had supported the film in the beginning. The new guys came in and wanted to prove the previous management's tastes were less than perfect, so they failed to support, in-oh-so-many ways, the filmmaker and project. The film, released after Puttnam's departure, quickly came and went. *The Big Picture* ended up as the invisible picture.

Other highlights at the festival included award-winning filmmaker Jon Else's *Yosemite: The Fate of Heaven*, coproduced by Sterling Van Wagenen and John Korty and executive-produced by Robert Redford. It tells the complex story of one of the nation's most spectacular and beloved national parks—perhaps loved to death in some people's minds—going through three million visitors annually and generating 25,000 pounds of garbage a day. Through a narration from the 1851 diary of Lafayette Bunnell, the contrast between the past grandeur of the natural state of the park and its more contemporary experience is vivid. In 1997, Jon Else produced, directed, and shot the highly acclaimed television series about the west and water, *Cadillac Desert*.

Brian Gibson's world premiere of *Murderers Among Us: The Simon Wiesenthal Story* marked one of the early appearances of an HBO-produced drama. The four-hour film was shown in two parts. Another HBO production making its world premiere was Richard Pearce's *Dead Man Out*. Produced by Forrest Murray (who also produced the *Spitfire Grill*), the film stars Ruben Blades as a death-row prisoner who, as a result of his incarceration, may have become too insane to execute. When he is interviewed by the prison psychiatrist, played by Danny Glover, the film opens up many questions of responsibility and free will and ultimately asks what is sane and what is insane.

Clint Eastwood executive-produced a documentary on the jazz legend Thelonius Monk, *Straight, No Chaser*. Directed by Charlotte Zwerin, shot by Christian Blackwood, and produced by Bruce Ricker, who had also produced the 1980's jazz film *The Last of the Blue Devils*, the film is an uncompromising look at this idiosyncratic piano player.

Monte Hellman's 1971 groundbreaker, *Two-Lane Blacktop*, starred Dennis Wilson of the Beach Boys fame, James Taylor, Warren Oates, and Laurie Bird.

F. W. MURNAU'S *SUNRISE* WITH THE UTAH SYMPHONY UNDER THE DIRECTION OF DAVID NEWMAN.

Universal Studios was kind enough to strike a new 35 mm print of the film, and it was a real tribute to the man described as "the thinking man's Sam Peckinpah."

Tony's choice of F. W. Murnau's 1927 silent masterpiece, *Sunrise*, accompanied by the Utah Symphony Orchestra under the direction of David Newman, as the festival's opening-night film truly set a benchmark for showmanship and created an unforgettably rich cinematic experience. The film was mesmerizing, a glimpse into the past and at the same time into moviemaking—in essence watching a film being scored live as it unfolds before you on the screen. It was a magical evening—in my mind, an unsurpassed opening night.

Michael Ventura curated an amazing collection of John Cassavetes's work, showing fifteen of his films that had helped to establish his place in the pantheon of filmmakers as perhaps the seminal figure in modern cinema. Films, such as *Edge of the City, Shadows, Too Late Blues, Faces, Husbands, A Woman Under the Influence, Opening Night,* and *The Tempest*, were meant to be seen in chronological order. Sadly, Cassavetes died from lung cancer just a week after the conclusion of the festival, which only underscored the rarity of the opportunity for a number of filmmakers to finally see difficult-to-find prints and celebrate one of film's true mavericks.

Another film maverick, Haskell Wexler, got rather feisty in a widely covered panel discussion titled "Have Independents Lost Their Social Conscience?" According to Todd McCarthy's *Variety* coverage of February 2, 1989:

> Seemingly in a particularly irreverent mood, Wexler insisted that "There truly

is an enemy, who for their own personal greed and power are willing to kill you. The big killers are out there running the show, and our job as filmmakers is to try to not let them get away with it.

Wexler also remarked that,

"The passion [for filmmaking] has to come out of our regular life. The danger in America isn't Communism, it's cancer. The big issue is trying to reverse the trends that are making us die too early.

The passion has to come out of the fabric of life, and if you do that in concert with other people, your artistic juices will be flowing, you'll be healthy, we'll be healthy."

However, I thought Anne Thompson, writing trenchantly for the *L.A. Weekly*, got it just about right:

It may be that the independents are just part of the ebb and flow of an industry system that keeps the studios dominant decade after decade. Scan a list of independent distributors and you'll find that most of them lasted a very short time before being victimized by mismanagement, undercapitalization, low clout with exhibitors and simple hubris. The same thing seems to be happening now. In the wake of the Wall Street crash and the disastrous product glut, those indie distributors who came to Park City looked very dour indeed.

While Park City proves there's no lack of talent among the independents, thus far the indie movement seems to be "all about first features," as producer's representative John Pierson puts it. The community provides little follow-up for filmmakers who want to continue to experiment and challenge established structures. (In its small way, Robert Redford's Sundance Institute is trying to fill this void).

Such conservativism is endemic. "I'd rather make a $4 million film with John Frankenheimer and Roy Scheider," claims Virgin Vision president Steven Bickel, "than a $1 million movie with no names and a good script." Bickel admits that before the fact, he "wouldn't consider" making a movie like *Bagdad Cafe*, a surprise indie hit.

If the independent movement wants to grow, it must trust the talent that is more than ready to spread its wings. The Park City festival proves the existence of many filmmakers with the necessary values to resist the lure of what sells. It's just that Hollywood is still really the only game in town.

Two other programs in 1989 were important revelations about the direction of Redford's interest. The Latin American program, called *Dangerous Loves*, was a collection of seven films, all based on short stories by Gabriel Garcia Marquez, and a tentative outreach toward the Soviet Union, where Redford had attended a festival in Moscow, occurred through the screening of Marina Goldovskaya's heart-wrenching litmus test of Gorbachev's new glasnost, *Solovetski Power*. It was the first film to present the horrors in the concentration camps on Solovetski Island just below the Arctic Circle, told by six survivors and former camp officials.

As Redford stated on the last Saturday of the festival, as reported by Todd McCarthy in the January 30 issue of *Variety*:

> I'm much happier than I was last year. We were at a crossroads last year. We could have gone for more celebrities and glitz, but we went after a certain kind of energy instead, and I feel that it's happened. The Soviet and Latin programs brought something new to it. The audience has been interacting with the filmmakers, who have been talking ideology, which is an approach to start turning things around. Those two programs mean a lot to me.

ALBERTO GARCIA AND TONY SAFFORD.

Despite the international emphasis of the festival, with initiatives in Latin America, the Soviet Union, and Tokyo, favorable press reaction, combined with bona fide hits coming out of the competition with *sex, lies, and videotape* heading the list made the 1989 festival a success over previous years. The other big announcement going into the festival appeared in the final paragraph of Tony Safford's introduction: ". . . it also brings to a close the too-short tenure of Executive Director Tom Wilhite. He will return to independent production. His fresh and challenging ideas, however, have been a tremendous inspiration to my work." This set the stage for ushering in the next Sundance regime—one whose fractures and divisions almost ended the dance altogether. It began with the hiring of Suzanne Weil, on eleven-year veteran of PBS, as the new executive director of the institute.

The 1990 festival was important for several reasons. With the many cinematic discoveries, several of which ended up with distribution deals, we had to demonstrate that 1989 wasn't a mere fluke and this trend had staying power. Try as he might, Tony had a hard time attempting to lower the expectations as the festival got started. As Tony Safford stated in *Variety* at the opening of the 1990 festival:

> My feeling is this is as strong as any year we've done, but odds are unlikely we can match last year's success. If people come up here expecting the next Palm D'Or winner, they'll probably be disappointed.
>
> I've always maintained that the responsibility of the festival is to reflect the best of the field. Clearly, some years are better than others, and, if it's an average year, it's our responsibility to reflect that.

Part of the new team brought in to help guide the festival included former volunteer driver and guest programmer of 1989's short-film program, Rogues Gallery, Alberto Garcia. Alberto, as the new competition director, represented a different sensibility; he was younger, wore a ponytail and granny glasses, and was almost pathologically shy. Yet his tastes ran to more unconventional and experimental fare at a time when commercial pressures were at an all-time high. Despite his introspective nature and dislike of being in public, he had a good rapport with filmmakers, who responded to his sensibility and behind-the-scenes manner.

As Tony and Alberto stated in their didactic introduction to the 1990 competition:

> . . . British critic and filmmaker Peter Wollen reflected that his understanding of "independence" goes back to the "salon of the independents" in nineteenth-century France, a modernist breakaway from academic painting that grew out of a refusal or rejection to be part of the mainstream. He concludes by saying that "independent filmmaking, particularly American independent filmmaking, still has a great deal to contribute" in this regard.
>
> What independents have to offer is an experience of the world incapable of being achieved by a mass-marketed cinema. Key to this experience, and what have pushed many films into the critical and popular limelight, are the ideas of **confrontation** and **interpretive ambiguity**.

I was always curious, in an article cowritten by Alberto and Tony, who contributed what? Was the writing Alberto's as the young, brash revolutionary, or Tony's as the seasoned veteran, bidding the event his farewell and finally revealing his true feeling? Yes, 1990's festival marked Tony Safford's swan song. Tony was moving on to the distribution arena to work as an executive with New Line Cinema. He could now afford to tell it like he really saw it.

As Alberto and he stated:

> "Cinema of rejection" may have a frightening ring to it for filmmakers, whose ultimate concern is to make their **next** film. Yet the challenge shouldn't pose a paradox. The mechanisms of filmmaking should be appropriated without assimilating the structures of the dominant cinema. As critic Armond White has stated, "Every filmmaker should ask why he or she is in this profession. If the answer is to be like any other filmmaker we know, he/she should think again. Resistance is the only politics I'd prescribe across the board."

I'm sure Tony went off to New Line thinking about all the formulaic resistance he was going to dish out. Except that he wouldn't be embracing the cinema of the rejected, he'd actually be doing the rejecting! Irony is a wonderful thing.

The ultimate irony is that the competition films actually were very strong in their own right without having to measure up to the ecstatic success of the previous year. The big scores came for not one, but two filmmakers from Flint, Michigan, Wendell B. Harris Jr. and Michael Moore. One was in competition and one out of competition, but had his film been in competition, it would probably have swept the awards.

Wendell B. Harris Jr.'s *Chameleon Street* seemed an odd choice for the grand prize. It is the incredible but true story of William Douglas Street, a black con man. With barely a high-school education, he impersonated a doctor, lawyer, journalist, and other professionals over a period of years. Harris playing the part of Street, wisely chooses not to pass moral judgment on him. Instead, he lets the humor and social irony reign supreme.

Unfortunately, after the festival, the film never saw the light of day again as Harris, on the advice of his family (his mother Helen B. Harris had executive-produced the film) decided to sell the picture to Warner Brothers after rejecting several less-lucrative offers, described by the filmmaker as "a backhanded compliment." Warner Brothers didn't actually want to distribute the movie to theaters. Instead, they were willing to pay a high price for the film to remake the story, starring Arsenio Hall. The $2 million film had a lot of blood, sweat, and tears in it. It had been rewritten thirty-six times and rejected by all the major studios, and its writer and director had played the lead. It was one of the more bizarre episodes involving a grand prizewinner and made *Chameleon Street* a fitting metaphor for what was happening to the festival itself. Its heart was clearly moving in the direction of a marketplace, despite the protestations of the organizers. It was no accident that Tony Safford's new employers, New Line Cinema, had the Hudlin brothers' $2.5 million *House Party* in the competition and set to open nationally on 800 screens.

Other dramatic highlights in competition included Hal Hartley's *The Unbelievable Truth*, which was being distributed by Miramax; Charles Burnett's excellent *To Sleep with Anger*, produced by Ed Pressman and starring Danny Glover in a fine performance; and Michael Roemer's *The Plot Against Harry*, which had actually been shot in 1969 and shelved for twenty years. Shot by Robert Young and associate-produced by Michael Hausman, the film had gracefully survived the test of time with deadpan earnestness and a colorful cast of characters.

Whit Stillman emerged with a moral tale of his own lost generation in *Metropolitan*, perhaps one of the best received and more successful films to come out of the festival in 1990; Robin Wright, Jason Patric, Barry Primus, Christina Harnos, and Rae Dawn Chong starred in Erin Dignam's *Loon*, another film that did some business; director Maggie Greenwald earned her stripes in *The Kill Off*, produced by Lydia Dean Pilcher and based on the dark novel of the same name by the legendary Jim Thompson; Norman Rene took a timely and enormously moving look at the people most decimated by the AIDS epidemic in *Longtime Companion*, executive-produced by Lindsay Law from *American Playhouse* and with a stellar cast, including Stephen Caffrey, Bruce Davison, Mark Lamos, Dermot Mulroney, Mary Louise Parker, and Campbell Scott. It won the coveted Audience Award.

One of the riskier films in competition and one of the best received was Everett Lewis's *The Natural History of Parking Lots*, best summed up by one of the characters in the film, "If Joseph Conrad were to write *Heart of Darkness* today, he would set it in the parking lot of a high school in the San Fernando Valley." The visually aggressive, black-and-white portrait of a young L.A. car thief generated high interest, if divided opinion.

At the same time, there were more than a few films that did not receive the accolades they had hoped for. Marjorie Skouras, who was on the Competition Selection Advisory Committee with me, said of Kurt Voss's *The Horseplayer*, it ". . . promises to be one of the most interesting films of 1990." Interesting is as interesting does. This was also the case with Anne Flournoy's *How to Be Louise*—it had the look of a more introspective Susan Seidelman film.

Shirley Sun's effort on the acclaimed book *Iron and Silk* was a case of execution not meeting expectation. The film, based on Mark Salzman's book and script and starring him, was richly photographed but stiff and formal—as though the author had lived the experiences in China, written about them, then was expected to re-create them once again for the camera. It just didn't have any life left.

W. T. Morgan (*The Unheard Music*) returned to the festival with his Sundance Workshop film *A Matter of Degrees*. Shot by Paul Ryan and produced by Roy Kissin and Randall Poster, the film stars Arye Gross, Judith Hoag, Tom Sizemore, and Wendell Pierce. It centers around a frustrated college student who yearns for the idealism and platitudes of more activist eras, gets hooked up in a crisis at the college radio station, and makes some discoveries about himself and the more personal side of politics. In the end, despite a great soundtrack by the Lemonheads, Throwing Muses, Fetchin' Bones, Miracle Legion, Yo La Tengo, and the Cavedogs, the film was trite and predictable and the arc the character traveled—a matter of degrees—was just too little and too late.

This was also the case with Andrew Lane's *Mortal Passions*, produced by Gwen Field, who had also produced *Patti Rocks*. It starred Zach Galligan, Krista Errickson, Michael Bowen, David Warner, and Sheila Kelley and was a sexy noir thriller—a perfect fit in a tight genre—but it just didn't seem to click with an audience looking for something more than a story full of sex and guns, no matter how interesting the performances.

Perhaps the most written-about film in the competition was Charles Burnett's finely honed drama *To Sleep with Anger*, executive-produced by Ed Pressman, Danny Glover, and Harris Tulchin and produced by Caldecott Chubb, Thomas Byrnes, and Darin Scott. It stars Danny Glover, Mary Alice, Paul Butler, Carl Lumbly, Vonetta McGee, and Richard Brooks and is a careful study of a family in south-central Los Angeles—familiar terrain for Charles Burnett—that must come to terms with its members and their feelings. An enigmatic stranger from the past, played with great vigor by Danny Glover, comes to visit. His intense presence sends the fragile family balance into chaos. There is something constantly lurking beneath the surface in this study of conflict and resolution that deftly shows itself in the chilling final act. It is a tour de force of dramatic dexterity that Charles Burnett achieves the effect with such a slow-burning fuse, but he is adept at setting the stage so that the emotional release of the confrontation is cathartic.

It was Danny Glover's signing onto the project that got the film made and his magnetic and powerful performance that got it seen. Charles Burnett—then the recent recipient of a MacArthur genius grant—is a soft-spoken and very thoughtful director whom I consider a friend. I'd been a supporter of his work, having played both *Killer of Sheep* and *My Brother's Wedding* in previous festivals. I was thrilled to see him getting the attention he so richly deserved. In the annals of black filmmakers, Charles Burnett is a unique and extremely important voice.

Finally, *Never Leave Nevada* was the one film I had vigorously supported for the festival because I found it hilarious and exactly the right film—one with a homemade vibe. It is irreverent, subversive, inventive, and full of likable performances by mostly nonprofessional actors. Written and directed by Steve Swartz and produced by Diane Campbell, it stars Swartz, Rodney Rincon, Janelle Buchanan, and Katherine Catmull.

Never Leave Nevada is an atomic, comic love story that celebrates the thrill of the open road, the joy of a new love, and two guys who travel around the country selling T-shirts and tube socks at antinuclear rallies. One of the guys is a cockeyed Jewish optimist, searching for love in all the wrong places and still smarting from a recent business setback. The other is a Hispanic cynic, a former child star of 1950s television and a born salesman. It doesn't take long for them to hook up with two local women, one a nurse who looks after the medical needs of the girls at Fran's Star Ranch, just down the highway, and the other is a half-Jewish transplant from Little Rock, who uses her haughtiness to supplant her naughtiness. What results is outrageously well-written dialogue that plays like an eighty-eight-minute stand-up performance by the writer/director delivered in a cardboard box. The sound quality on the 16 mm print probably kept the film from doing much, which was a shame because it really was a funny, off-the-wall film. Blown up to 35 mm with remixed sound, it could have traveled the *Stranger Than Paradise* road to fame and fortune. Instead the filmmakers retreated back to Texas, then on to Los Angeles, where I lost track of them.

The documentary competition was chock full of returning filmmakers. But with Michael Moore's smash film *Roger and Me* playing as a regional premiere with Michael's ubiquitous and disquieting rebel presence sucking up a lot of the available press space about documentaries, the competition films produced no market breakouts.

Mark Kitchell's *Berkeley in the Sixties* won the Audience Award as well as an Academy Award nomination; the grand prize was split between Stephanie Black's

H-2 Worker, a study of the exploitation of Jamaican sugarcane workers in Florida, and Pat O'Neill's *Water and Power*, a profound photographic memory built out of optically layered images that tell the story of transformation.

Special Jury Prize went to Ellen Bruno for her beautiful transportive look at a deeply troubled Cambodia from a Buddhist perspective in *Samsara: Death and Rebirth in Cambodia*. Lisa Leeson and Claudia Hoover's *Metamorphosis: Man into Woman* received the Filmmaker's Trophy. It is an amazing film about a transsexual's journey between identities.

Other highlights of the doc competition included Ralph Arlyck's sardonic look at the impact of living a modern life, *Current Events*; veteran Deborah Shaffer's *Dance of Hope,* about eight tenacious women's struggle to raise human-rights issues in Chile at the end of General Pinochet's dictatorship; Anne Bell and Deborah Dickson's gracious portrait, *Dancing for Mr. B: Six Balanchine Ballerinas;* George Butler's (*Pumping Iron*) controversial look at the male ritual of hunting, *In the Blood*; Karen Thorson's emotional and eloquent portrait, *James Baldwin: The Price of the Ticket*; Mickey Lemle's space-doc entry *The Other Side of the Moon*; Amalie Rothschild's artful *Painting the Town: The Illusionistic Murals of Richard Haas*; Kenneth Bowser's tribute to the irreverent film director, *Preston Sturges: The Rise and Fall of an American Dreamer; !Teatro¡*, about an agitprop theater group in Honduras, by Ruth Shapiro, Edward Burke, and Pamela Yates; Joel Freedman's excellent portrait of the Western Shoshone sisters, the Danns, trying to hold onto their ancestral land in *To Protect Mother Earth*; and Susan Korda and David Leitner's searing psychological portrait of a country and its citizenry, *Vienna Is Different*.

The last film of note in the documentary competition was particularly poignant. *Mr. Hoover and I* was the final film of the passionate iconoclast Emile de Antonio. He died suddenly at the age of seventy—just before the festival started—and, in fact, the documentary competition was dedicated in his honor. Since de Antonio was maker of such seminal films as *Point of Order, Rush to Judgment, In the Year of the Pig,* and *Underground, Mr. Hoover and I* is a fitting final film because it concerns a drama played out over thirty years between the filmmaker and the FBI—particularly with J. Edgar Hoover—who de Antonio describes as "one of the most dishonorable people in the whole history of this great country." As Laurence Kardish of the Museum of Modern Art's film program stated in the festival dedication:

> Emile de Antonio, the paradigmatic independent American filmmaker, raised the process of inquiry to a popular democratic art. He contended and informed, and over the decades while doing so, he changed our idea of how an effective documentary film could look. He revealed that under the images and pronouncements of our most public figures complex social motives and political relationships lay like a deep pool of water, perhaps unfathomable, troubled by wind and sharks.

Besides the tributes, 1990's festival had the pleasure of hosting Richard Lester, known for zany British comedies such as the Beatles' *A Hard Day's Night, The Knack,* and *How I Won the War*. A celebration of Melvin Van Peebles's films included *The Story of a Three-Day Pass* and *Sweet Sweetback's Baadasssss Song*. A new film out of Kazakhstan, *The Needle*, was accompanied by actor and musician Viktor Tsoi jamming after the screening on the Egyptian Theatre's stage, which turned out to be a melancholy memory because it was his only concert in the United States. He was prematurely killed the following year back in the former Soviet Union.

There were other highlights in a program of special screenings, including John Woo's United States premiere of *The Killer* with Chow Yun-Fat; Eliseo Subiela's *Last Images of the Shipwreck;* Michael Apted's rousing documentary on Soviet underground rock musician Boris Grebenshikov's first opportunity to travel, live, and record; and Jane Campion's mesmerizing feature debut, *Sweetie.*

Another big internal change at the 1990 festival, along with Tony Safford's departure and Alberto Garcia's appointment as the competition director, was the introduction of young programming associate John Cooper; at subsequent festivals, he would program short films as a separate program, an innovative addition.

In the end, attendance went up to 35,000 tickets sold, with a 20-percent increase in press attendance, and an estimated 5,000–7,000 visitors to the small town of Park City. The year was noted for the impressive presence of strong black films with *House Party, Chameleon Street, To Sleep with Anger*, and the Van Peebles's retrospective leading the way.

One other noteworthy thing was that the festival underwent yet another permutation of its name. In 1990, it was called the funny-sounding "Sundance/United States Film Festival." In Tony Safford's final act, he announced at the conclusion of the festival that in the future it would be known simply as Sundance Film Festival. I guess Tom Wilhite was gone but not forgotten, and I think this name will finally stick, with or without the definite article.

GARY BEER.

CHAPTER 9

Premiere Magazine and the Urge to Purge

In the summer of 1991, Peter Biskind wrote a story for *Premiere: The Movie Magazine* which rattled more than a few cages at Sundance. The revealing and very critical article suggested that all was not right in the land of Sundance; as the lead said, ". . . there's trouble in them thar hills."

The ugly truth was that there was a sizable deficit left over from Tom Wilhite's reign, which doubled, according to the article, to nearly $1 million under Suzanne Weil's limited tenure. Her first act, before she flew off for a Japanese vacation, was to fire Maria Schaeffer, who had been vice president and general manager of the institute for four years. Cinda Holt, who took her complaints about Suzanne Weil directly to Gary Beer and her complaints about Gary Beer directly to Redford, was not getting satisfactory answers about what was going on internally in the organization, and she and other personnel were growing increasingly frustrated, leaving the staff to wonder what was next.

All of this infighting and bickering among various camps inside the organization was only compounded by an edict given to the staff by Redford: the Salt Lake City offices would be closing and the staff would have to commute to Sundance, at least an hour drive each way for most employees. Although the offices were new and Sundance beautiful and secluded, in the dead of winter the drive could prove long and hazardous. Luckily, there were enough complaints that the policy was never implemented.

ROBERT REDFORD WITH SUZANNE WEIL.

The article suggested there were inherent conflicts within the many Sundance interests. They ranged from Redford's alleged poaching of Norman MacLean's *A River Runs Through It* from the makers of *Heartland*—director Richard Pearce, Annick Smith, and writer Bill Kittredge—when their option (provided by a Sundance development loan for $15,000) ran out and Redford jumped in to snatch it up; to Redford's falling out with Sterling Van Wagenen, whom Rockefeller Foundation executive and Sundance board member Howard Klein suggested in the *Premiere* article should have avoided producing *The Trip to Bountiful*, stating, "Sterling was serving a lot of masters, among them his own ambitions. He was unable to resist the conflict of interest that was open to him."

However, fellow board member, screenwriter Tom Rickman, feels that the conflict of interest was minimal. "Sterling would have to have taken a vow of celibacy," he says, not to have taken advantage of the contacts that came his way. In fact, one former staffer thinks *The Trip To Bountiful* represents the best Sundance has to offer, the opportunity for creative networking. But not everyone looked at it that way.

Redford's rupture with Sterling also involved a book he and the late John Earle had optioned from Utah historian and writer Maureen Whipple, *The Giant Joshua*. I'd had the great pleasure of meeting Whipple when she was in her seventies. Wrapped up in a blanket, she spent the evening telling stories and sipping on a little red wine on a camping excursion to the Shivwits Indian Reservation in the mid-

1970s. My group of college friends had kind of informally adopted her since she was a real outcast in her St. George, Utah, community, after the publication in 1948 of *The Giant Joshua*. The book is the story of a young, sixteen-year-old pioneer woman who is introduced to the rigors of a polygamist marriage when she is forced to marry her much older "uncle," who helped raise her when her own parents were killed in an Indian attack. In 1948, the book had made the *New York Times'* best-seller list, second only to Ernest Hemingway's *For Whom the Bell Tolls*. She was a marvelous storyteller, rich in the lore of the local culture, both Native and pioneer. *The Giant Joshua* had been one of the first scripts at the Sundance June Lab. John Earle and his wife, Denise, had written the draft of the script, which I recommended for selection. Several years and drafts later, when it came time for Sterling to direct the film, with Michael Hausman attached to produce and Vanessa Redgrave interested in playing one of the older wives, the project, just weeks away from preproduction, was abruptly cancelled by the financial backers who had just weekended with Redford. The implication was clear and drove a wedge between the two men. According to the *Premiere* article:

> Denise Earle [after her husband's death] was the loser in the jockeying between Redford and Van Wagenen, and she is bitter. "Redford never wanted Sterling to go out on his own," she says. "He only wanted him to do his thing, be his gopher." To this day the project has not been produced.

Sterling remained on the board of directors for Sundance, but was now listed as a producer for Ian Cummings's Utah-based production company, Leucadia Film Corporation. Again, according to the *Premiere* article:

> *The Giant Joshua* not only pitted Redford against Van Wagenen, but if Denise Earle's account is accurate, it also put him in competition with the very independents Sundance was set up to nurture. Sundance is a minefield of potential and actual conflicts of interest. The institute was never supposed to be a source of projects for Redford or of its other principals. But sometimes the lines got blurred.

As one Sundance insider put it in the article, "It's hard to run a finishing school in the middle of a whorehouse."

One of the clearest conflicts of interest, which persists to this day, is the one between the institute and festival, on the one hand, and the resort and the Sundance Group on the other. Originally it was thought that the resort would help support the institute and its programs since it was for profit. But because the resort wasn't a big moneymaker, it turned out that the institute, with its myriad workshops, gave more than half its annual lab budget (about $225,000 in direct costs), as quoted in the article, to the resort for cottage rental and food service. Thus, the nonprofit institute actually helped support the for-profit business.

According to the Biskind article,

> "Some staffers also resented the fact that Redford gave so little of his own

money to the institute. Of Sundance's annual budget, which had grown to $2.7 million by 1990, Redford donated only $50,000 a year, and this was often earmarked for bills the institute owed to the resort."

The result was a tax write-off for money that went from one pocket to the other. Again, according to the *Premiere* article:

> "There was nothing illegal about any of this," says Johann Jacobs, a former Sundance financial officer who argues that the problem was not so much [Gary] Beer [who, by then, was vice president of the institute and one of Redford's closest advisors, deeply involved in the launching of the Sundance Catalog and accused in the article of behaving like a studio head with his expense account] but that "it was never clear where the differences were between the institute, the resort and the Sundance Group (a separate entity set up to develop commercial business opportunities for Redford)."

When Redford returned from Sydney Pollack's production of *Havana* in Santo Domingo to learn of the institute's dire financial condition, he stated, "I just couldn't have it." By the fall of 1990, Suzanne Weil was gone. She claimed, "I had a chance to mess it up, but I didn't have a chance to put it together again." That was when Gary Beer effectively took over management of the institute. As Redford stated in the Biskind article:

> If there is a leadership problem at Sundance, it's my responsibility to find someone who can run it. I haven't done it. It's as simple as that. But there's somebody who has moved into the picture right now who I think has a very good concept for raising a lot of money: Gary Beer.

Not long after that, Cinda Holt,

> . . . the director of program administration and an eight-year veteran, had resigned. She had complained to Redford about Beer in the past, and reliable sources say her resignation was not voluntary. According to Alberto Garcia, festival competition director, "Some of the firings were completely political. I would wish, if I'd spent years of my life with a nonprofit arts organization, to get a nice good-bye rather than a hefty boot."

She became the newest member of the "Sundanced Club."

The 1991 festival saw the announcement of Geoff Gilmore's selection as the new program director to replace Tony Safford. Alberto Garcia was to run Independent Film Competition, with the input of the Selection Advisory Board, of which I continued to be a member. Nicole Guillemet was now the managing director of the festival, replacing Cinda Holt, Michelle Satter had continued to successfully negotiate the treacherous shoals of Sundance politics and stay quietly in charge of the Feature Film Program, and Gary Beer was effectively running Sundance, with Saundra Saperstein continuing in the increasingly important role of media director for the festival.

I purposefully tried to stay in the background of the 1991 festival to get some kind of compass direction from Geoff Gilmore. On some level, I also trusted Alberto Garcia's rebel underground streak, and the thoughtfulness of my fellow committee members: Laurence Kardish, curator of the Department of Film at the Museum of Modern Art; director Billy Woodbury (*Bless Their Little Hearts*); Karen Arikian, director of the Independent Feature Project in New York; and Robert Hawk, from the Film Arts Foundation in San Francisco.

DIRECTOR JILL GODMILLOW WITH FESTIVAL MANAGER CINDA HOLT.

The 1991 festival got off to a terribly unfortunate start, when the opening-night film, Lasse Hallstrom's *Once Around* (produced by Amy Robinson and Griffin Dunne from a script by Malia Scotch Marmo, who had met and worked together at Sundance, starring Richard Dreyfuss, Holly Hunter, Danny Aiello, Laura San Giacomo, and Gena Rowlands) coincided with the first salvos of the Gulf War and the announcement that Tel Aviv had just been bombed by Iraq. The tension that night from the distraction of knowing we were entering a war with Iraq was palpable. Holly Hunter acknowledged it, and a moment of silence was gracefully observed. The heightened sense of politics and human drama ran like a steady current throughout the festival.

Highlights from the 1991 competition included Jon Jost's return with his most accessible film to date, *All the Vermeers in New York*, directed, shot, and edited by Jost and produced by Henry Rosenthal, about a stock trader and a young French actress. Julie Dash's exquisite *Daughters of the Dust*, a film clearly ahead of its time, is so sumptuous in its costuming, color, and lyricism that it is a revelation. The film captures the unique culture of the Gullah, African Americans living on the islands off the South Carolina coast who are descendants of freed African slaves, and won the Cinematography Award. Keith McNally's *End of the Night,* shot by Tom DiCillo and edited by Ila von Hasperg, who had worked with Rainer Fassbinder, is about a long descent into the night by an insurance salesman whose wife is expecting. Joseph Vasquez's *Hangin' with the Homeboys*, distributed by none other than Tony Safford's new employer, New Line Cinema, has the distinction of being the only independent film actually picketed by disgruntled IATSE members at its screenings in Park City for its failure to hire two union editors.

Other films in the dramatic competition were *Iron Maze*, directed by Hiaroki

Yoshida and starring Jeff Fahey and Bridget Fonda; *The Juniper Tree* by Nietzchka Keene; Jane Spencer's much-anticipated *Little Noises*, starring Crispin Glover and Tatum O'Neal; *A Little Stiff*, a $10,000 feature by Greg Watkins and Caveh Zahedi about the filmmaker's obsession with a girl in college; Robin Armstrong's *One Cup of Coffee*, a sentimental baseball story that won the Audience Award and then quietly disappeared; Yvonne Rainer's mostly experimental *Privilege*, which won the Filmmaker's Trophy; Nina Menkes's *Queen of Diamonds*; Jon Jost's second film in the competition, a feat no one else has ever pulled off, *Sure Fire*, shot in Circleville, Utah, about a Mormon land speculator, a film I assisted with; and Don Boyd's film *Twenty One*, starring Patsy Kensit, Jack Shepherd, Patrick Ryecart, Maynard Eziashi, Rufus Sewell, and Sophie Thompson, which received praise from the *L.A. Times'* critic Sheila Benson; *Enid is Sleeping*, directed by Maurice Phillips and starring Elizabeth Perkins and Judge Reinhold as two inadvertent murderous lovers, premiered at the festival and was worth more than a few laughs.

A few films that emerged from the rather blasé 1991 competition were Hal Hartley's *Trust*, starring Adrienne Shelly and Martin Donovan; nineteen-year-old Matty Rich's *Straight Out of Brooklyn*, starring George T. Odom, Anne D. Sanders, and Lawrence Gilliard Jr.; and Todd Haynes's *Poison*, inspired by the writings of Jean Genet. The film tells three different stories where deviant behavior and retribution—physical, psychological, and karmic—play a key role. Although a dark and polarizing film, it surprisingly won the grand prize.

As far as the premieres went, Stephen Frears's *The Grifters*, with Anjelica Huston, John Cusack, and Annette Benning, was a success; Brent Capra's *Mindwalk*, with Liv Ullman, Sam Waterston, John Heard, Ione Sky, and Emmanual Montes, also struck a harmonic chord, described as *My Dinner with Andre* for three; and John Sayles returned with the world premiere of his film *City of Hope*, starring Vincent Spano, Tony Lo Bianco, Joe Morton, and Angela Bassett, about an urban housing construction project and the shifting sands of politics and corruption. As Laurence Kardish stated in the program guide:

> That an American filmmaker, without studio financing but with much ingenuity, willpower, and a remarkable cast, can still realize such a provocative work of intertwined layers and major dimension is the most positive signal that the independent cinema in this country remains alive and fearless.

Perhaps the most successful film to come out of the film festival was one I supported but had only played a small part in obtaining. Richard Linklater, from Austin, Texas, had made a remarkable film featuring 105 of his favorite friends and neighbors, an experiment where each character leads fluidly to the next, much like life, especially if one happens to be young, friendly, and unemployed. I first saw *Slackers* in the offices of Tom Bernard and Michael Barker, at Orion Classics in New York. They popped a tape in the VCR, and off I went to Slackerville, U.S.A. It was a great ride. From the first few moments, I sensed I was watching something quite unlike anything I'd seen before. Though the camera didn't hurry, it did roam to find the next set of characters with which to spend time, and each was more interesting than the last. It was as though the film was choreographed to take place in one long take. An utterly unpredictable film, it featured a standout performance by a woman hawking Madonna's urine sample in a small jar and many of the other non-professional players were also memorable.

I knew immediately that the film was perfect for the festival. To prove his point, just after he'd finished the $23,000 16 mm version of the film, Richard Linklater booked it into a theater in Austin, where it played for eleven weeks, broke the house record, and sold out its first twenty performances. Based on that success, he felt confident enough to send a tape to producers rep John Pierson, who had Orion Classics interested within a week. They put up finishing money and blew the film up to 35 mm.

I guess I wasn't the only one to notice the film's merits because it established Richard Linklater's career, which has continued to be challenging, built out of autobiography, slices of life, and tidbits of local history. It is very cool he has remained so iconoclastic, thoughtful, and in touch with his peers. He has stayed in Austin but let Hollywood pay for a few films, and I think that was a smart move: stay connected to what got you to the dance in the first place. Richard Linklater has understood that concept, like Victor Nunez, Rob Nilsson, and a handful of others.

Months after *Slackers* had come out and Madonna's urine sample had been written about in *Time* magazine, I called Tom Bernard because I knew he was into playing practical jokes on people. Doing my best impersonation of an old Jewish lawyer, I asked for Mr. Tom Bernard's office. When the receptionist asked who was calling, I answered, "Tell him Madonna's attorney is on the line." When I was put on hold, I could imagine the pandemonium I'd created in his office. After a moment, Tom came on the line, very serious: "May I help you?" I was cracking up but in my best litigator-out-for-a-fight voice, I said, "I understand you're out pedaling Madonna's bodily fluids!"

He got kind of flustered. "Have you seen the movie?"

"Of course I've seen the movie; I saw it in your office," and with that I couldn't keep a straight face any longer. There was a sigh of relief from Orion Classics that I could hear all the way to Utah.

The documentary competition in 1991 also had a strong collection of films in the wake of *Roger and Me*. One film in particular broke out into the marketplace, Jennie Livingston's *Paris is Burning*, the film about "voguing" and the subculture that has found strength and meaning from the world of empty fashion images through "Drag Queen" balls. Made through three years of filming and interviews, the film struck an emotional chord with audiences in its exuberance and poignancy.

It shared the grand prize for documentary with Barbara Kopple's rousing *American Dream*, her five-years-in-the-making story of the Hormel meatpackers' strike in 1986 in Austin, Minnesota, which went on to win the Academy Award in March for best documentary. *American Dream* swept all the documentary awards at the 1991 festival, also winning the Audience Award and Filmmaker's Trophy. No other film has ever done that.

Other highlights from the 1991 festival included the Maysles brothers' follow-up film *Christo in Paris*; Ric Burns's *Coney Island*; Jan Oxenberg's *Thank You and Good Night*, the clash of humor and pathos that accompanied her family's dealing with Grandma Mae Joffe's illness and eventual death; and a screening of Luis Bunuel's 1967 groundbreaking *Belle de Jour*, starring a sublime Catherine Deneuve. The best film I saw at the 1991 festival had to be the unforgettable *Raspad*, by Soviet filmmaker Mikhail Belikov, an epic and chilling fictional account of the human and environmental decay left in the wake of the Chernobyl nuclear disaster. It was a profoundly moving cinematic experience, which should have been required viewing but inexplicably disappeared after the festival. The film's failure to gain widespread U.S. distribution underscored one of the problems inherent in putting on such a large and eclectic film festival. Pretty soon the festival has such a mishmash of programming splinters that it loses its focus, and it is very easy for the press and public to miss what should have been a very important and widely seen film. *Raspad* still haunts my soul, but I wish anyone trying to find it good luck.

Competition director Alberto Garcia got it just about right in his dramatic competition article in the program guide:

> Last year, the industry, the press and moviegoers alike flocked to Park City in search of *the* film that would ignite things in 1990. Callers tried to pry out tips and hints on which selection this might be. Indeed it is this anticipation of discovery that makes the festival exciting, but it is also this fever-pitch mentality that breeds the hype that billows the hot air that melts the snow that ruins the skiing and makes Park City feel like Los Angeles on one of its chilly days; all this detracts from the spirit of celebration. While no "son of Soderbergh" may emerge this year, there was a diverse group of extraordinary films to view, talk about, and be inspired by.

By 1991, a festival Fast Pass was up to $900. Package B, the preferred option to attend the last half of the festival, was $400. Also, for the first time, the festival expanded to include a Salt Lake City program, playing ironically at Trolley Corners, the very theaters where the festival had started. I guess the more things change, the more they remain the same.

One of the prominent things that did not remain the same, mirroring the staff changes, was the relationship between Sundance and the once-ubiquitous *Premiere Magazine.* As Chris Hicks reported in his January 27, 1991, wrap-up in the *Deseret News:*

> *Premiere* magazine, which had free copies all over Park City during the past two festivals . . . was nowhere in sight this year. The latest issue includes a negative story about the Sundance Institute and the magazine was withdrawn as a sponsor—and its $10,000 contribution returned. In addition, the article's author, *Premiere* executive editor Peter Biskind, resigned from the festival advisory board citing "conflict of interest" and canceled his festival ticket package and press credentials. (He told *Variety* he was going to Acapulco to interview Martin Short and didn't want to take two back-to-back trips.)

The other unique thing about 1991 was that it marked the tenth anniversary of the institute. Although Redford had publicly acknowledged his disdain for anniversaries and despite the trials and tribulations, the institute had ten years of experience under its belt, had an excellent collection of people to manage it, had produced amazing work, had acquired a sterling reputation, and had really made its presence known, both as a place of experimentation and exhibition. But more importantly, it was a festival for supporting a kind of film built first out of the craft of the screenplay and then from the whirlwind created by the talent who pulled together to make it reality. Creating relationships that led to producing good, honest, intelligent, heartfelt work clearly had an impact not only on Hollywood but, increasingly through Redford's personal design and interest, on the world stage as well. The unique blend of Redford's passions, personality, and place, all came together to make it so. As producer Amy Robinson of *Once Around*, said, "Redford began the institute ten years ago because he had the smarts, the sense of humor, the fortitude, the guts—and the real estate."

It was certain that the next ten years would present many new challenges, far different from the earlier ones. But in many ways the scenario would remain remarkably the same. It is still damned hard, no matter how much money you have, to make a good film—long, short, fiction, nonfiction, color, black-and-white. It all comes down to a properly structured, well-written script; inspired casting, which should help assure noteworthy performances; and finally, good pacing and tight editing, all of which is harder to accomplish than one might think. Really, when I think about it, it's a miracle movies ever get made, especially great ones. No matter what kind of mud can be slung Sundance's way (and it's really small, like dirt clods), no one can deny that it has been a major force, probably the principal factor in advancing the idea of independent film, along with the films themselves. That has become one of the real concerns with the growth and popularity of the festival: if people were worried about Sundance "going Hollywood" in 1990, how do they feel about 1997 or 1998?

Geoff Gilmore came to Sundance from ten years as the head of television and film programming at the UCLA Archives. While there he had programmed 800 to 900 films and 4,000 to 5,000 television programs, ranging from independents to mainstream. He had also consulted with a number of film festivals, including Los

Angeles, Hawaii, San Francisco, Berlin, and Venice. As he stated in an interview with Chris Hicks of the *Deseret News*:

> The Sundance Film Festival is a wonderful festival. It has an exceedingly good reputation and it is certainly one of the five most important festivals in the United States. It is the major film festival for American independent cinema.

Geoff went on to describe his working relationship with Alberto Garcia, the holdover competition director, handpicked by Tony Safford, "Last year Al did the competition with Tony's cooperation and I'm working with him essentially in the same way, perhaps a bit more than what Tony did. I'll probably see more films than Tony did." I had an inkling how Al might feel about that. But Geoff was a presence to be reckoned with. The best way to do it, I determined, was engage him full force.

The 1992 Sundance Film Festival was highlighted by a strong contingent of both documentary and dramatic films, and my voice in the selection was automatically increased when the two advisory committees were combined into one. Besides myself, the committee consisted of Robert Hawk from the Film Arts Foundation; Laurence Kardish from the Museum of Modern Art; Marian Luntz, film program director from Houston's Museum of Fine Art; film critic and writer B Ruby Rich; and publicist Norman Wang, then with Renee Furst and Associates. I was delighted to once again have a small say in documentary selection.

One of the extraordinary films I advocated was Lech Kowalski's *Rock Soup*. Shot vérité style by Doron Schlair in 1988, the film describes a day in the life of a group of New York's Lower East Side homeless who have banded together in a ragtag family and live in cardboard boxes and discarded wooden pallets in a small neighborhood park. They miraculously start an outdoor soup kitchen, which they call the Rainbow Soup Kitchen. The recipe for rock soup, as delivered by kitchen leader Kalif Beacon, in a star-spangled chimney sweep's hat, is simply to start a fire, put a kettle of water on, bring it to a boil, throw in some large rocks, and before you know, people are stopping, sniffing, and offering to add their own ingredients. Before long, hopefully, rock soup turns into a hearty meal. You never know when the recipe might come in handy.

The kitchen is being supported by significant donations from area restaurants and a very resourceful tribe of collectors when the residents discover they are going to be evicted to make way for a senior-citizen housing project. The unfortunate result is a pitting of the elderly against the homeless. The chronicle portrays the demise of the enterprising soup kitchen, and it is disheartening to think that most of these people went back to their solitary existence, really a national disgrace that continues today. It is as though the homeless are victims of some sort of natural disaster—think of it as an emotional tornado—they wander aimlessly, trying to cope; they are wiped out, living among the rubble of their own lives, but no one is coming to their rescue. As a black man in the film says, while he washes himself in the steaming morning air, "I feel like I'm in another country." Unfortunately, this country still exists in our cities, and the patrons of the Rainbow Soup Kitchen are more numerous than ever, each with a story to tell. The film is as pertinent today as it was a decade ago, perhaps even more so.

The other documentary film I championed was Robert Epstein and Jeffrey Friedman's *Where Are We?: Our Trip Through America*. Originally shot on video by the accomplished Jean de Segonzac and transferred to film, *Where Are We?* is a travelogue across America, made by the Academy Award–winning filmmakers responsible for *Common Threads*. "Where are we?" is the standard question of weary travelers on the highway, and that includes the filmmakers, who set out in a van to discover an America they really haven't known before. Using open-ended questions to very ordinary folks, such as "What do you do here?" and "What are you afraid of?" and "What are your hopes for the future?" the filmmakers discover the responses don't always match the circumstances.

Where Are We? is a road map into the psyche of heartland America, which reveals a people often limited by the vision they have of themselves, much like glimpses into lives, including our own, that go by like a roadside blur at sixty-five miles per hour. There's a visit to an obsessed Elvis fan, whose husband has erected an elaborate miniature of Graceland on their front lawn. The people we meet range from a gay marine, who is planning to come out, and presumably did because of the film, to the middle-aged mobile-home salesman making his sales pitch to a young couple looking for their first home in the tornado-prone South. The kaleidoscope of random portraits of American culture are not entirely complimentary. As one smiling old man says after learning the filmmakers are from California, ". . . they might run you back . . . no, we like people from other countries."

Other highlights in the documentary competition included undoubtedly the highest-budgeted film, Errol Morris's *A Brief History of Time*. This extraordinary portrait of world-renowned physicist Stephen Hawking, the wheelchair-bound (from Lou Gehrig's disease) genius responsible for unlocking some of the universe's most precious secrets, was rumored to have cost upward of $2 million (quoted in *Variety* as $5 million). The costs included the reconstruction of a larger and more elaborate office for Dr. Hawking on a soundstage in London, as well as other backdrops

ERROL MORRIS FROM THE EARLY YEARS OF THE FESTIVAL.

for all the other interviews. Although exquisitely done and a genuine success commercially, the film could have been chosen to play out of competition. Having a documentary with such a large budget winning the documentary competition effectively skewed, or more precisely screwed, the other entries.

The other unqualified hit was Joe Berlinger and Bruce Sinofsky's *Brother's Keeper*. The film was cobbled together from weekend shoots while the filmmakers held down full-time jobs. *Brother's Keeper* relates the compelling case of the Ward brothers, all over sixty, all illiterate bachelors who have lived in a two-room shack without an indoor toilet, telephone, or running water their entire lives in central New York state, a mere two-hour drive from Manhattan. Their lives are shattered on June 6, 1990, when Delbert, one of the brothers, awakens to find another brother dead in bed next to him. After he allegedly confesses to suffocating his brother Bill, an agonizing ten-month trial ensues, and the town that has previously shunned the reclusive family rallies to their defense, at the same time elevating a possible case of euthanasia into the nation's spotlight. In this detailed, intimate, and compelling telling of the story, the filmmakers succeed in answering many, but certainly not all of the questions in the case, including guilt or innocence. They also succeed in creating a very sensitive portrait of a family of isolated individuals operating well under the radar of rural America.

Brother's Keeper, along with Errol Morris's *The Thin Blue Line* and Nick Broomfield's *Eileen Wournos*, went on to help establish the primacy of contemporary criminal trial stories as effective film vehicles in the marketplace. The national media was naturally interested in the subject, since it reflected a deeper analysis of newsworthy events that was both provocative and entertaining.

Unfortunately, Michael Apted's *Incident at Oglala*, which played in a special screening at the 1992 festival, failed to alter the misguided history of the case. The film was executive-produced by Robert Redford, who had taken a long-term interest in the case of Leonard Peltier, the Native American who had been railroaded as the killer of two FBI agents and a fellow Native American on the Pine Ridge Reservation in South Dakota in 1975 in the now famous standoff. It was hoped the film would prompt a reexamination of the circumstantial evidence and result in a new trial for perhaps the most celebrated political prisoner in this country. Unfortunately, Peltier remains in federal prison, despite the best efforts of the filmmakers.

In another genre, the personal documentary, Camille Billops in *Finding Christa* tells the heart-wrenching story of giving up her four-year-old daughter for adoption because her lover refuses to marry her, and she is young, black, single, and has some ambition to be an artist. When she puts Christa up for adoption, it is with the understanding she may not see her again.

When Christa reaches adulthood, with the help of her compassionate foster mother, she tries desperately to find her birth mother, wandering the streets and dreaming of her. With assistance from ALMA, an organization that helps adoptive children find their natural parents, she finally tracks down her mother, who lives and works in New York City. What results is a life-affirming portrait of three independent and spirited black women. The courage of the filmmaker and her family to expose their own problematic laundry and, in the end, lead the audience to new understandings, was formidable.

The documentary jury noticed, and the film went on to split the grand prize with *A Brief History of Time*. The two illustrate an interesting disparity, one with a budget of millions and featuring a recognized international genius, and the other built out of straightforward interviews and old photographs, and with a decidedly homemade feel. Each was profound in its own, very different way.

The documentary competition was loaded with personal visions of the filmmaker's own worlds. Alan Berliner's exquisitely illuminating *Intimate Stranger* focuses on the reassembling of his maternal grandfather's past, which, with each revelation, causes even more questions, to the point where it acquires universal meaning about the pursuit of the American dream at the expense of personal relationships within a family. The questions are still poignant even several decades after the grandfather's death.

Marcos Williams's *In Search of Our Fathers*, documents his seven-year journey to find and meet his father. Although the film is a personal journey of discovery, as its title suggests, within the African American community, it achieves greater resonance as an examination of the way children are raised in the modern family.

James Danaqyumtewa, a seventy-four-year-old Hopi filmmaker, along with Swiss artist Agnes Barmettler and Swiss filmmaker Anika Schmid, made the extraordinary *Techqua Ikachi: Land—My Life*, a film that the elders of the Hopi village Hotevilla decided to make to record their oral tradition to leave as a legacy to their children. The result is a unique exploration of Hopi lifeways that paints a picture of endurance and resistance against overwhelming odds.

The other type of documentary in the 1992 competition was a unique blend of the resurgent travelogue, often dismissed as a joke of film history, and a critical examination of cultural issues. Marlon T. Riggs's provocative *Color Adjustment: Blacks in Prime Time* looks at the way African Americans have been portrayed historically on television. Robert Mugge's *Deep Blues*, is a musical tour de force of the Mississippi Delta and its blues tradition. Lucille Carra's *The Inland Sea*, is an examination of the "old Japan," as seen through the eyes of Donald Richie, an American authority on Japanese ways, and a portrait of this nearly landlocked sea garden and natural paradise. Les Blank's *Innocents Abroad* follows a busload of American tourists as they careen through the highlights of European culture. Stephen Olsson and Scott Andrews's *Last Images of War* is the startling antiwar statement built out of the photographic images of four photojournalists, American Jim Lindelof, British Andy Skripkowiak, Russian Sasha Sekretaryov, and Japanese Naoko Nanjo, all of whom were killed while on assignment in Afghanistan. Finally, Trinh T. Minh-ha's *Shoot For the Contents* looks past the travel guides of China via the small villages the filmmaker encountered in the optimistic days before Tiananmen Square.

The dramatic competition was no less compelling and also largely drawn from the filmmaker's personal experiences but grafted onto a more classic narrative structure. A film I joined Larry Kardish in supporting was *Black and White*, about a young female Soviet émigré, Lisa (Elena Shevchenko), and her volatile situation when she is taken under the wing of an apartment super, Roy (Gilbert Giles, in a winning performance), who is black, shy, decent, and tentative about his attraction to her. The film was written and directed by Boris Frumin, himself a Soviet émigré filmmaker. Although the film is in English, has an American cast, except for Elena Shevchenko, and was shot entirely on location in New York, it was edited in St. Petersburg, Russia, because Frumin was finally allowed to reenter his homeland and finish a film he had been forced to abandon, ironically named, *Errors of Youth*.

Allison Anders's excellent solo debut *Gas, Food and Lodging*, is the small-town, big-dreams story of a teenage girl, Shade (Fairuza Balk), and her quest to find a man for her single waitress mom (Brooke Adams), sort out her own romantic desires, and deal with her jaded older sister, Trudi (Ione Skye), who has been sexually wounded and overcompensates due to her fear of male abandonment. The result is a tender and authentic working-class tale of survival, love, and finding meaning just off the freeway in rural New Mexico. The film was a close contender for a prize at Sundance but finished just out of the money. It did, however, really launch Allison Anders's career, a woman who had admirably gotten herself off welfare and attended UCLA film school.

Alexandre Rockwell (*Hero*) returned with his enormously popular entry at the festival, *In the Soup*, starring the irrepressible Steve Buscemi, combined with the volcanic Seymour Cassel and backed by strong performances from Jennifer Beals, the director's talented wife, and Will Patton. The film centers on a young, frantic East Village director, Adolpho Rollo, who is down to his last dime when he places an ad in the paper to sell his 500-page screenplay to the highest bidder.

None other than Cassel shows up as Joe, a small-time hood looking for the perfect dupe to use in his petty scams. It turns out, despite Adolpho's best efforts to the contrary, to be a match made in heaven, as each character discovers something in the other that complements the stew. *In the Soup* is a riotously funny, black-and-white film that makes one wonder how low a filmmaker will sink to reach his dreams.

The film won the coveted grand prize, but somehow never was able to connect, from a distribution angle, with an audience I'm certain would very much enjoy it.

LORY SMITH FLANKED BY RON HENDERSON OF THE DENVER INTERNATIONAL FILM FESTIVAL AND ACTOR SEYMOUR CASSEL.

It helped to resurrect the acting career of Cassavetes's friend and talented colleague, Seymour Cassel, in a performance crafted out of pure acting joy and a dynamic physical presence.

Neal Jimenez and Michael Steinberg's *The Waterdance*, based on Jimenez's screenplay, is the autobiographical story of three men who must suddenly come to terms with their own paraplegic paralysis as a result of accidents when they find themselves face to face in a rehabilitation clinic, wheelchair-bound and without much hope for the future. Starring Eric Stoltz as Garcia, William Forsythe as the racist biker, Bloss, and, Wesley Snipes as the jive-ass Raymond, the film also benefited from strong and tender supporting performances by Helen Hunt and Elizabeth Peña. The relationships modulate over the course of their adjustment as wheelchair fights replace fists, fantasy replaces passion, and humor masks an utter sense of loss and despair. The end result is an honest and moving tale of courage and bonding and an unsentimental portrait of triumph over tragedy. The film rightly won the Audience Award and helped kick Neal Jimenez's career into high gear.

Anthony Drazan's *Zebrahead*, produced by Jeff Dowd, Charles Mitchell and William Willett, and executive-produced by Oliver Stone and Janet Yang, starring Ray Sharkey; Michael Rapaport, in a career-discovering performance; N'Bushe Wright; Deshonn Castle; and Ron Johnson. It's the inner-city story of a racially mixed group of high schoolers who are struggling with their relationships, their idealism, and their sense of family, tribe, and community. The title is an African American slang term for a white kid who has taken on the vestiges of black culture. Zack, a white Jewish kid, played by Rapaport, is immersed in the rhythms of black culture, in part due to his father, played memorably by Ray Sharkey, the ratty owner of a record store. Zack's best friend is black, and when his friend's cousin moves into the neighborhood, sparks begin to fly. Standing in the afterglow is an angry young man appropriately named Nut by the kids. A carefully detailed story with uniformly strong performances that build to an effective emotional climax, *Zebrahead* won the Filmmaker's Trophy.

Tom DiCillo's directorial debut was the quirky, visually interesting *Johnny Suede*, starring a young Brad Pitt as an undertalented rock 'n' roll wanna-be, who finally must confront his options. Catherine Keener plays his eventual love interest, Calvin Levels is his animated sidekick, and Nick Cave turns in a hilarious performance as Freak Storm, a down-on-his-luck rocker, with plenty of advice to dispense. Despite the cast and subject, the film really didn't perform as hoped in the marketplace.

On the heels of 1991's discovery of gay-themed films in *Paris is Burning* and *Poison*, 1992's program also contained several gay films, including Tom Kalin's *Swoon*, which went on to considerable commercial success and is a fictional account of the Leopold and Loeb murders of 1924; Christopher Münch's *The Hours and the Times*, also a fictional portrayal of real people, in this case John Lennon and Beatles manager Brian Epstein on holiday for a weekend in Barcelona. The film won a special jury prize even though it was playing out of competition and was technically ten minutes shy of being a feature film.

Finally Greg Araki's *The Living End*, is the outrageous contemporary story of two dissimilar gay men who both discover they are HIV-positive and decide they have nothing to lose as they vent their disillusionment on the American wasteland. This provocative study turns the conventional male "buddy" film on its proverbial head by fully examining the sexual aspects of gay attraction. *Butch Cassidy and the Sundance Kid*, it isn't. But there is no denying Greg Araki's imaginative defiance.

For the life of me, I couldn't understand why several films were in competition, let alone at a film festival. Either tediously self-indulgent or simply like a bad cable movie, the films I questioned included Rico Martinez's *Desperate*, which pretty much explains it all; Paul Mones's somber *Fathers and Sons*, starring Jeff Goldblum as a former director now running a bookstore, who jogs regularly along the boardwalk to exorcise his "inner demons" and attempts to reconcile with his son after his formerly neglected wife dies of cancer. Unfortunately, Jeff Goldblum doesn't run far enough in this inauthentic clunker. *Jo-Jo at the Gate of Lions* is one of those enigmatic, poetically charged, murky films that takes itself oh so seriously, as though youth angst were a new subject just discovered by the filmmaker in film school. The same is true of the technically ambitious *Star Time*, by Alexander Cassini, about a man's search for normalcy through his favorite television show, which has just been cancelled, when who should suddenly appear out of the ether but a television con man named Bones.

Finally, one of the most egregious selections ever put into competition is the formulaic *Poison Ivy*, by Katt Shea Ruben, starring Drew Barrymore, Sara Gilbert, Tom

Skerritt, and Cheryl Ladd, about a femme fatale who seduces her best friend's father, then kills the mother to take over the household. As the uncredited program note pathetically stated, "*Poison Ivy* is a young girl's introduction to the darkest extremes of human nature." With a name like Ivy, what's a poor girl to do? It was so bad it was laughable.

I found these misplaced films a major source of aggravation as I wondered how a festival dedicated to "independent" film could make such choices when there were so many more qualified films that actually deserved to be shown. When I questioned Alberto or Geoff, or my fellow committee members, no one was ever able to come up with a satisfactory explanation. It was either a capitulation to political pressure from some quarter, or someone had forgotten to watch the films all the way through, which I found highly unlikely. In either case, I wasn't alone in my feelings. As *Variety's* Todd McCarthy said of *Poison Ivy*, ". . . it certainly has no place at a film festival."

Finally, two very interesting, very violent, and very controversial films with clear connections to Hollywood emerged as clear winners at the box-office after the festival but failed to move the jury, festival audiences (except perhaps out of the theater prematurely), or the attending press. Jeff Stanzler's *Jumpin' at the Boneyard*, starring the stellar cast of Tim Roth, Alexis Arquette, Danitra Vance, Kathleen Chalfant, and Samuel L. Jackson, is set in the Bronx and takes place over the course of a single day, as two brothers sift through their various disappointments after one catches the other trying to rip off his apartment to support his substantial crack addiction and beats the living daylights out of him. Executive-produced by Lawrence Kasdan, the depiction is unsparingly graphic but nothing in comparison to its rival by an unknown director who used to work in a video-rental store, named Quentin Tarantino.

Reservoir Dogs is a fusion of ultraviolence, pulp drama invested with black humor, over-the-top writing, and performances unleashed by an imaginative and smart director, who was clearly making his calling-card announcement to the Hollywood establishment that he was a force of nature to be reckoned with. It didn't hurt that the film was coproduced by Harvey Keitel, which helped the young filmmaker gain access to a cast that included Keitel, Tim Roth, Chris Penn, Steve Buscemi, Laurence Tierney, and Michael Madsen. But despite the film's eventual acclaim, the press didn't immediately warm to the subject. As *Hollywood Reporter's* Duane Byrge said, "*Reservoir Dogs* is just plain brutal . . . its relentless intensity will likely claim many screening victims." *Variety's* Todd McCarthy said in his review:

> Accomplished as all these individual elements are, however, there is a strong sense of this as an audition piece for the director, an occasion for a new filmmaker to flaunt his talents but apply them to no ends other than that. Undeniably juicy, with its salty talk and gunplay, the film is nihilistic but not resonantly so,

giving it no meaning outside the immediate story and characters. Pic is impressive but impossible to love.

Apparently the jury agreed, as the film was a topic of major discussion, but ultimately was awarded no prizes, much to the consternation of Tarantino, who proceeded to bad-mouth the festival and eventually withheld *Pulp Fiction* from screening at Sundance. To my knowledge, the guy hasn't been back. Apparently he holds a grudge just as long as he holds a violent angle. Perhaps his loss is our gain. I've always been suspicious of people who seem so full of themselves and so outspoken in their effort to attract attention.

That was certainly not the case with Alberto Garcia. Painfully shy but with a radical youthful exuberance and a tendency toward subversiveness, Alberto was someone to whom I felt I could talk. He always seemed eager to gauge my opinion on films and, in fact, had sent me Carl Franklin's intense film *One False Move*, which I watched, recognized as a provocative piece of work, but didn't feel I could support because of its violence. He respected my take, and obviously others on the committee agreed because we didn't play the film. While others have rallied to the film, and it may have been a mistake not to have played it, I just couldn't bring myself to be its advocate.

This was to be Alberto's last year with Sundance. He left at a high point, and I always appreciated the direction in which he had tried to nudge the competition. He got out of film programming and went into sound recording, working on various projects, including a film or two with Gregg Araki. Every now and then I see his name in credits and hope he is much happier sitting at a Nagra with headphones on and actually contributing to the creative side of filmmaking.

The other significant change coming out of the 1992 Sundance Film Festival was a new official sponsor in the form of *Entertainment Weekly*, which happily stepped into the void created by *Premiere's* abrupt departure. As the publisher of the magazine, Michael J. Klingensmith, stated in the program guide:

> It is with a great deal of pleasure that *Entertainment Weekly* magazine joins the ranks of sponsors of the prestigious Sundance Film Festival. This association with the best in independent filmmaking is indeed an honor, and one which we hope to nurture over the years.

Entertainment Weekly is still nurturing the relationship for all it is worth. Someone from *Premiere* attends Sundance every year, to cover the festival, but it isn't Peter Biskind.

Caryn James of the *New York Times* wrote a funny article about people's most vivid impression of attending the festival. Spalding Gray, whose *Monster in a Box* made its U.S. premiere at Sundance, stated:

> So what do you do in a little town where you either have to ski or go to the movies? Where there are so many movies you feel like you're in New York City?

Renee and I ended up going to the movies, and I really don't like to see too many movies in a row because I get all mixed up. Also I tend to get depressed when I go to movies during the day.

Eric Stoltz was right on when he stated:

> This is like being in the midst of a Fellini. I walk down the street, and I'm surrounded by people of all shapes and sizes and colors—producers, actors, writers, directors. There's a constant flow of strange people, and they all have colds, they all have the flu, and they all insist on shaking your hand. So all I think of as I walk down the street is "When can I wash my hands?" Certain viruses can live longer on the hands of producers, and you're constantly shaking their hands. So I'm trying to wear my gloves as much as possible.

ROBERT REDFORD AND LOUIS MALLE.

Finally, writer and director Paul Schrader, whose film *Light Sleeper* made its world premiere at Sundance in 1992, said after learning that his car had been towed when he and the actor Willem Dafoe had parked on a strip of grass to make their screening at he Egyptian Theatre, "This part of the country, I don't know why, it just sort of brings out the Gary Gilmore in me. I just want to go over to a 7-Eleven and shoot somebody." He was finally reconciled when the apologetic police informed him and Dafoe that they shouldn't feel too badly because Clint Eastwood's car had been towed the year before.

The festival wrap-up showed that attendance had risen another 10 percent, selling just under 40,000 tickets. Corporate donations also increased by an amazing

53 percent over the previous year, according to Sundance executive vice president Gary Beer. A Fast Pass cost $900; Package A, $300; and Package B, $400. There were 33 films shown in competition out of 250 submissions and the program included nearly 80 films.

And Redford lightheartedly confessed to Caryn James about Paul Schrader's car, "It was me who towed that car. We're desperately in need of funds, and we'll take revenues any way we can get them." The word went out that, for a change, the popular films had won all the awards at Sundance.

PARK CITY'S MAIN STREET DURING SUNDANCE FILM FESTIVAL—AN EXERCISE IN SELF-PROMOTION.

CHAPTER 10

Young Versus Old, Slamdance Versus Sundance

The watchword going out from the 1993 festival was that twenty-something filmmakers had emerged center stage, showing off brash talents housed in very youthful mortal coils. Todd McCarthy wrote a fascinating piece in *Variety*, just after the festival, to blunt the criticism that twenty-something filmmakers couldn't possibly have much to say about life experience, nor the requisite cinematic skills to say it.

> At the Sundance Film Festival this year, there were a notable number of films directed by exceedingly young directors. Jennifer Lynch of *Boxing Helena*, Rob Weiss of *Amongst Friends*, Robert Rodriguez of *El Mariachi,* Tony Chan of *Combination Platter*, Bryan Singer of *Public Access*, and Leslie Harris of *Just Another Girl on the I.R.T.* are all reportedly between twenty-four and twenty-seven years old.

McCarthy quoted an old friend of director Frank Capra, Dr. Carl Anderson, a Nobel Prize–winning physicist from CalTech, who suggested in Capra's autobiography that the mixture of brain activity and personal audacity seems to make the mid-twenties a particularly fertile time in many disciplines. "It's the age when the combination of knowledge and brashness is the most potent," observed Anderson. "At twenty-six a student is flush with up-to-date learning, yet is rebel enough—and full of beans enough—to defy the conservative, scientific establishment, and to come up with some wild guesses."

Capra himself went on to name great figures from history for whom twenty-six was a critical age—from Alexander the Great to Napoleon to Lincoln to Shakespeare and Charlie Chaplin. He reminded readers that Orson Welles was twenty-five when he directed *Citizen Kane*. McCarthy then listed a formidable collection of directors who made their first features in their late twenties, and concluded with:

> . . . of course, all of the above are pikers when compared to Bernardo Bertolucci, who made his first feature film at 21, and William Wyler, Francis Ford Coppola and Rainer Werner Fassbinder, who did the same at 23.

The point here is that it's never been particularly unusual for directors to get their starts at an age when they have often been among the youngest people on the set. Precociousness, brashness, arrogance, and unearned ego have always been part and parcel of the directorial package, along with talent, so it shouldn't be seen as a remarkable phenomenon that a number of directors, at any given time, are in their mid-twenties.

McCarthy went on to presciently caution:

> The dark side of this obsession with age is that, all too often, especially in the New Hollywood, the promising first or second film turns out to be the ultimate achievement. Many directors now or approaching middle age—you can supply the names as well as I can—made their marks with some genuinely exciting or interesting films back in the 1970s and 1980s, but more recently have been getting by with what can only be called hack work. . . .
>
> One telltale sign is when a director who started by writing or co-writing his or her films essentially drops that part of the job, which is another way of saying that some creative death occurs when you start doing projects other people want you to do rather than films you simply have to make.
>
> Inevitably, as always, some of the directors at Sundance this year will be happily sucked up into the system and add their names to the roster of efficient industry assembly-line workers. Others, with more on their minds than their bank accounts, will steer a more independent course and possibly carve more idiosyncratic careers. It's very often harder to make a second film than a first, and the sophomore efforts of this year's young crop will probably tell us more about where they intend to go than did their initial outings.

As usual, McCarthy's analysis was right on. A pertinent example is the trajectory of Robert Rodriguez's career. After the much ballyhooed, and inaccurate, statement that *El Mariachi* had been made for the ridiculous sum of $7,000 (of course, in that form the film was unreleasable and Columbia Pictures ultimately had to kick in several hundred thousand dollars to blow the film up to 35 mm and redo the sound mix), it was announced at the festival that Rodriguez would direct a $6 million remake of the film. It was the first time, to my knowledge, that a filmmaker had used an independent film as a vehicle to drive directly through the gates of Hollywood, where he was swooped up by the establishment to make it all over again under very different financial conditions. My question is: Which version is more interesting to watch: the 16 mm handheld version, shot often in single takes over the course of two weeks without sync sound; or the big-time mainstream movie of the same story? It is apparent that some people can do much more with much less.

GABRIEL GARCIA MARQUEZ, ISABELLA ROSSELLINI, DAVID LYNCH, AND ROBERT REDFORD.

That was certainly not the case with the controversial *Boxing Helena*, directed by Jennifer Lynch, the twenty-four-year-old daughter of David Lynch, himself no stranger to controversy. The film had received a great deal of pre-festival publicity because of the lawsuit filed by the producers against actress Kim Basinger, who had backed out of her verbal commitment to the picture just four weeks before production. Madonna had done the same thing before Basinger.

But the real hubbub centered around the film's bizarre story about a sexually alluring woman and her infatuated suitor, an orthopedic surgeon who removes her arms and legs and keeps her as a torso in a coffin-like box. It was a disturbing film labeled "a black comedy," except by the end, very few people were laughing. *Boxing Helena* starred Julian Sands, whose comment at a press conference during the festival—"I wanted to f—k the corpse"— further outraged film critics. Sherilyn Fenn's courageous performance was the only plus; it was nothing short of piercing.

One clear pattern was developing within the realm of independent films, at least the examples that appeared at the festival. They employed emerging stars in their casts, or other recognizable older cast members in secondary roles, to help secure financing from home-video rental markets. Many films at the 1993 festival revealed that trend: Everett Lewis returned to the festival with *An Ambush of Ghosts*, starring Stephen Dorff, Geneviève Bujold, and Bruce Davison; Michael Steinberg returned with *Bodies, Rest, and Motion*, starring Bridget Fonda, Phoebe Cates, Tim Roth, and Eric Stoltz; Rob Weiss brought *Amongst Friends*, starring Patrick McGaw and Mira Sorvino; Jeffrey Levy's *Inside Monkey Zetterland*, starred Steven Antin, Patricia Arquette, Sandra Bernhard, Sofia Coppola, Tate Donovan, Rupert Everett, Katherine Helmond, Bo Hopkins, Ricki Lake, Debi Mazar, and Martha Plimpton; Rod McCall's *Paper Hearts*, starred James Brolin, Sally Kirkland, and Kris Kristofferson; and Keva Rosenfeld's *Twenty Bucks*, featured Linda Hunt, Brendan Fraser, Gladys Knight, Elizabeth Shue, Steve Buscemi, Christopher Lloyd, David Schwimmer, and Spalding Gray in cameo roles. I was generally resistant to these calculated films, which seemed somehow like hybrids between Hollywood films and what I thought of as independent films. They had story lines that were at times innovative and probably wouldn't get made in establishment Hollywood, but at the same time they were more like experiments for the nearly rich and famous. I don't like acting lab experiences committed to film, financed by elements of the Hollywood system, and pushed into the marketplace under the rubric of "independent film."

DAVID LYNCH, DR. RUTH WESTHEIMER, AND ISABELLA ROSSELLINI AT THE RIVER HORSE CAFE.

But there were also some real gems straight from the independent heart of fine filmmakers. Tony Chan's excellent *Combination Platter*, shot in his parents' Chinese restaurant on weekends and after hours; Steve Gomer's *Fly By Night*; Jon Jost's return with *Frameup*, starring veteran stage actors and actual husband and wife. Nancy Carlin and Howard Swain; Leslie Harris and her Miramax-distributed *Just Another Girl on the I.R.T.*; David Williams's emotionally touching *Lillian*; Edward Barkin's love-triangle drama *Rift*; and finally the two films that shared the grand prize at the 1993 festival, in a perfect counterpoint to each other, twenty-something Bryan Singer's *Public Access*, a visually and thematically interesting film about a young man's sinister presence in a small town via the public-access channel, and festival veteran Victor Nunez's exquisitely realized *Ruby in Paradise*, a film I had discovered and championed from the beginning.

Ruby in Paradise is the coming-of-age story of Ruby Lee Gising, played to perfection by the young Ashley Judd, a young woman who, as she puts it, has managed miraculously to escape the hills of Tennessee "without getting pregnant or beat up." She travels to the "redneck Riviera" on the coast of Florida to begin her new life in retail sales at a tourist gift shop and sort out her complicated feelings about her self-worth.

All the while she is testing the waters of relationships, first with the handsome, jerk-off son of her employer, played with smarmy enthusiasm by Bentley Mitchum, and then with the more honorable but disillusioned Mike, who works at a tree nursery, played with intelligence and empathy by the excellent Todd Field. By this point in the film, I was actually pulling for Ruby and Mike to succeed in their tender mercies for each other, but filmmaker Victor Nunez leaves the film's denouement clearly in the hands of Ruby, as she abandons the budding relationship to find her own independence and voice.

Ruby in Paradise is one of the most moving, subtle, honest, and life-affirming films I've seen to date, and it did move into the marketplace to critical and moderate financial success. Victor Nunez had emerged triumphant, after an eight-year wait since his *A Flash of Green*, with his integrity intact. As he said to Duane Byrge in the *Hollywood Reporter*, "It's too late for me to get discovered. I go to Sundance because I believed in small films made outside of the mainstream. Also, we're hoping we'll come out of Sundance with a distribution deal."

Fortunately, it wasn't too late for Ashley Judd to be discovered. At the closing night, as I was congratulating Victor Nunez and his producer, Keith Cofford, I asked Ashley Judd if she realized she was going to be touted as one of the acting discoveries at the festival. She demurred her answer, but perhaps more effectively answered the same question to Donna Parker in the *Hollywood Reporter*. "When you're investing your heart and soul, your reward isn't monetary," said Judd, who admitted her ego had gotten out of hand since winning accolades. "When that happens, I call 1-800-EGO-DEFLATE, that's my mother," she joked. She is the youngest daughter/sister of the former country-western singing duo, Naomi and Wynonna Judd.

I couldn't have been happier for Victor Nunez and the well-earned response to *Ruby in Paradise*. It was validation once again, for the kind of films I thought our festival should be championing.

In many ways, the documentary competition outweighed the dramatic one for positive audience response. With two films also sharing the grand prize, as well as having similar production histories, comparison to the dramatic films was inevitable.

The grand prize was shared by *Silverlake Life: The View from Here* and *Children of Fate: Life and Death in a Sicilian Family*. Both films had been started by one filmmaker and for some reason taken over by another, who carried the project to completion. In the case of *Silverlake Life*, when Mark Massi and Tom Joslin discovered they had AIDS, Tom, a former USC film professor and director, decided to document their experiences on videotape from their diagnoses to their ultimate deaths. The film, which was completed by their friend, Peter Friedman, is difficult to watch, but it put the AIDS epidemic into the realm of personal journal. It was an unforgettable journey.

Children of Fate was originally shot by Robert Young in 1961, documenting for an NBC white paper the poverty and despair of a Sicilian family. Deemed too controversial at the time, it was never broadcast and was shelved by the filmmaker until it was rediscovered by his son Andrew and his filmmaking partner and wife Susan Todd, some thirty years later. Andrew and Susan went back to Sicily to get an update on the families depicted in his father's footage.

The combination of the original and updated footage made for a powerfully dramatic cinematic experience, intensified by the realization that these people's lives were real then and now and that they hadn't changed much over the course of three decades. As my friend and fellow Competition Selection Advisory Board member Robert Hawk stated in the program guide, "Searing and unforgettable, the thirty-year arc of *Children of Fate* leaves an indelible imprint on the viewer."

It was also a very rewarding experience to see the accomplished Robert Young beaming with pride at the achievement of his son, a kind of passing of the cinematic torch from one generation to the next. *Children of Fate* was nominated for an Academy Award in 1993.

Another unique documentary, again which I had championed and brought to the festival, was *On The Bridge*, made by the wonderful Frank Perry, a friend and colleague I'd made while serving on various juries at the Aspen Film Festival. Frank was well known for creating the groundbreaking *David and Lisa*, in 1962, for which he had received an Academy Award nomination. He had also made the accomplished *Play it as it Lays*, the seldom-seen but delightfully funny *Rancho Deluxe*, and the highly regarded *Diary of a Mad Housewife*, as well as the acclaimed *Mommie Dearest*, originally a miniseries for television documenting the severe relationship of Hollywood actress Joan Crawford and her daughter.

What would turn out to be Perry's final film was the touching and fascinating documentary *On the Bridge*. It is the revealing portrait of a cancer patient in search of remedies and illumination about the meaning of life and death and everything in between. The thing that made it such a courageous and valuable piece of work was that the cancer patient was none other than Perry himself. As Geoff Gilmore put it so succinctly in the program guide:

> His introspective observations are fascinating, humorous, moving and insightful. There is an uncanny lack of self-pity. Indeed the resoluteness with which he faces the various stages of his illness would be inspiring if this work was attempting to be merely sentimental or melodramatic. Instead, the effect is a thought-provoking and ultimately touching realization of the preciousness of life, which leads us to profoundly respect both the man and the filmmaker.

It was a fitting tribute to a man of enormous talent and range.

Frank Perry lost his battle with cancer later in the year, but we all won something in his intimate probe of the mysteries of life, which he was brave enough to share. I was proud to have had the opportunity to get to know the man and call him a friend.

Another fabulous documentary made by a friend was Jerret Engle's *Something Within Me*. Directed by Emma Joan Morris, *Something Within Me* is the heartwarming story of St. Augustine's School of the Arts, set in the hardness of the South Bronx, a school where the curriculum emphasizes rigorous musical training as a mandatory component of the students' education. At a time when arts disciplines were being eliminated from many schools' core studies, and even their list of extracurricular activities, this program administered by committed educators and parents alike is a refreshing relief from the steady diatribe of negative stories about the state of education in America. Hopefully it is also a guidepost for the future. The film's optimistic point of view is conveyed by the students themselves, where hope is supported by discipline, and the musical magic of self-expression is the inspiration that leads to a freeing of the children's spirit.

The film touched all our souls. It was the epitome of what education should be all about: to work toward an understanding and mastery of a subject that promotes general curiosity and enthusiasm for life. What makes *Something Within Me* particularly meaningful is that none of these kids demonstrate any particular talent for music, nor is it the expectation that any of them will ultimately become professional musicians. The principle is that the forum of music, and, by implication, the arts in general, can foster the value of educational accomplishment, increase the individual's sense of self-worth, and plant the inner knowledge that, given hard work and encouragement from others, these children can succeed at anything they set their hearts and minds to. *Something Within Me* deservingly won the documentary Audience Award and the Filmmaker's Trophy as well as a commendation for merit from the jury.

Another very popular documentary was Bill Couturie's *Earth and the American Dream*, financed courageously by HBO and one of the most visually memorable documents in the 1993 competition. The film chronicles the white man's pursuit of the American Dream and the environmental disaster that has historically been left in his wake. Concentrating mostly on mass production and the resulting mass destruction, *Earth and the American Dream* is an evocative red flag raised over the course of human pursuits that resonates with cautionary warnings remaining largely unheeded. But the film also underscores the inherent value of documentary films in our culture by serving as a historical clarion call, set in a specific context by a formidable cinematic talent.

The remaining films in the documentary competition broke into the familiar genres of place and personality. Nora Jacobson's *Delivered Vacant*, eight years in the making, focuses on the gentrification of the traditionally blue-collar Hoboken, New Jersey; Tiana Thi Thanh Nga's *From Hollywood to Hanoi*, recounts the filmmaker's journey back to her Vietnam roots; Roger Weisberg and Jean de Segonzac's wonderful *Road Scholar* features poet and NPR commentator Andrei Codrescu in a search for what makes America from the comfort of a red Cadillac convertible on the open road; Bill Day and Terry Schwartz's unorthodox eco-documentary *Saviors of the Forest* brings a sense of humor and irony to the edges of the rain forest; and Barbara Hammer's erotic, political, and personal exploration of gay mores and their traditional portrayal in cinema makes *Nitrate Kisses* an assemblage of images sometimes difficult to watch because of their unfettered in-your-face graphic quality but full of impact nonetheless.

On the personality side of the documentary equation were Nick Broomfield's questioning documentary on the nation's first purported female serial killer, *Aileen Wuornos: The Selling of a Serial Killer*; Barry Minott's gritty labor portrait *Harry Bridges: A Man and His Union*; Jerry Aronson's labor of love *The Life and Times of Allen Ginsberg*; Susan Munoz and Erica Marcus's stirring documentary on Palestinian journalist Raymonda Tawil, *My Home, My Prison*; and finally Susan Steinberg and Susan Lacy's polyphonic documentary of prodigious singer/songwriter *Paul Simon: Born at the Right Time*.

There were other notable highlights and a couple of true misadventures, too, in the premieres and special screenings at the 1993 festival. Mike Newell's *Into the West* was the opening-night film. Although I had spent several days with the amiable British director, scouting for locations throughout Utah on an earlier film of his, *Amazing Grace and Chuck*, and in fact, had been present to watch and encourage him to consume his first Hostess Twinkie at a little filling station near Paradise, Utah, and then try to explain the concept of shelf life, *Into the West* was the only opening-night film that, because of illness, I was ever unable to attend.

The film was written by Jim Sheridan *(My Left Foot)* and starred Gabriel Byrne and the always excellent Ellen Barkin, and is about a family of Irish boys living in the tenements of Dublin who bond irrevocably with a magnificent white horse their grandfather has brought home to the apartment. The film was very well received and set the stage for the following year's Mike Newell encore with the even-more-heralded *Four Weddings and a Funeral*. Newell is a very nice man who also happens to be a great director who makes wide-ranging, intelligent, well-acted films, employing that wry British sensibility that betrays an English-speaking, but clearly European, take on story, plotting, pace, and design.

The U.S. premiere of Sally Potter's wildly exotic adaptation of the Virginia Woolf novel, *Orlando*, was one of the great visual treasures of the festival. The riveting film stars the translucent Tilda Swinton, as well as Lothaire Bluteau, Billy Zane, and Quentin Crisp, and is the story of the changing sexual identity of a seemingly ageless character over the course of 400 years. It was an unforgettable and utterly transporting film experience and received a full ten-minute standing ovation after the screening in the Egyptian Theatre as Potter climbed the rickety stairs to the stage. As she said to Bernard Weinraub of the *New York Times*:

> One of the things we're saying here is that men and women have far more in common than we've imagined, that the differences between us have been grossly exaggerated and made the basis for huge pain, grief and misery. Women have difficult lives, but men have difficult lives, too. What I'm trying to say here is that endings are beginnings. . . . In order to come into the present, you have to give up the past, let go. It sounds simple but it's very hard to achieve in most of our lives. We're all driven by our histories.

Anybody who hasn't seen *Orlando* should rent it and put it on the largest screen available. It is an exquisite cinematic tour de force.

Sadly, such was not the case for the world premiere of *Silent Tongue*, a film by the sometimes-brilliant and always-daring playwright, screenwriter, director, and usually interesting actor, Sam Shepard. *Silent Tongue* endured one of the most poorly received screenings I've ever had the misfortune of sitting through, as it premiered in the jealously guarded 7:00 P.M. slot at the Egyptian Theatre. The end of the week was when Package B holders arrived, the main Hollywood heavy hitters. It was an excruciating experience to watch an interesting cast, including Alan Bates, Richard Harris, Dermot Mulroney, River Phoenix, and Sheila Tousey, stumble around in the dirt as a ragtag group of dysfunctional frontier people, with a collection of sideshow oddities, headed by the alcoholic leader of the Kickapoo Indian Medicine Show and a Native American ghost, thrown in for good measure. The result was an over-ambitious mishmash of dusty set pieces, particularly uncinematic in its staging, visual design, and structure.

During the unfortunate screening, with Sam Shepard and Jessica Lange in attendance, the film elicited unintended snickers and even laughs at the preposterously overblown dialogue and plot and the way-over-the-top performances. I actually felt sorry for Shepard when he was finally coaxed to the stage by Geoff Gilmore to take questions and answers following what everyone knew had been a disastrous screening. After a couple of minutes of torturous questions from a mind-numbed audience, which he answered mostly with "yeps" and "nopes," he was mercifully allowed to leave the stage.

It probably didn't help that Gilmore's program notes had overhyped the film and raised expectations, stating, "This is that rarest of cinematic achievements: a film which can be applauded for its artistry, for its intellectual content, for its emotional power and for its message. . . . Shepard's accomplishment is no less than a redefinition of the western." Unfortunately, the film's message was as mumbled as the director's answers at the Q and A. Fortunately for Shepard's filmmaking career, the film was never heard from again. A "silent tongue" was the best they could have hoped for.

Speaking of silence, Canadian Guy Maddin's fascinating experiment in re-creating German expressionism, *Careful*, told the story of a snowy mountain town where everyone had to whisper to keep a disastrous avalanche at bay. It was extreme filmmaking, in its use of various color-film stocks, a scratchy soundtrack, and its authentic "old talkie" quality, a perfect fit for Park City in the midst of winter, as it had been in the fall for the Telluride Film Festival.

But by the conclusion of the 1993 Sundance Film Festival, there wasn't much whispering going on; all that was left was the shouting. As David Ansen said in his festival wrap-up for *Newsweek*:

> It was an irritating but not uncommon sight at the 1993 Sundance Film Festival; a guy in a movie theater whispering into his cellular phone as the lights go down. Agents and lawyers were crawling all over the snowy streets of Park City, Utah, this year; it was said William Morris Agency alone had 25 reps in place, scouring the festival for the next breakthrough twenty-something filmmaker. What was once the most laid-back, un-Hollywood film festival—designed by Robert Redford's Sundance Institute to showcase American independent film—has become a tension-filled auction block, with long waiting lists for the hot screenings and nervous young filmmakers whose futures are on the line.
>
> As it turned out, the real story of Sundance '93 was the renaissance of first-rate documentaries. . . . The dealmakers may have had a disappointing year, but the real goal of the Sundance Film Festival was fulfilled: to celebrate the stubborn, maverick and often not-for-profit visions of the independent moviemaker.

Comparisons to other festivals were inevitable. Victor Nunez, cowinner of the dramatic grand prize, was quoted in the *Washington Post*:

> The New York and Toronto film festivals used to be wonderful places for American independents. But no more. Both are now overrun by the big movies, particularly European ones, and the buzz at these festivals is usually about which big star is being flown in that day for interviews. It's hard for an independent with a low-budget film and no money for publicity, to compete for attention.

Actor John Turturro, in attendance to premiere his debut film *MAC*, concurred, "The difference between Sundance and other festivals is that the studio head and the first-time director are invited to the exact same parties."

But with 55,000 tickets sold, up 34 percent from 1992, and both A and B packages sold out for the first time, even with the Carl Winters School (now the Park City Library Center) adding a loathsomely uncomfortable 300-seat theater, the twenty extra screenings wedged into the schedule, and the advent of 8:00 A.M. press screenings 200 of the 500 international media people now attending, the festival appeared to have reached the saturation point.

Gary Beer had done a masterful job of attracting substantial new corporate funding, reported by Duane Bryge in the *Hollywood Reporter*, as being 70 percent more than the previous year. With upscale sponsors like Mercedes Benz, AT&T,

Entertainment Weekly and champagne-maker Piper-Heidsieck helping to make up nearly 50 percent of the festival's now $1.2 million annual budget, the fear was that the festival was too crowded, too corporate, and way too cozy with the Hollywood establishment. As Pat Wechsler reported in a wrap-up for the *Washington Post*: "Presumably, the sponsors are aware that even the most defiantly independent filmmakers might just leave Sundance with a greater appreciation for champagne and a Mercedes."

But, in fairness, the festival had reached some sort of synthesis of previously clashing cultures. Instead of being an outsider organization looking in under the tent, we were now clearly seated front and center. In 1993, two small references proved we had finally driven the idea of our film festival deep into the consciousness of the media-obsessed country. One was when Alex Trebeck, on the popular game show *Jeopardy*, provided the "answer"—"It is the annual event, held each January in Park City, Utah, sponsored by Robert Redford." The participants all hammered hard to supply the "question" that was on the tip of their collective tongues, "What is the Sundance Film Festival?"

The other occurred in Robert Altman's very inside look at the comings and goings of Hollywood in his loopy send-up, *The Player*. When the slimy studio executive played by Tim Robbins runs into John Cusack, playing himself, he asks if Cusack is going to Telluride this year. Cusack says he plans to go to Sundance instead.

As I sat in the darkened theater in Salt Lake City, a smile crossed my face for what had just occurred in a piece of throwaway dialogue. But I also thought it was an unfortunate and inappropriate pitting of one festival against another. I'd been attending Telluride's excellent film festival every Labor Day for over ten years and had worked with festival codirector Tom Luddy on a film project. I considered both him and the festival great friends. But there was no denying, Sundance was now part of the national lexicon, an insider's and outsider's reference. It had become the most important ten days on the calender for studio executives and people making films in their basements, with only their guts, instincts, and raw talent as their guideposts. They all shared the notion that, come the third week of January, if you had anything to do with movies, Park City, Utah, was the place to be seen and heard.

The 1993 festival also introduced Catherine Schulman to the staff, taking over for Alberto Garcia as associate programmer. She, like Alberto before her, was a talented person receptive to strong conversations about various films' merits, which in my mind was essential to the selection process. Frank discussion was more important than ever because of the exponential increase in festival entries coupled with the demand for screening slots by companies looking to launch new films. Add to this heady mixture enormous pressure from the press for new film discoveries, the heat-seeking mission of film business interests looking for the next Steven Soderbergh, and a burgeoning public awareness of this new and different type of film experience, compound it with the limited number of competition slots available for the past dozen years, and it all added up to an opportunity for someone else to come along and exploit the near misses that had almost made it into Sundance. I could feel it coming in my bones.

Between the 1993 and 1994 film festivals, I initiated a dialogue with Geoff Gilmore about either expanding the number of films in competition to keep abreast of the burgeoning number of entries and the many excellent American independent films that we were not able to include in the program, or developing a new program to incorporate these other films. It had always been a bone of contention for me that our festival purported to be a festival celebrating American independent film, but it was so full of foreign films, premieres, tributes, and special screenings. In any given year, approximately 30 percent of the festival consisted of American independents and the rest was a mishmash of cinema from other parts of the world.

Now don't get me wrong; some of my greatest cinematic experiences during the festival included these other films, especially the foreign ones. And there was a concerted effort on behalf of festival programmers to find parallels to American independents in the far corners of the globe. But at a time when our entries were increasing severalfold each year, I felt strongly that we could not keep the number of competition films static. To continue was to put a hammerlock on the kinds of films deemed worthy to enter the marketplace. As one of the cultural gatekeepers, I thought it was imperative that our festival remain as open and exploratory as possible, even if that meant playing some films that had moments of brilliance but were fundamentally flawed.

Other members of the programming staff were not as receptive to this idea as I had hoped. My primary focus all along had been advocating American independent films. It was still an uphill battle for American independent filmmakers, and I thought we needed to remain steadfast supporters. Also I was constantly reminding anyone who would listen that they were the group of talent who had brought us to the dance in the first place and we needed to have some kind of loyalty to them, a responsibility that outweighed spreading the message around the world. I was keenly aware, at the same time, that it would only take one, perhaps two, off-years in the production of quality American independents to seize up our festival and the independent-film movement like an overheated engine that has run out of lubricant. By spreading the focus of the festival out over a wide range of similar world cinema, we could always hedge our bets when the cycle might sputter. But regardless of these possibilities, I was determined to remain the strong, pure advocate of American independents.

I faxed Geoff Gilmore my concerns about enlarging the competition, and we discussed the festival's problems. One was budgetary, because the festival brought in and housed a representative for each film in competition, which was expensive. A larger problem concerned the inability of the national juries to physically see more competition films during the film festival. They were already maxed out with screenings. The only alternative would be either to have them watch many of the films in competition without benefit of a real live audience, which would be unfair to the films, or to have the entire competition prejudged and the decisions made before the festival even started, which would eliminate the sense of expectation and drama inherent in the horse race of a competition unfolding *during* the week.

Gilmore was understandably resistant to my proposal and said he would discuss the dilemma with Redford. I stressed that failing to address the problem would open the door for another festival to come in and scoop up the also-rans for which we couldn't find room. I remember my specific line, really a refrain, "We could make a festival just as interesting as the one we're putting on out of the films we recognize have merit but can't find room for." In many ways, I thought it would be an even more interesting festival because even flawed films can teach many valuable lessons to others coming down the pike. Going into the 1994 festival, however, my suggestions went unheeded.

The 1994 Sundance Film Festival started out with a bang and ended with what some might argue was the proverbial whimper. The big bang was supplied by a sizable earthquake that rocked Los Angeles in the early morning hours three days before the opening of the festival. The earthquake knocked things off shelves, cracked foundations, and sent people spilling out of their beds. Everyone from Los Angeles arrived at Sundance with an earthquake story, and the joke going around during the early days of the festival was that there were a lot of angry spouses who were left behind to clean up the mess. To show just how important attendance at the festival was, according to managing director Nicole Guillemet, the earthquake resulted in only three cancellations. Not even an act of God could come between the pilgrimage to a cinematic mecca and the pilgrims, philistines though they might be. When the mountain won't go to Mohammed, Mohammed must go to the mountain. And in many ways, that was the story that emerged from the 1994 film festival. Was Hollywood co-opting these talented independent filmmakers, or were the independent visions molding the Hollywood establishment in their own image? There were more than a few contradictory examples in the 1994 festival.

First and foremost was the return of the prodigal Coen brothers with their big-budget, megalomaniacal *The Hudsucker Proxy* as a last-minute world premiere. Slotted in the prized Package B premiere slot on the last Thursday, the film went over like a hula-hoop demonstration at a skateboarder convention. Obviously, a great deal of money was lavished on the Joel Silver production, and it did have splendid production design, thanks in large part to the inspired work of the very talented Dennis Gassner, but the film, starring Tim Robbins, Paul Newman, and Jennifer Jason Leigh, lacked emotion or personality beyond the rather melodramatic performances. Joel Silver was known as a producer who blew things up, and of course the Coens were filmmakers who tore convention down, so it was an odd marriage of sensibilities that never quite jelled. As reported in *Entertainment Weekly*, when the Coen's were asked by the press if they sold out, in their dry-witted manner, between incessant tokes on filterless cigarettes, Joel answered unequivocably, "Yes." And Ethan chimed in without missing a beat, "We're trying to sell out." Added Joel, "Isn't everyone?"

Even in the guise of a Joel Silver megaproduction, even with Paul Newman playing in an out-and-out comedy, the Coens' subversive reading of a familiar genre couldn't hide their talent nor the out-of-whack worldview that will undoubtedly serve them the rest of their careers. *The Hudsucker Proxy* is just an expensive and failed blip along the way. So much time, money, and effort for such an inconsequential piece of fluff. If I had had to listen to Jennifer Jason Leigh's over-the-top, shrill, nasal, machine-gun line delivery one more minute, I would have fled from the theater. Then again, every filmmaker should be allowed to make missteps, even if they cost enough to make twenty independent films! Fortunately, the festival had an outstanding crop of independent features and documentaries to underline the point that these films and the attention paid them by the press and the paying public were literally transforming our national cinema. In the documentary category, undoubtedly the highest flying of them all was Steve James, Fred Marx, and Peter Gilbert's four-and-a-half-year labor of love, *Hoop Dreams*. The film won the coveted Audience Award in spite of its three-hour running time or perhaps because of it. It was an incredible emotional roller-coaster ride through the lives of two families of the Chicago-area high school basketball standouts, William Gates and Arthur Agee, and after it was egregiously overlooked by the Academy Awards documentary committee, there was serious discussion about it even being nominated as the best picture of the year. As a tearful Fred Marx said at the festival awards ceremony, "We poured so much of our lives into this film for so long, to see that what came from the bottom of our hearts touched your hearts is very gratifying." Steve James continued "For us this is particularly meaningful. We have a three-hour documentary and the fact the audience voted it the best couldn't be more perfect. . . . We want people to see it."

See it they did, as the film broke out into theaters all around the country before its ultimate broadcast on television. But *Hoop Dreams*, distributed by Fine Line Features wasn't the only documentary coming out of the festival to receive national distribution. Jyll Johnstone and Barbara Ettinger's tough and tender film about their respective childhood nannies, *Martha and Ethel*, was the first film of the 1994 festival to get a distribution deal when it was picked up by Marcie Bloom at Sony

Pictures Classics. It is one of those rare films that pushes all sorts of buttons in men and women about child care and the tension between feminism and child rearing. The stories of the two different nannies—an elderly black woman from the South; a feisty, bowlegged, rather-severe, elderly German woman—are told from the first-person frame of reference of the filmmakers and their families. It is a wonderfully rich film that really does, as Sony Pictures Classics' copresident Tom Bernard, puts it, "have some kind of mojo working for it"; audiences really connected with it.

The distribution deal was personally rewarding to me because I had seen the film in New York in September at the Independent Feature Film Market and had become a strong advocate. In fact, Jyll Johnstone called to tell me first that Sony Pictures Classics had made an offer on the film and to seek my advice from a pay phone at a gift shop in northern California. I was delighted and further gratified when my fellow programmer and soon-departing colleague (to Samuel Goldwyn) Catherine Schulman pulled me aside at a festival party and told me how important my support had been for getting the film in the competition. It was my tiny bit of vindication, to have been the champion for the first film to announce a distribution deal at the festival.

The documentary competition had other highlights. One was Connie Field and Marilyn Mulford's powerful *Freedom on My Mind*, a delineation of one of the most dramatic chapters in the American Civil Rights movement, which won the grand prize. It seemed fitting because years before I had programmed Connie Field's excellent *Rosie the Riveter*, and I was happy to see her doing well. Andy Young and Susan Todd returned with *Lives in Hazard*, a look at gang life initiated by Edward James Olmos in connection with his directorial debut, *American Me*, the film that prompted death threats by rival gangs.

Two of the most visually stunning films I've ever seen were part of the 1994 documentary competition, and both were shot in black and white. Arthur Elgort's *Colorado Cowboy: The Bruce Ford Story*, won the Cinematography Award for Morton Sandtroen, with his elegant composition and lively visuals. Gianfranco Rosi's eerie and profound look at the riparian and human life along the banks of the mystical Ganges River in *Boatman* is another haunting film experience that one never forgets.

Also unforgettable is Steven M. Martin's oddball *Theremin: An Electronic Odyssey*, the popular documentary that proves again that truth is stranger than fiction in its tribute to inventor and physicist Leon Theremin, the Soviet émigré who invented one of the first electronic instruments. The theremin is an odd musical instrument—and difficult to control, let alone master. It produces eerie sounds when a hand is waved over it. It was used by musicians ranging from Edgar Varese, to John Cage, to The Beach Boys in their "Good Vibrations" period. The film won the Filmmaker's Trophy for its unique subject matter and eloquent execution.

Other documentaries, all excellent, traveled more traditional paths in theme and subject. Arthur Dong's *Coming Out Under Fire* and Gregg Bordowitz's *Fast Trip, Long Drop,* both deal with gay issues, specifically of coming out while in the military and coping with the discovery that one has AIDS.

Women's issues were also well represented in 1994's documentary competition: Lucy Massie Phenix's *Cancer in Two Voices*; Academy Award–winners Allie Light and Irving Saraf's with *Dialogues with Madwomen*; Soraya Mire's provocative *Fire Eyes*, about the taboo subject of female genital mutilation; Gini Reticker and Amber Hollibaugh's *Heart of the Matter*, an examination of AIDS and women's sexuality; and Bethany Yarrow's *Mama Awethu!*, a portrait of the remarkable women of Cape Town, South Africa, who struggle in the midst of apartheid.

The dramatic films in competition were no less compelling. Without a doubt, the breakout film was the lowest-budgeted film of the lot and the riskiest in terms of content and performance. In the tradition of *Stranger than Paradise*, Kevin Smith and Scott Mosier's outlandish *Clerks* is in black and white. As the film's poster created by its distributor Miramax says, "Just because they wait on you doesn't mean they like you." Extremely well written, *Clerks* has enough insouciance to last a lifetime, a fact not lost on filmmaker Kevin Smith, who insisted he had to be back to work on the Monday after the festival at, of course, the convenience store where the film had been shot after hours.

Clerks emerged winner of the Filmmaker's Trophy, and producers rep John Pierson negotiated a distribution deal over three orders of potato skins at The Eating Establishment across the street from the Egyptian Theatre after the film's final performance. Also present were Harvey Weinstein and another executive from Miramax, who sealed the deal with his own blood, having gotten a nosebleed in the midst of negotiations. I'm not certain Kevin Smith ever showed up for work, but *Clerks* did go on to do actual business for Miramax and set Kevin Smith and Scott Mosier up in the movie business, a far cry from their previous gig.

Several other standout films in competition also received distribution. *Go Fish,* Rose Troche and Guinevere Turner's lesbian film, known in some circles as the "dyke *Slacker* picture," is also a gritty low-budget black-and-white effort and was picked up by Samuel Goldwyn Company, again repped by John Pierson, in a deal made the first weekend of the film festival.

Scott McGehee and David Siegel's austere, visually compelling and thematically inventive *Suture*, also in black and white, which won the Cinematography Award for Greg Gardiner, had already been picked up by Samuel Goldwyn after its premiere at Telluride earlier in the fall. That's where I had seen Lodge Kerrigan's *Clean, Shaven*, a difficult-to-watch but compelling portrait of a paranoid schizophrenic as he self-mutilates his way down the highway to his eventual victim.

David O. Russell's outrageous and beyond-quirky, mother-and-son-implied incest drama *Spanking the Monkey* was picked up by Ira Deutchman, for Fine Line Pictures, in the back of Z Place just before the film won the Audience Award at the awards ceremony. The unknowing ushers kept insisting the two of them take their seats, but they were still able to hammer out the details of a deal before the announcement of the film's award. Moments later, it looked like a marriage made in heaven.

That was the way of the festival. Futures were made and creative relationships formed in the frenzy of a crowd in the stuffed hallways and living rooms of condos, the preferred site of the late-night parties. The only invitation anyone needed was the address of the unit, or even its general direction, and an ability to find a parking place and trudge through the star-speckled, cold night to step inside the belly of the beast.

Jessica Seigel described the scene in the *Chicago Tribune:*

> On the first floor of the spacious condominium with the incredible view, movie industry schmoozers stood buttock to buttock, crammed so close there was barely enough space to nibble a shrimp. "It has its positive side. They have to talk to you because they can't move," said Lisa Beth Kovetz, a writer who made contact with numerous industry types to whom she will send her screenplay after returning home. "I accomplished more in three days here than in three years back in Los Angeles."
>
> Emerging from the pack of bodies that had inadvertently trashed a fax machine during a fete thrown by the William Morris talent agency, directing hopeful David O'Neill remarked that experiencing the Sundance party scene was like being inside a heart attack. "I feel like a piece of fat," he said, "stuck to an artery wall." That pretty well sums up the experience.

Tom Noonan's surprise grand prizewinner *What Happened Was . . .* showed off the acting talents of the only two people in the film. Noonan, in a change from his chilling bad-guy roles in bigger films like *Last Action Hero*, is a paralegal who is invited over for a dinner date by a secretary in the office, played in carefully modulated rhythms by Karen Sillas in a wonderful performance that solidified her career. The film paints an achingly realistic portrait of two lonely people desperately trying to connect, but the evening leads ultimately only to a better understanding of each other's interests and vulnerabilities. Their mutual failure at intimacy and sadness cries out like the electric-light glow in an Edward Hopper painting. The two become emblematic of the culture at large, lonely people walking around carrying attractions and wounds at the same time. As Emmanuel Levy said in his *Variety* review, "Both Noonan and Sillas give startling performances as the bruised, isolated individuals. This film should establish Sillas, who has done splendid work for Hal Hartley (*Trust, Simple Men*) as a dramatic actress of the first order."

Karen Sillas also starred in Deidre Fishel's film *Risk*, but didn't generate the same kind of notices from that very uneven film. That just underscores the chances actors must be willing to take in the low-budget world of independent filmmaking: Sometimes the film works, and sometimes it doesn't, and it's not easy to predict.

Miramax was already signed to distribute Boaz Yakim's fine film *Fresh*. The film starred Sean Nelson, Giancarlo Esposito, Samuel L. Jackson, and N'Bushe Wright. It earned an acting acknowledgment from the national jury for its young lead, Sean Nelson, who plays a quiet, wise, and sympathetic drug-dealing youth desperate to escape his environment. Samuel L. Jackson does a nice job as his speed-chess-playing absentee father.

The jury also commended the acting talents of young Alicia Witt and Renee Humphrey, female leads in *Fun*, the teenage drama about two girls who kill an elderly woman for kicks. Directed by Rafal Zielinski, *Fun* was one of the sleeper hits during the festival, as was Peter McCarthy's *Floundering*, starring an incredible cast that included James Le Gros, John Cusack, Ethan Hawke, Steve Buscemi, and Billy Bob Thornton.

Paul Zehrer's *blessing* was also a very well-received film about a dysfunctional farm family, starring Carlin Glynn, Melora Griffis, Guy Griffis, Garret Williams, and Clovis Siemon. Dysfunctional families seemed to be one of the emergent themes of the festival in general. Kelly Reichardt's *River of Grass* and Adrian Velicestu's *The Secret Lives of Houses* both also spoke to the family as the core of feeling.

At least Richard Glatzer's *Grief*, perhaps an unfortunate title in the context of all the realistic films in the program, and Alan Jacobs's *Nina Takes a Lover*, the last-minute replacement for Kayo Hatta's *Picture Bride*, which ran into postproduction problems, were lighthearted efforts. But as usual, in a serious film festival, humor was in short supply. As John Brodie reported in *Weekly Variety:*

> Audiences here in the Rockies were treated to such moments as *Clean, Shaven's* schizophrenic hero slicing his fingernail off with a pen knife; *Fun's* two teenage girls killing an old woman for kicks; *Killing Zoe's* Eric Stoltz asking a prostitute for permission to urinate on her; and *The Minotaur's* eponymous hero ordering a gin enema from room service after strangling a beauty queen in a bathtub shaped like a champagne glass.

We couldn't be accused of being in the "granola movie" business any longer, that much was certain.

But there were redeeming social values in many other premieres and special screenings in the festival. Eric Stolz showed his range in Dan Algrant's popular *Naked In New York*. Other noteworthy films were British director Iain Softley's sweet tribute to the Beatles, *Backbeat*; Swedish director Ake Sandgren's 1920s coming-of-age delight, *The Slingshot*; Australian John Duigan's delightfully libertine *Sirens*, starring a bare-breasted Elle Macpherson; Ben Stiller's directorial debut, the good-natured *Reality Bites*, starring the always-interesting Winona Ryder and Ethan Hawke; Andrew Fleming's *Threesome*, with Lara Flynn Boyle, Stephen Baldwin, and

Josh Charles; Ilkka Jarvilaturi's Estonian feature *Darkness In Tallin*; Vietnamese Tran Anh Hung's *The Scent of Green Papaya*; Canadian Francois Girard's *Thirty-Two Short Films About Glen Gould*; and a program of films by and about Native Americans, which was of particular importance to Redford. It included Canadian filmmaker Alanis Obomsawin's *Kanehsatake: 270 Years of Resistance*, and Vermont filmmaker Jay Craven's *Where the River Flows North*, beautifully shot by Paul Ryan and starring Rip Torn and Tantoo Cardinal.

WINONA RYDER AT THE EGYPTIAN THEATER.

When I saw Jay Craven's film at the Carl Winters School, I was perplexed why it wasn't in the competition, because it was a nicely realized and very regional effort. It underscored the different programming philosophies between Geoff Gilmore and myself, and Tony Safford before him. I always felt the festival was skewed to the higher end of the independent food chain, and I apparently wasn't the only one. As Claudia Eller and Alan Citron reported in the *Los Angeles Times*:

> Steven Soderbergh, whose *sex, lies, and videotape* was the toast of the 1989 Sundance Film Festival, is sitting in a corner of a typically over-packed party, grumbling about the "encroachment of commerce" eclipsing art at this important annual showcase for independent movies. . . . Soderbergh takes a sip of beer and observes, at the risk of sounding arrogant: "Since 1989, it's never been the same.

At that time, when he emerged as one of the hottest young filmmakers around, Sundance "wasn't overrun by agents—it hadn't become a deal market, a sales place," Soderbergh says. The shift, he says, came in 1990 when "suddenly this festival became this feeding frenzy, and it was no longer about art."

Program director Geoff Gilmore tried to blunt those criticisms, when he said to Caryn James in the *New York Times*, "It's not like I'm trying to become Cannes West here. To some degree, the distinction between studios and independent films is becoming more and more gray, and we're reflecting that."

The increasingly important and well-attended shorts film program, put together by program associate John Cooper, was a good case in point. As Cooper stated in *Markee Magazine*, to writer John Bernstein, "In many respects the short film selection is a microcosm of an ideal independent film community, and in turn an optimistic forecast of what's to come." The shorts program consisted of many terrific films, often directed by people from other areas of filmmaking, like producers, writers, editors, and designers who wanted to test the directing waters. There were also many films directed by actors taking their turn behind the camera for a change, including Daryl Hannah, Matthew Modine, Ethan Hawke, Peter Weller, and Rob Morrow. In fact, some of the most interesting work at the festival was in this program.

In fairness, I should mention that I, too, had my first short film in the program, *Three Things I've Learned*, written by former *New York Time*s and *New Yorker* magazine writer Michael Kelly. It went on to play in fourteen other international film festivals and was sold for broadcast all around the world. When I formed the small subchapter S corporation to use as the production company for the film, I named it Epicenter Films. When the opening credit came up on the screen at Sundance, with the Los Angeles earthquake fresh in everyone's mind, the name actually got a chorus of groans and then a titter of laughter.

Another interesting short film starred an emerging actor by the name of Billy Bob Thornton, who was also its screenwriter. It was directed by George Hickenlooper and titled *Some Folks Call It A Sling Blade*. Years later, of course, Billy Bob Thornton, unhappy with the short, expanded it into a feature film he directed called simply *Slingblade*.

Robert Redford had a good way of dealing with the shots taken at the festival about the double-headed nature of the beast we'd created—part art, part commerce. According to John Bernstein in *Markee Magazine*:

> Redford is also optimistic about the future. He acknowledged the possibility that he may be launching a Sundance cable channel that would feature independent work, but wouldn't go into any details. As for the festival itself, his objectives are unchanged. "This will continue to be a festival specifically for the filmmaker. What we meant to do when we started was to form a marriage between independent film and the main part of our industry, and that remains true today. In terms of the growth issue, we remain committed to keeping our scale."

Redford also admitted to *Variety's* Todd McCarthy something that particularly piqued my interest:

> What might be an interesting experiment would be to take the films that either came in late or we didn't select, and say we're going to have a second festival for these films, and see what people think. Still, with the success of the festival, there's increasingly more and more disgruntled people, and the problem is going to get even worse.

It was a prophetic statement, for sure enough, in the midst of the 1994 film festival, an ad hoc underground festival was hatched under Sundance's very nose. A group of disgruntled independent filmmakers showed up with their own films, rented a room and a projector, and before I could say "action," Slamdance was born.

SUNDANCE PRAYER CIRCLE.

Chapter 11

In the Nick of Time

In 1994 Slamdance was in essence a sour-grapes organization of three guys: John Fitzgerald; Dan Mirvish, rumored to be related to Robert Altman; and Shane Kuhn. Dan and Shane had had films we'd all seen at the Independent Feature Film Market in New York in the autumn. Although Dan's film *Omaha* did have some moments, our committee didn't find it strong enough and we passed on it. Likewise with Shane's *Red Neck*. I remember both of the films, and they were terribly uneven efforts. Not even in a very weak year would we have been able to include them. But the resourceful filmmakers showed them in Park City anyway, and the event, despite its rather aggressive slam at Sundance, began to slowly gather momentum.

There was a model for such an assault on a film festival. It occurred in 1968 at the Canne Film Festival, when French filmmakers, unhappy with the festival's official selections, stormed the Palais in a protest. They were led by a young Francois Truffaut, and the result was the creation of the Director's Fortnight, which became a mainstay of the annual French festival. This process has been duplicated throughout much of cultural history. A group of people start a radical idea; after it becomes a success, the idea suddenly seems mainstream, and others step up to push it further toward the radical. But it didn't make the organizers of Sundance very happy.

Certainly, the first year's smattering of films at Slamdance didn't advance the idea of independent film as art. They were simply a group of filmmakers, miffed at their exclusion, who were eager to show their films in whatever setting they could provide in Park City and to expose their work to the press and industry in attendance. Given the resourcefulness of most hard-core independent filmmakers, it should not have come as a surprise that someone would eventually organize such an event. The question was whether Slamdance had made enough of a ripple in 1994 to have the momentum to return in a more organized and perhaps more legitimate form.

As 1995s festival approached, Slamdance announced that it would in fact be returning, with John Fitzgerald putting together a small program of films left out of Sundance. I called John. He was more than a little surprised, perhaps even a bit defensive, to hear from someone on the selection committee of Sundance, let alone the guy who had started the independent-film competition. I explained that I had been one of the people who had specifically passed on the films Slamdance had played the previous year, and that in general I wasn't opposed to the idea of an alternative festival in the midst of Sundance.

I did offer some advice, however. I told John that in order for Slamdance to succeed, it needed to stop attacking Sundance. Anyone familiar with the history of Sundance should applaud its creation and success, not malign it. As long as Slamdance was seen as a sour-grapes event, it would never succeed. I suggested strongly that Slamdance should make a consolidated effort to acknowledge the inroads made by Sundance and position itself as a complementary event to strengthen independent film. It was an approach Slamdance had already thought about, and my underscoring only encouraged it.

My motivation for making that phone call was twofold. I was increasingly feeling like the lone voice in the wilderness on the selection committee, with so many competition slots going to films with huge budgets and Hollywood sensibilities. My interest still focused on empowering individuals with the means to make their own films in their own towns and giving them a chance to hook up with an audience who might be interested in seeing their work.

The other reason for talking with Slamdance was that I thought if it continued, the likelihood would increase that Sundance would either have to expand the competition or create a new program, as I had been lobbying, to include more of the kinds of films I was advocating. I did not mean to be disloyal to the festival I had worked so long and hard to create. My criteria have always been: is it good for the filmmakers? I came to the conclusion that it was. Probably Geoff Gilmore wouldn't see it that way, but my motives were pure, and I thought if it all worked out, it would help independent film and ultimately the Sundance Film Festival. The subsequent events indicated that my intuition was correct, but not without some monkey wrenches thrown in along the way.

MIRAMAX PRESIDENT HARVEY WEINSTEIN WITH GEOFF GILMORE AND NICOLE GUILLEMET.

It was ironic that the 1995 film festival had to cope with perhaps one of the leanest years for independent films we had ever experienced. As the pressure continued to mount from all quarters—press, public, industry, and sponsors—1995 really represented a regrouping year. Geoff Gilmore and Nicole Guillemet noted in their introduction to the festival:

> In some quarters, growth is regarded as an unequivocal virtue, but at the Sundance Film Festival, it's viewed as a mixed blessing. Indeed over the past five years, as the program has expanded, as audiences have doubled and redoubled, as sponsorship has increased, and as media attention has become more intense, the questions, "What is this festival, and who does it serve?" have come up more and more often. And the fact is, there is no longer any simple, black-and-white answer.
>
> The basic truth remains that we are a filmmaker-driven festival, and everything we do focuses on reflecting that belief. The Festival now serves a number of constituencies, including the industry—both Hollywood and independent (and more recently, international buyers and sellers); media and press; filmmakers and artists, both established and neophyte (as well as other parts of the independent production community); sponsors and supporters of the Festival; and of course the general public, both local and national.

No small credit for the festival's success goes specifically to Managing Director Nicole Guillemet. She has always been a tireless and open-minded organizer of all the logistics that go into making the festival a world-class event. She has continually refined the operations to respond precisely to problem areas, making adjustments and improvements every year. She and her excellent staff, including the calm at the center of the storm, Jill Miller, the director of administration and the person most responsible for ticketing improvements, all deserve great kudos for their grace under pressure and flexibility to meet new challenges.

Although 1995s program did include some notable films, the most interesting ones came not from the slightly expanded competition, but from special screenings, premieres, and foreign features, many of them from returning Sundance alumni. Richard Linklater's return *Before Sunrise*, was the opening-night premiere, a very romantic yet intelligent film that combined the down-to-earth talents of Ethan Hawke with those of the ephemeral Julie Delpy. Two people experience a meeting of the mind, heart, and soul through an all-night conversation as they wander the lush lit streets of Vienna before they must part company in the morning. It was a difficult film to accomplish, with such a pared-down narrative, but Linklater and his talented cast were more than up to the task of endowing it with real humanity and honest romance.

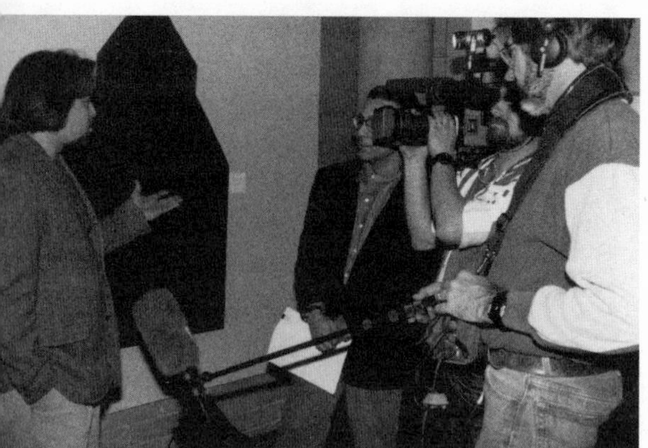
MEDIA FRENZY IS A BIG PART OF SUNDANCE.

Perhaps the most well-received film at the 1995 festival was Bryan Singer's return with the explosive and unpredictable *The Usual Suspects*. Produced by Singer and Michael McDonnell, written by Christopher McQuarrie, production-designed by Howard Cummings, and shot by Newton Thomas Sigel, the plot-twisted crime story starred Kevin Spacey, Chazz Palminteri, Kevin Pollak, Stephen Baldwin, Gabriel Byrne, Pete Postlethwaite, Suzy Amis, and Benecio Del Toro. To this day, I think its script and execution make it one of the most imitated films of the past decade. Amazingly, in the Q and A, following the premiere in the Egyptian Theatre, Bryan Singer admitted the script had been written in about three weeks and the film shot on a very tight twenty-four-day schedule. Although his previous film, *Public Access*, which split the grand prize with Victor Nunez's *Ruby in Paradise* in 1993, never found a distributor, *The Usual Suspects* clearly put Bryan Singer's talent front and center.

This was also the case with my old friends, Gregory Nava, as screenwriter and director, and his lovely wife Anna Thomas, as cowriter and producer, of the emotionally grand *Mi Familia (My Family)*. The film was executive-produced by Tom Luddy, Francis Ford Coppola, and Guy East and featured a stellar cast in Jimmy Smits, Esai Morales, Eduardo Lopez Rojas, Jenny Gago, Elpidia Carrillo, Constance Marie, Lupe Ontiveros, and Edward James Olmos in one of the finest Latino ensembles ever assembled. The multigenerational story, set in Los Angeles, evokes such a sense of nostalgia and longing as it precisely articulates the triumphs and tragedies of one family striving

REDFORD SPEAKS WITH FILMMAKER GREGORY NAVA.

for success and authenticity amidst the cultural richness and reduced circumstances in their daily lives. The film was beautifully designed by Barry Robison and shot by Ed Lachman, and received a lengthy standing ovation after its premiere, with the entire cast and production team called onstage. It was a triumph for Greg and Anna, two extraordinary filmmakers and longtime friends of the festival. I was moved to tears as I gave Greg a big bear hug while the enthusiastic audience exited the theater. It is a powerful film that will expand an understanding of the individual and collective history of a culture.

Todd Haynes returned with *Safe*, another controversial film. Produced by Christine Vachon and Lauren Zalaznick, with James Schamus, Lindsay Law, and Ted Hope as executive producers, the film is a careful examination of one woman's survival in a toxic world. Played to perfection by the luminescent Julianne Moore, she is an upscale and uptight woman of means whose world is turned upside down by a bewildering set of symptoms and maladies, caused by fumes and chemical reactions in her insular environment. After her disappointing encounters with modern medicine, which fails to diagnose her life-threatening ailments, she seeks out the refuge of a New Age retreat, where people who have been similarly poisoned by modern toxicants have gone to find a tolerable coexistence. The result is that her repressed emotional life also opens up, and for the first time in her life, separated from her shallow existence, she feels safe. It is a thought-provoking film, made entirely watchable by Moore's remarkable performance, and further delineates Todd Haynes's odd point of view. *Safe* was not an unheralded success at the festival nor in the marketplace, but it is consistent with Haynes's previous work and just as notorious.

The same can be said about Gregg Araki's return with *The Doom Generation*. The first film he made in 35 mm with SAG actors and a full crew. *The Doom Generation* still covers his familiar terrain of disenfranchisement and sexual politics. Its Day-Glo sensibility and Quickie Mart ultraviolence combine with mosh pit roots to form an anthology of youthful disintegration. The film even features a cameo by Hollywood madam Heidi Fleiss as the ultimate social commentary on the sad state of contemporary hypocrisy.

Although peppered with interesting work, the documentary competition really had only two breakout films. Terry Zwigoff's *Crumb*, which was picked up for distribution by Sony Pictures Classics, is the bizarre portrait of cartoonist and cult hero Robert Crumb, best known for his pop art "Keep on Truckin'" and *Fritz the Cat* incarnation, which champions a politically incorrect feline. A peek into the family closet of the artist shows why he turned out the way he did and is an eye-opening commentary on a dysfunctional upbringing. The film won the Grand Jury Prize and was produced by Zwigoff's friend Lynn O'Donnell, whom he credited with inventing a compelling structure for the film, and who was to die prematurely from breast cancer within the year.

The other standout was Douglas Keeve's *Unzipped*, a look behind the curtain of the New York fashion scene through the eyes of world-renowned designer Isaac Mizrahi. Hoping to duplicate some of the notoriety and theatrical success of *Paris Is Burning*, Miramax picked up the film for distribution after negotiations fell apart with Fine Line Pictures, which thought it had a deal until the film split the Audience Award and the film's financier, publishing behemoth Hachette Filipacchi, owner of *Elle* magazine, wanted to change the terms.

Heather MacDonald's *Ballot Measure 9*, the film that goes behind the headlines of Oregon's 1992 ballot measure to deny civil rights protection for gays, which went down to defeat, was the cowinner of the Audience Award. B Ruby Rich, in her festival program note, said of *Ballot Measure 9*, ". . . this just might be the next training manual on how to rescue the soul of America."

One of my favorite documentaries was Michel Negroponte's haunting *Jupiter's Wife*. Initially shot with a video camcorder and based on a chance encounter between the filmmaker and a homeless woman living in Central Park, the film is the unforgettable journey of one woman's descent into madness, where she becomes both victim and heroine of her own dense plotting. The more one discovers about the subject of the film, the more questions are raised. Are we witness to the hallucinatory wanderings of an articulate imagination, remarkable coincidence, or, as Maggie Cogan, who thinks she is the god Jupiter's wife, puts it, "all the cosmic gizmos that are directing traffic on planet Earth?" The film has all the dramatic payoffs of a fiction film but is even more riveting because, by the end, viewers know it is all true.

There were other memorable documentaries, including Marlon Riggs's *Black Is . . . Black Ain't*, the filmmaker's search for black identity, finished by his production team after his death from AIDS; Meg Partridge's *Dorothea Lange: A Visual Life*, the intriguing portrait of one of the most celebrated photographers of the twentieth century; music producer Don Was's *I Just Wasn't Made for These Times*, his tribute to the just barely living legend Brian Wilson, who was on hand at the 6,000-foot elevation of Park City, to perform a set on the piano at a Riverhorse Cafe private party; Andrew Behar's *Tie-Died: Rock 'n' Roll's Most Dedicated Fans*, which celebrated the subculture of Deadheads, who used to pilgrimage on tour with the Grateful Dead; and David E. Simpson and Billy Golfus's *When Billy Broke His Head . . . And Other Tales of Wonder*, the story of disabled activist Billy Golfus and his video instructor, who take on the world in various acts of civil disobedience to highlight the struggle of the disabled to live and be productive.

The dramatic side of things in the 1995 competition was certainly less inspiring. Out of the eighteen features, nearly one-third arrived with distribution already in place. Distributors understood that making deals in the midst of the fury of

Sundance was not as advantageous as requesting screenings of the films before or just after the selections were made in late November. They did, however, recognize the value of *announcing* the deal at Sundance and using the festival more as a launch than a proving ground for the film.

Probably the biggest news came from neophyte writer, actor and director Edward Burns, and his debut film, fresh from the lab, *The Brothers McMullen*. Unbeknownst to many in attendance, the film had been cleverly tied up by Fox Searchlight Pictures's president Tom Rothman. He had seen a two-and-a-half hour rough cut and put up some finishing money in exchange for a first look at the completed film, a move that proved to be prescient in the light of *The Brothers McMullen* winning Sundance's grand prize.

The other film that received considerable attention, distribution, and some success in the marketplace was Tom De Cillo's *Living in Oblivion*, the comedic send-up of independent production starring Steve Buscemi as the harried director coping with all the chaos surrounding his East Village, low-budget debut film. In many ways, *Living in Oblivion* was like the sequel to Alexandre Rockwell's *In the Soup*, with the same guy still playing the part of the filmmaker in the skinny, wiped-out form of Steve Buscemi; he was just a little farther down the road. Sony Pictures Classics picked the film up in the final hours of the festival, based in large part on audience reaction, although other distributors saw it as a narrow theme and market.

As usual, the triumvirate of Michael Barker, Tom Bernard, and Marcie Bloom scored another winner in this follow-up to DiCillo's *Johnny Suede*, a film that he used as his model for the script of *Living in Oblivion*, poking gentle fun at the persona and performance of Brad Pitt. It provided an interesting object lesson for the insider crowd, one that is undoubtedly lost on the general audience. Film lovers should rent two of the movies and watch them back to back: a Steve Buscemi night with *In the Soup*, followed by *Living in Oblivion* or a Tom DiCillo night with *Johnny Suede* and *Living in Oblivion*. Either way, the films seem to inform one another.

Kayo Hatta's picturesque *Picture Bride,* a holdover from the 1994 competition when it failed to materialize in time, is the story of a Japanese emigrant in Hawaii in the early 1900s. The film was all ready to be distributed by Miramax and had played in a lightly altered version in Cannes the previous May.

Matthew Harrison's lean *Rhythm Thief,* a fictional look inside the New York underground-music scene was also well received, despite its ultra-low budget and black-and-white cinematography. It had already played at the Montreal, Toronto, and Boston film festivals before arriving at Sundance.

But what became apparent during discussions of the 1995 Sundance Film Festival was that commerciality didn't necessarily dictate that a given film was a sellout to Hollywood, or conversely that "difficult" independent film couldn't actually do some business in the marketplace. As John Brodie wrote in *Daily Variety*,

> . . . many of the creators of pix such as Gramercy's *Cold Blooded* and Miramax's *Picture Bride* bristled at the suggestion that getting a distribution deal is somehow analogous to selling out.
>
> "This whole fru-fru about commerciality and budget levels is a lot of bullshit," says James Mangold, director of *Heavy*. "Think of this in a music context; there are no Mariah Careys or Billy Joels here. Everyone here is making an intense movie that was probably hard to get made because it didn't fit into some kind of cookie cutter." Mangold doesn't have a distributor for *Heavy*.
>
> Wally Wolodarsky, the writer and director of *Cold Blooded* took a lighter touch when addressing the issue of whether box-office potential and independent filmmaking are mutually exclusive.
>
> "To be aligned with a money-grubbing independent distributor . . . that was the goal all along," quipped the former *Simpsons* producer. "I was hoping to make a film that no one liked or no one understood."

Despite the jocularity, the point remained: What were some of these films doing in a festival dedicated to independent film? When I saw Nick Gomez's slick *New Jersey Drive*, I was furious. I ran into Geoff Gilmore at Ichiban Sushi in Park City, and I'd had just enough saki to be vocal. I suggested that *New Jersey Drive* was an okay film, and to play it if he liked, but its apparent budget of five to six million dollars didn't exactly make it an "independent" production, and I felt it had no place in the competition. Geoff was taken aback by this and claimed not to know what the budget was for the film. He found me later in the festival, suggested the budget was even higher, and admitted the film probably shouldn't have been in the competition.

It was a telling conversation because it underscored our differing ideas of what constituted an independent film. It seemed for the first time Geoff was getting an idea of what I was talking about. Even if a film's budget was raised independently, which is becoming increasingly rare, it didn't mean the filmmakers were out to blaze an original trail. They were following in the footsteps of many others on the path to fame and glory. Ed Burns's *The Brothers McMullen*, in hindsight and in light of his subsequent films, is the perfect example of what I was protesting against. It became not so much an original cinematic statement consistently adhered to over the course of a career, but rather a loud calling card that served as an entree to the Hollywood big boys. It wasn't exactly what I'd had in mind when I started the competition.

By 1995, things were way beyond the control of anyone associated with the film festival, including Robert Redford. As he stated to Todd McCarthy in *Variety*, the festival "is going to increase by itself because it has become its own perpetuating force." We'd created a monster, and we all knew it. But the question emerging from the 1995 festival was whether we could tweak the monster into more provocative directions.

In a funny way, the foreign films helped lead the way at the 1995 festival. Australian P. J. Hogans's *Muriel's Wedding* was a highlight I'd seen at Telluride. It has a wonderful payoff to a very wry and funny story. New Zealander Lee Tamahori's hard-edged *Once Were Warriors*, portrays an impoverished Maori family that comes to terms with their brutish circumstances when one woman makes a stand for them.

Perhaps the most impressive film I saw at the 1995 festival was Milcho Manchevski's assured debut, *Before the Rain*. It is an excruciating playing-out of Macedonia's long-buried ethnic hatreds, but told with some very human faces. It is without a doubt one of the most powerful visual and dramatic films I've ever seen. To discover it was made by a twenty-something filmmaker was to announce to the world a significant cinematic talent had arrived on our shores. The film was a tour de force that also won the Golden Lion at the Venice Film Festival in 1994.

The new British film industry was also well represented in 1995 at Sundance. Antonia Bird's debut feature *Priest* created quite a stir, as much as Peter Chelsom's *Funny Bones* struck a humorous chord, particularly because of cast member Jerry Lewis's presence at the festival. Mike Newell was back with another Hugh Grant offering, *An Awfully Big Adventure*, a slight but humorous look at relationships within a theater company, set in England's quiet desperation following World War II. The film had a particularly strong performance from Alan Rickman, who played the visiting headliner for the troupe.

Benjamin Ross's *The Young Poisoner's Handbook*, the darkly humorous tale of a brilliant schoolboy's predilection for testing poisons on his friends and family, was apparently loosely based on an actual event. Rounding out the British invasion was *Shallow Grave*, Danny Boyle's wicked tale of a group of housemates in search of a new roomie, which leads to their eventual disintegration.

Maria Maggenti scored big time with *The Incredibly True Adventure of Two Girls in Love*, which Fine Line was set to distribute. Canadian filmmaker Bruce McDonald's Native American slacker tale, *Dance Me Outside,* received a very positive buzz during the festival, as did the Russian delight, Yuri Mamin's 1993 effort *Window To Paris*, being distributed quite successfully by Sony Pictures Classics.

Finally, the raucously popular, formerly impossible idea, *Park City at Midnight,* was selling out every evening's performance, as clear an indication of the growth of the festival as any. Outrageous films in 1995s midnight program included my friend Trent Harris's wildly speculative comedy about Mormons, sex, and space aliens, *Plan 10 From Outer Space*. The film stars the fine Stefene Russell; the loyal Karen Black, who also appeared in Trent Harris's debut feature, the cult classic *Rubin & Ed*; and the local performance legend Gyll Huff as the hilarious ponytailed

Porter Rockwell, known in Mormon circles as "Brigham Young's avenging angel." People literally burst out of their seats with enthusiasm at the conclusion of the screening, having been primed for the film by an action-packed private party put on by the film's producer, Walter Hart. It featured the first of its kind live Internet broadcast of the actual party, as well as caged disco dancers, a live Tongan marching band and a raffle of Trent's mother Mae's world-famous hot sauce.

ROBERT REDFORD AT CLOSING NIGHT CEREMONIES.

Another popular midnight screening was Bruce LaBruce's feel-good movie of the year, the vaguely autobiographical, triple-X-rated *Super 8 1/2*, a kind of existentialist tome of a declining porn star, featuring "talents" like Liza LaMonica, Chris Teen, and Dirty Pillows.

The 1995 festival ended up setting box-office records, despite an uneven program of films in competition, the mainstay of the event. Fortunately much of the slack was taken up by other programs, leading to more than $750,000 in gate receipts. Attendance was higher than ever, and the maxing out of venues remained a major problem for a festival bursting at the seams. Key to the future of the festival was the record number of independently produced films submitted for the competition. Over 300 feature-length films were received from which to select the thirty-three dramatic and documentary films.

As Geoff Gilmore admitted to Todd McCarthy in *Variety*,

> It used to be that you'd look at a group of 25 films and be able to turn off most of them before they were over. Now, more and more have a quality to them and it makes the decision-making more competitive. There were at least 40 to 45 films on our short list this year, whereas last year there were maybe 20.

It was a telling comment, not lost on organizers and participants of the alternative Slamdance, which started the week out at the University of Utah, then moved to Park City to show their eleven films in the conference rooms at Prospector Square. The guerrilla event claimed to be the perfect venue for "the kinds of films and filmmakers who begged for film stock, scoffed at permits, hired undiscovered actors and still owe their parents, friends, parent's friends and friend's parents thousands of dollars." Who could disagree with that?

Apparently the powers that be were more than a little annoyed by this upstart event, attempting to ride their coattails to success. I suppose I was one of the few insiders who wasn't troubled by the coexistence. I continued to have problems getting the kind of films I supported into the festival program, so I shared the frustration of many filmmakers around the country, who felt Sundance had a predilection for films that could bridge the gap between personal vision and commercial appeal. Based on Geoff Gilmore's comments about the extended short list of entries, I again suggested we needed to come up with another program, one that would confirm our commitment to independent filmmaking.

As 1996 approached, standing in the crowded foyer of the Angelica Theaters, on Houston Street in New York to attend the annual fall pilgrimage to the Independent Feature Film Market, Geoff informed me that he had finally convinced Redford of the merits of such a program and said it would be called First Cinema to help draw attention to interesting debut films. It was an idea I felt needed some refinements.

There had long been the feeling, especially from distributors; producers reps, including John Pierson and Jeff Dowd; entertainment attorney Tom Garvin; and the press, specifically *Variety's* Todd McCarthy, that independent filmmaking was mostly about first features. If a filmmaker wasn't successful on the first go-round, chances of making a second and third film diminished.

It was largely true, but it sent a chilling message into the community: Distribute or die. I had always felt that if the festival had proven one thing, it was that audiences could be developed for these film experiences, which translated into paying customers and helped return money to filmmakers and their investors. It really shouldn't matter if the film was the filmmaker's first or third effort. Promoting independent filmmaking as strictly a one-time occurrence unnecessarily limited the options to make interesting films whose core was personal vision and the passion to make it a reality.

I also told Geoff I thought First Cinema was a weak name for the program. Once I got back to Utah, I faxed him my suggestions for the program, along with a name that I thought moved the focus away from first feature films and at the same time sounded uniquely national. My suggestion for the name of the program I'd lobbied so hard to get was simply American Spectrum.

Thank God, it resonated in Los Angeles. The 1996 festival would launch this important rededication to American independent filmmaking. It would open up at least an additional twenty program slots for these films and deepen the festival's focus and influence. I couldn't have been happier, even though I never got credit for my contribution. That wasn't really important to me. I knew this program might be my final and most important suggestion, and the benefit to independent filmmakers was all the solace I needed. Slamdance had unwittingly served the festival very well.

It turned out that 1996 was a banner year, perhaps the banner year for independent filmmaking reaching a pinnacle in the intensity and amount of acquisition deals. It was the year when Lee David Zlotoff's *Care of the Spitfire Grill* got a $10 million advance from Castle Rock Entertainment, and a late-night shouting match ensued between Miramax's Harvey Weinstein and Jonathan Taplin, president of production for Pandora Cinema, in a restaurant on Park City's Main Street over who had made a deal for Scott Hicks's Australian film *Shine*. They were clearly the next big breakthrough films, heralding a new era of what distributors might pay in the frenzy of the festival for movies that worked for audiences at Sundance.

Although the *Shine* shouting match and the *Care of the Spitfire Grill* deal sucked up most of the festival's substantial publicity, it happened to be a fabulous year for films, especially with the advent of American Spectrum, which became an instant hit. It was a particularly strong year for documentaries, as well as dramatic features in competition, and special screenings.

All things considered, it was a fortuitous decision to create American Spectrum because the number of submissions for competition more than doubled for the 1996 festival to over 700 with approximately 500 dramatic features and 200 documentaries. It was an unbelievable statistic to all of us. It was also a daunting task for the committee to get through all the films. As was the tradition, each committee member received Fed Ex'd boxes of submitted tapes, which we plowed through. Then we turned in notes recommending screening the films in the festival, turning them down, or opting for further consideration. The tapes were then shipped to another selection committee member for review.

It was a good system, which at least guaranteed that each film would be reviewed by at least two people. The problem was in trying to have a conversation with the entire committee. All the conversations occurred in a vacuum, monitored apparently only by the Los Angeles office, which consisted of an excellent staff of Geoff Gilmore, John Cooper, Lisa Viola, Christian Gaines, and Trevor Groth. Fellow committee member Robert Hawk and I had figured out long before that joining forces on some films we agreed on made the battle easier. But I never had a conversation with many other members of the committee until perhaps after the festival was under way and we happened to be standing next to each other at a party. I enjoyed having conversations about the films I'd seen because our screening process had so much riding on each of the entries. I felt a tremendous responsibility not to miss a great film out of fatigue, other distractions, or the sheer volume of entries. I wanted to hear other people's voices.

Unfortunately, in an understandable effort to protect the staff from recriminations from disgruntled filmmakers who hadn't been selected, it was decided none of the Sundance programmers would discuss any of the submissions with the filmmakers themselves. In one sense, I understood the need for protection, but in another I thought it was an unfortunate turn of events, which inevitably had to affect the whole gestalt of the festival. Over the course of eighteen years, I'd learned from and valued conversations with filmmakers even when I hadn't liked their films. To remove that dialogue seemed unfortunate. It was self-censoring in a way that didn't serve the interests of filmmakers. I began to get reports from filmmakers who felt Sundance had offended them by not returning phone calls to discuss a submission or rejection.

But the 1996 festival was so full of quality films, one could understand the sheer human limitations of the programming staff to address each submitting filmmaker individually. It would be hard enough to speak directly about film included in the chock-a-block full program, let alone the ones that had been turned down.

To quote festival stalwart Todd McCarthy in *Variety*:

> . . . this year, the festival, now in its second decade under the control of the Sundance Institute, has definitely crossed the threshold from peppery middle-weight to imposing heavyweight able to hold its own with any other festival on the map. It didn't hurt that 1996 saw an unusually high number of strong entries that kept demanding cinephiles more stimulated than discouraged all week.
>
> But the sheer quantity of films, people and industry activity combined with record levels of media presence and sometimes paralyzing snow to create a circus-like environment that, for the first time, began to resemble Cannes. About 115 films, roughly 60 of them new, were screened at the festival, which was attended by about 9,000 people.
>
> In terms of quality, Sundance 1996 underscored that American independent cinema is flourishing on the production side, even if there is an increasing pinch in distribution and exhibition opportunities for offbeat work. Plenty of filmmakers no one had ever heard of before last week experienced career and life turning points during the festival, meaning that Robert Redford's mantra that Sundance is "for the filmmakers" has been fulfilled for another year.

What a year it was! In the dramatic competition, *Bandwagon*, a winning film about a group of guys putting a band together, put former drummer John Schultz on the map; Stanley Tucci and Campbell Scott's fictional tale of two brothers running an Italian restaurant, *Big Night*, went on to considerable success; Brad Anderson's *The Darien Gap* was an interesting personal journey disguised as a road movie; Jim McKay's excellent *Girl's Town*, starred Lili Taylor, Bruklin Harris, and Anna Grace; Mary Harron's *I Shot Andy Warhol,* also starring Lili Taylor, garnered most of the hip press at the festival; sisters Julia and Gretchen Dyer's captivating, *Late Bloomers* was a warm and humorous lesbian-awakening story; Alexander Payne's *Meet Ruth Stoops*, starred Laura Dern as a glue-sniffing druggy who is homeless and pregnant and becomes an unwitting symbol in the tug of war of reproductive rights after a night in jail with some pro-lifers fresh from a demonstration; Nicole Holofcener's *Walking And Talking*, starring Anne Heche and Catherine Keener, arrived late for its first screening under the arms of producers Ted Hope and James Schamus, who'd been delayed coming in from New York by a blizzard; Todd Solondz's *Welcome To The Dollhouse*, which won the grand prize, went on to substantial critical and popular success; and *The Whole Wide World*, starring Vincent D'Onofrio and Renee Zellweger, proved there is hope for festival programmers as filmmakers, since director Dan Ireland had been one of the programmers of the Seattle Film Festival.

Add to this the amazing documentary competition with films like Rob Epstein and Jeffrey Friedman's *The Celluloid Closet,* an examination of homosexuality and its portrayal in the movies; Susan Todd and Andrew Young's *Cutting Loose*, a look behind the scenes in New Orleans' colorful Mardi Gras; Beth and George Gage's incredible *Fire on the Mountain*, a film about World War II's Tenth Mountain Division, composed of a group of hearty individuals who had mastered the art of skiing to use in a surprise attack force, and who, later in life, formed the backbone of the U.S. ski industry; and Melissa Hacker's heartfelt *My Knees Were Jumping: Remembering the Kindertransports,* the story of her mother's experiences being separated forever from her parents in Nazi Germany, an agonizing decision made to save her life. I was so moved when I saw the film alone in my office that I broke down and cried as I left a message on Melissa's answering machine, telling her how powerful her film was.

Then there were Joe Berlinger and Bruce Sinofsky's follow-up effort, *Paradise Lost: The Child Murders at Robin Hood Hills*; Iara Lee's look at artificial environments duplicating and taking the dangers out of nature in *Synthetic Pleasures*, produced by festival veteran George Gund; and Jeanne Jordan and Steven Ascher's remarkable tale of her parent's farm in crisis, *Troublesome Creek: A Midwestern*, truly one of the greatest, most touching, poignant films I've ever seen. It won the Audience Award *and* the grand prize in 1996. Finally, Leon Gast's chronicle of the Mohammed Ali–George Foreman heavyweight fight set in 1974 in Zaire, *When We Were Kings*, went on to win the Academy Award for best documentary of 1996.

American Spectrum's inauguration was announced in the program guide simply.

> The steady increase in the overall number of Festival feature-film submissions has galvanized Sundance's commitment to providing American independent filmmakers with a showcase where these films can be seen. Thus the American Spectrum was created to give new works by emerging filmmakers the recognition they deserve.

Although there was some trepidation on the part of filmmakers who'd had their hearts set on being in competition, we all knew it would be a program of extreme diversity that would become one of the important components of the festival. I knew it would quickly become a hot ticket, because it gave audiences and press an opportunity to look deeper into the totality of independent film.

American Spectrum exceeded our expectations with films like John Walsh's *Ed's Next Move*, a gentle and well-written and performed romantic comedy, starring Matt Ross and Calliope Thorne; Todd Verow's *Frisk*, based on the infamous novel by Dennis Cooper; Scott Silver's *johns*, starring Lukas Haas and David Arquette as street hustlers; Stacy Title's wicked social satire *The Last Supper*, with an amazing cast, including Jason Alexander, Cameron Diaz, Jonathan Penner, and Nora Dunn; Lisa Krueger's *Manny And Lo*, the story of three misfits whose lives come together in a most interesting kidnapping; Miranda Smith's elegant and haunting testament to her father's painful legacy, *My Father's Garden*, which advocates a return to organic farming in the face of agribusiness's dependency on chemicals; Eric Bross's assured debut film *Nothing To Lose*, with a star-making performance by Adrien Brody; and Steven Bognar's *Personal Belongings*, an ironic film about his father's hasty departure from his beloved Hungary as Soviet tanks rolled in during the summer of 1965 and his subsequent return after the end of the cold war. The film also describes the disintegrating condition of his parents' marriage.

Bryan Gordon's delightful *Pie in the Sky*, starred Josh Charles, Anne Heche, John Goodman, and Christine Lahti; L. M. Meza's *Staccato Purr of the Exhaust* had the most mysterious title at the festival; and Neil Abramson's stunningly courageous film *Without Air*, was the most Casavettes-like film I'd seen in a long time. It is the story of a sad blues singer and stripper, played with conviction by Lori Crook because it is all based on her life, re-created and improvised into a dramatic story, which gives the film a gritty authenticity missing from most narrative works.

Finally, the premieres and special screenings included Hal Hartley's *Flirt*; Kenneth Branagh's pleasant *A Midwinter's Tale;* Eric Schaeffer's *If Lucy Fell*; Scott Hicks's immensely popular *Shine*, which was nominated for an Academy Award as the best picture of the year; Alan Taylor's *Palookaville*, with winning performances by Vincent Gallo, William Forsythe, and Lisa Gay Hamilton; Philip Haas's meticulous *Angels and Insects*, based on the A. S. Byatt novella *Morpho Eugenia*; Gary Walkow's strange adaptation of the Dostoevsky novella *Notes from the Underground*, starring Henry Czerny and Sheryl Lee; Kevin Bacon's directorial debut *Losing Chase*, starring Helen Mirren, Kyra Sedgwick, and Beau Bridges; Robert Young's *Caught*, starring veteran Edward James Olmos, Maria Conchita Alonso, and Arie Verveen; Bruno Barreto's *Carried Away*, starring Dennis Hopper, Amy Irving, and Amy Locane; and Al Pacino's fascinating presentation of Shakespeare's *Richard III, Looking for Richard,* with a lot of his acting buddies, including Winona Ryder, Alec Baldwin, Aidan Quinn, and Kevin Spacey. It was a truly marvelous collection of films, which all came together in the same year.

As Todd McCarthy's wrap-up in *Variety* suggested:

> The success and magnitude Sundance has now achieved leaves little doubt that it could easily become the key international film event of the year if it so

desired and if its setting allowed for the possibility of growth. If one discounts the Cannes market, which has become increasingly marginal in recent years, Sundance now premieres about the same number of films as the Riviera event. More significantly for the press and distributors, it now appears that Sundance at least equals Cannes as a place where new filmmakers are discovered and U.S. distribution deals are made, and this without any sort of market apparatus.

The point wasn't lost on Slamdance. Greg Mottola's *The Daytrippers*, executive-produced by none other than Steven Soderbergh and starring Hope Davis, Parker Posey, Stanley Tucci, and Campbell Scott, won Slamdance's jury award, and Marc Foster's *Loungers* won its audience award. Slamdance reported attendance of approximately 5,000 people. As festival director John Fitzgerald said to John Brodie in *Variety*, "Our films were every bit as strong as those on the Sundance slate. And the fact that offers have been made for many of our titles supports that idea." No matter how it was sliced, American independents were all over Park City.

The program introduction to the 1997 festival from Nicole Guillemet and Geoff Gilmore outlined the dilemma faced by the plethora of emerging filmmakers coping with the changing face of the marketplace. With over 800 feature films submitted to Sundance in 1997:

> The bad news is that most of these productions will never see the theatrical light of day, and only a small percentage of them will enjoy even broadcast, cable, or video release. The competition for distribution is increasingly intense, and the task of the Sundance Film Festival is truly formidable.
>
> But is our primary function to serve as a "gatekeeper" as some have declared? We don't believe it is. . . . We remain focused on what's creative and artistic even in the midst of the overshadowing struggle for distribution. The success of the film festival should not be based on what or how many films make it into the marketplace.

The challenge to independent filmmakers was compounded by an additional festival decision that really upset the applecart, namely that competition films needed to be premieres. Despite the festival's declaration and Redford's assertion that it was there to serve the filmmakers, I thought the decision worked at cross-purposes. Restricting the competition to premieres meant that a film couldn't have played at any other domestic venue, no matter how few people may have seen it. The result was that anxious filmmakers were forced to put all their eggs into the Sundance basket. Many other national film festivals were outraged by the move, as were many filmmakers, who had passed up other screening possibilities to hold out for Sundance, only to discover they didn't get in and had missed all other possible festival exposure for the entire year.

I thought boxing in the films that way was unnecessary. It was really an outgrowth of what I can only describe as an institutional ego. The only constituency it served was the festival itself. It meant that press, industry, and distributors were guaranteed films they'd never seen before, but many decent, rejected films would miss helpful exposure through other festivals, as well as bookings on the heels of successful festival runs. I expressed my extreme displeasure with the move to no avail. The festival was throwing its weight around, and no one seemed to want to stand up against the new giant on the block. The new policy only served to raise anxiety levels among filmmakers, their investors, and distributors about whether they were going to be playing at Sundance or not. Several filmmakers withdrew films after being invited to other festivals when they realized it could screw up their shot at Sundance.

In the wake of 1996's banner year, 1997 had a very tough act to follow. With the underperformance in the marketplace of films that had received record-breaking advances, with *Care of the Spitfire Grill* leading the pack, savvy distributors either locked films up in advance of Sundance or arrived in Park City very tight fisted. The word was out: Don't get caught in the feeding frenzy of the festival. Sony Pictures Classics copresident Tom Bernard got it just about right when he told *Variety's* John Brodie, "There will be an unprecedented number of acquisitions people with money to burn, and they aren't going to leave empty-handed. We will probably see films get acquired this year that might have been passed over in previous years."

Part of the reason for this phenomenon was that producers were not letting distributors have a peek at their films beforehand, as they had done in previous years, so that they might create a market frenzy at the festival. Producers lie awake at night dreaming of just such a bidding war for their prized film. Distributors, on the other hand, were increasingly using the festival for other purposes, either launching their films to the press and public, forming relationships with talented people for future work, or setting up coproduction arrangements with people in attendance. It was the classic immovable object meeting an irresistible force. In the end, there would be more purchases but for much less money in 1997.

Erica Potter, a First Look vice president of marketing, said to Steve Gaydos in *Variety*:

> I know everyone will say they're not going to spend a certain amount, but if you want a picture and three others want the same film, depending on how important getting that film is to your overall strategy for the coming year, you have to be prepared to go outside the plan you made in advance. This has been developing the last two or three years. For instance, we bought *johns* out of the American Spectrum last year.

Randolph Pitts, CEO of Lumiere Pictures, added, "Taking last year as an example, the most interesting films were in American Spectrum."

American Spectrum again boasted an interesting collection of films, and with over 800 submissions to the 1997 festival, setting a new record once more, the program proved to be a vital release valve for the mounting pressure of so many strong films being made just as the marketplace was shrinking. Highlights included Finn Taylor's *Dream With The Fishes*, produced by Johnny Wow and Mitchell Stein; Constance Marks' *Green Chimneys*, about abused and rejected children at a treatment facility that is also a working farm; Julie Davis's *I Love You . . . Don't Touch Me!*, a kind of female version of Woody Allen's world; Tony Vitale's *Kiss Me, Guido*, produced by Ira Deutchman and Christine Vachon; Stephen Kay's *The Last Time I Committed Suicide*; Sarah Jacobson's scrappy *Mary Jane's Not a Virgin Anymore*; Jay Chandrasekhar's consistently funny debut *Puddlecruiser*; Ross McElwee's fascinating *Six O'Clock News*; Miquel Arteta's very well received *Star Maps*; Mark Schwahn's delightfully down-to-earth *35 Miles from Normal*; Michael Oblowitz's *This World, Then The Fireworks*; Ross Marks's *The Twilight of the Golds*; and finally, William Gazecki's *Waco: The Rules of Engagement*, which was nominated for an Academy Award as best documentary of the year.

The competition films were just as interesting, if peppered with a few more recognizable names. They included: Alex Sichel's *All Over Me*, written by her sister, Sylvia, and filled with the spunk of Riot Grrrl culture; Hannah Weyer's *Arresting Gena*; Jill Sprecher's *The Clockwatchers*, also written with her sister, Karen, and starring the ubiquitous Parker Posey. Ira Sachs, talented son of the Park City iconoclast, showed up with the beautiful debut, *The Delta*; Tim Blake Nelson's *Eye Of God*; Mark Waters's *The House of Yes*, the film that garnered an acting nod from the festival jury for Parker Posey; Morgan J. Freeman's *Hurricane*, which shared the Audience Award with Theodore Witcher's *love jones*; Neil LaBute's very successful and politically incorrect *In the Company of Men*; Bart Freundlich's *The Myth of Fingerprints*; Andrew Shea's *Santa Fe*, produced by Larry Estes and written by Mark Medoff and Andrew Shea; and Jonathan Nossiter's grand prizewinning *Sunday*, a sad tale of middle-aged impostors, reinventing their lives for one radiant Sunday, when a one-time actress, played by Lisa Harrow, mistakes a middle-aged man, played by David Suchet, for a famous movie director, and he is only too willing to oblige the delusion.

The documentary films in competition were not as strong as the previous year, with no film really breaking out into the marketplace. The grand prize went to Jane Wagner and Tina DiFeliciantonio's *Girls Like Us*, while the Audience Award was won by Monte Bramer's *Paul Monette*: *The Brink of Summer's End.* Other highlights included Arthur Dong's *Licensed to Kill*; Macky Alston's *Family Name*; Laura Angelica Simón's *Fear and Learning at Hoover Elementary;* veteran documentary filmmakers Pamela Yates and Peter Kinoy's *Poverty Outlaw*; Michael Uys and Lexy Lovell's *Riding the Rails*; and finally, the film that had the longest title, gathered the most press, and merited a special jury award, Kirby Dick's *Sick: The Life and Death of Bob Flanagan, Supermasochist*.

Premieres and special screenings heralded a number of festival veterans returning with accomplished work, rededicating themselves to the craft of superb storytelling and deep characterizations as the basis for strong films. First and foremost was my friend Victor Nunez's triumphant return with *Ulee's Gold*, the film that was to propel Peter Fonda to an Academy Award nomination as the salt-of-the-earth beekeeper and grandfather; Greg Araki's *Nowhere* was his fourth film in five years at the festival, a remarkable record perhaps only challenged by Jon Jost. David Lynch world-premiered his *Lost Highway*, and Kevin Smith redeemed his career, after the disappointing teenage departure *Mallrats*, with the world premiere of *Chasing Amy*, produced by Scott Mosier and executive-produced by John Pierson, whose Independent Film Channel program *Split Screen* had been passed over by the Sundance Channel and premiered its opening segment at the renegade Slamdance Festival.

Hoop Dreams director Steve James premiered his dramatic film *Prefontaine*, about the famed long-distance runner. Richard Linklater premiered *subUrbia*, written by Eric Bogosian. Vondie Curtis Hall wrote and directed *GRIDLOCK'd*, starring Tim Roth and the now-deceased rapper Tupac Shakur as two addicts trapped in the bureaucracy of treatment and urban life. Errol Morris premiered his *Fast, Cheap & Out of Control*, proving once again to be the master of cinematic invention and just plain weirdness. Tom DeCillo also returned to the festival with his enchanting *Box of Moonlight*, beautifully shot by Paul Ryan. The film starred John Turturro, Sam Rockwell, and Catherine Keener in a nostalgic story about a very under-control man suffering mild hallucinations, who goes back to find a childhood vacation spot to figure some things out, only to encounter the literal embodiment of childhood exuberance in a character named Kid, who's broken down by the side of the road and is running around in a Davy Crockett outfit and making the best of it. It is an interesting film, with great but very different performances by John Turturro and Sam Rockwell, which didn't get enough attention upon its release.

To top it all off, the world cinema program had at least eight films that were standouts. Undoubtedly the biggest discovery at the festival was the British film *The Full Monty*, written by Simon Beaufoy and directed by Peter Cattaneo, a film that translated all across the spectrum of demographics for Fox Searchlight Pictures, now headed by Lindsay Law. Another British hit, which I'd seen at Telluride was Kevin Allen's outrageous *Twin Town*, being distributed by Gramercy Pictures. Miramax's large slate included Australian Peter Duncan's *Children of the Revolution*; Jan Sverak's *Kolya*, nominated for an Academy Award; the Japanese delight, *Shall We Dance?* written and directed by Masayuki Suo; and Chen Kaige's *Temptress Moon*. Sergei Bodrov's superb *Prisoner of the Mountains* was a clear winner, as was Australian Emma-Kate Croghan's *Love and Other Catastrophes*.

All in all, 1997 was most noted for the maxed-out facilities festivalgoers encountered on every level. Despite upgraded public transportation, record numbers of cars were towed, and the temporary screening rooms set up in the ballroom of the Yarrow Hotel really left something to be desired. As Todd McCathy suggested in his *Variety* wrap-up, ". . . if Sundance were an NFL team, they'd demand a new stadium or move out of town."

Slamdance mounted a strong program, including Michael Davis's very original film *Eight Days a Week*, which received the Audience Award. It was ironic, because I'd had a long-running dialogue with Michael Davis, after seeing his film in New York at the Independent Feature Film Market the previous fall and becoming an instant supporter. Frustrated by my inability to get the film into the festival programs, I encouraged Michael to submit the film to Slamdance. Producers rep Jeff Dowd was concerned Geoff Gilmore might hold a grudge against films and filmmakers who played at Slamdance, Michael decided he wanted to show his film wherever he could, and it ended up being a good decision, I think.

The other funny thing that happened in 1997 was that with nearly 1,000 submissions, Slamdance found itself in the position of having to reject huge numbers of films to make its modest program. That resulted in even another renegade festival appearing on the scene. It was called Slumdance because it was held in the basement of the building that formerly housed Debbie Fields's Cookie College. For a first-time event, it got plenty of press. There was no doubt in anyone's mind that this thing was completely out of control.

The 1998 festival was memorable for at least two things. First and foremost was the completion of the 1,300-seat George S. and Dolores Doré Eccles Theatre, a state-of-the-art facility that was just barely finished in time to accommodate the festival. It came just in the nick of time, a major pressure-release valve for the bursting-at-the-seams event. The other thing that helped reduce the congestion on Park City's Main Street was moving the festival's offices a couple of miles away to Shadow Ridge, near the Park City Ski Area.

While it has always been true that in Park City, ironically, a person could never really park and there truly is no city, the introduction of meters on Main Street and in Swede Alley, behind Main Street, also reduced the amount of traffic, which was heralded as a good move by hassled residents. Many locals have to trudge through the snow to retrieve their mail from the Main Street post office, and the festival's massive presence made that journey a pain in the derriére. While there has always been an uneasy relationship between the festival and the town and its year-round residents, statistics indicate that during the course of the ten-day event, approximately $18 million is spent in Park City and environs. The impact on what used to be the slowest week of the winter season has been telling.

People in Park City often wonder why we can't move the festival to a really slow time, like April, when the ski season comes to an end. The answer is obvious and important. Falling in January, Sundance begins the festival season. The January date also positions the festival to be able to screen many premiere films shot over the past spring or summer that are finished just in time for Sundance. For Sundance to move to any other time of year would cause major repercussions. The addition of the Eccles Theatre, and moving operations off Main Street should make Sundance a slightly more tolerable neighbor—unless, of course, one happens to be a time-share owner who has a vacation during the third week of January. If the time-share owner lives next door to a condo that is hosting a late-night party or he/she is trying to get into one of the town's overflowing restaurants, a problem might arise. But then again, how many times does one get to see so many beautiful, recognizable people, all dressed in black?

Ken Brecher had become the executive director of the Sundance Institute in 1997, having come from the Mark Taper Forum in Los Angeles. He was the first executive director since Suzanne Weil had left, and the responsibilities for the institute and festival had fallen on the shoulders of Gary Beer, who was by 1998 president and CEO of the Sundance Group, responsible for overseeing all of Redford's myriad interests. But Beer's days at Sundance were also numbered. After the 1998 festival, despite the enormous success of all Redford's interests, Beer's departure was imminent.

The 1998 festival was memorable for several other reasons. According to Tom Bernard at Sony Pictures Classics, for the first time he was actually interviewed by filmmakers who had films at Sundance as though he was a prospective employee. This was a big turn of events in the methodology of finding a distributor. I think he found the experience less than thrilling, but it also said volumes about the expectations some people had for the success of their movies.

There were plenty of strong movies; that much is certain. But the sense of purpose and passion had been somehow inextricably altered. The festival had grown into something altogether different than when it started. It had become a behemoth serving so many masters that on some level it lost its soul. It was so full of movie experiences that even a great film like Michael DiJiacomo's *Animals* could get lost in the process. To be certain, 1998 will go down as one of the great years for innovative films, but the festival had become so influential that is was much more market oriented and less personal. Long gone were the days of wide-open parties; now the late-night events were full of people very familiar to each other, having all been given invitations, and some small part of the magic seemed to slip into the cold mountain air of Park City.

Tom DiCillo premiered *The Real Blonde*. The Coen brothers returned with *The Big Lebowski*, a riotous film based on the character of Jeff Dowd, played by Jeff Bridges, which almost didn't make its screening. Everyone associated with the film forgot to arrange for the print to arrive in Park City and it had to be flown by chartered jet into nearby Heber City, arriving about an hour late for its screening. It was worth the wait. Boaz Yakim returned with *A Price Above Rubies*, starring the emergent Renee Zellweger. Brazilian filmmaker Walter Salles scored one of the early hits at Sundance with his *Central Station*, which was scooped up by Sony Pictures Classics as a preemptive buy just before the festival started. Ted Demme's taut film *Snitch*, starred Denis Leary, Billy Crudup, and Famke Janssen. David Mamet premiered his *The Spanish Prisoner*. Timothy Hutton premiered *Digging to China*, his feature film directorial debut. Michael Moore and his Flint entourage arrived with *The Big One*. Don Roos premiered his wry and comic debut film, *The Opposite of Sex*, featuring a gem of a performance by Christina Ricci.

The dramatic competition was highlighted by a number of first features. Tommy O'Haver's *Billy's Hollywood Screen Kiss*; hotheaded actor Vincent Gallo's *Buffalo 66*, which also starred Christina Ricci; Lisa Cholodenko's *High Art*; Saul Rubinek's darkly funny *Jerry and Tom*; Darren Aronofsky's *π*; Chris Eyre's evocative *Smoke Signals*, which was written by Sherman Alexie and won the Audience Award; Jimmy Smallhorne's *2by4*; Kip Koenig's *How to Make the Cruelest Month*; Benson Lee's *Miss Monday;* and Meg Richman's *Under Heaven*. All were directorial debut films.

Additional films in the dramatic competition included Brad Anderson's follow-up to *The Darien Gap* with *Next Stop, Wonderland*, featuring Hope Davis and Alan Gelfant; animator extraordinaire Bill Plympton's *I Married a Strange Person*; Laurie Weltz's *Wrestling with Alligators*; and Marc Levin scored big with his cinema vérité jailhouse-poetry film *Slam*, which won the grand prize and prompted audiences to explode with spontaneous applause in the middle of the film.

CHRIS EYRE, DIRECTOR OF *SMOKE SIGNALS*, RECEIVING HIS AWARD.

Documentary films in competition were equally impressive, if less explosive in the marketplace. Highlights included Anne Makepeace's personal film about trying to conceive a child in *Baby It's You*; Katharina Otto's models on the rise in *Beautopia*; Penelope Spheeris's revisitation of postpunk culture in *The Decline of Western Civilization, Part III*; Steve Yeager's impressive romp through the world of John Waters in *Divine Trash*; Liz Garbus and Jonathan Stack's memorable film on prison life, *The Farm*, which split the grand prize with Todd Phillips and Andrew Gurland's *Frat House*, a telling look inside the ritualistic Greek system; and Julia Loktev's *Moment of Impact*, about her father's fate after being hit by an automobile.

Jeff Dupre's *Out of the Past* won the Audience Award, which was fitting because it focused on an incident in Salt Lake City when a high school student attempted to form a gay club at school, sending shock waves throughout the conservative community. The result was the banning of all extracurricular clubs, a blanket way of dealing with the issue. Iara Lee took a look at the electronic music scene in

NICOLE GUILLEMET AND GEOFFREY GILMORE.

Modulations; Ellen Bruno's *Slavegirls* studied Burmese girls sold by their families into prostitution in Thailand, and Barbara Kopple returned with her magnificent *Wild Man Blues*, a behind-the-scenes look at Woody Allen as he tours Europe with his clarinet, Dixieland jazz band, and Soon Yi.

American Spectrum also had some standout films. Michael DiJiacomo's *Animals* is the only film I've ever seen that uses the device of a short film to precede the feature leading into the feature by depicting the same characters as younger people. I was absolutely blown away by the aesthetic of this film and cannot believe that someone hasn't picked it up and demanded it be screened all over the world. Lynn Hershman Leeson's *Conceiving Ada* starred the inimitable Tilda Swinton; Bob Gosse, one of the cofounders of the low-budget outfit The Shooting Gallery, landed his debut *Niagra, Niagra*; and Garret Williams brought his interesting film *Spark*, produced by Bob Potter, Lynn Holst, and Ruth Charny, about two African Americans whose car breaks down on the edge of the desert.

GEOFFREY GILMORE. WOULD HE HOLD A GRUDGE AGAINST FILMMAKERS WHO SCREENED AT SLAMDANCE?

Perhaps the most controversial no-show at the 1998 festival was Nick Broomfield's documentary on Courtney Love and Kurt Cobain, *Kurt and Courtney.* Even though Nick was on the jury and was a festival veteran, when Courtney Love threatened to sue Sundance if it showed the film, supposedly over some music rights, the festival caved in to the pressure and canceled the screenings. Other festivals were quick to step up and promise to play the film despite threats of legal action.

The 1998 festival was noted for being a better-run, better-managed, and better-projected event. Of course by now, attendance was huge, with films being shown in Salt Lake City, Ogden, and Provo, at the Sundance resort, and on every available screen in Park City. Press attendance was massive, and the clippings about the festival in the press room stood over a foot tall. The program continued to be of the highest quality. It was clear that not only had Hollywood influenced the independents but the independents had influenced Hollywood. In fact, in many ways they had taken it over.

One of the last nights of the 1998 festival, my filmmaker friend Monty Diamond, who was looking for finishing funds for his shot-and-assembled feature, *Peroxide Passion*, and I were trudging through the snow to an anonymous condo where we'd been invited to a William Morris party. When we arrived, a young agent was at the door turning people away because the condo was overcrowded. Monty was looking for another William Morris agent, so she let him in, and I said, "I'd just as soon hang out on the porch and smoke my cigar, rather than cram myself into the hallway of the condo." I stood outside in the cold night air, with the stars twinkling brilliantly in the crisp Utah sky, and watched this young agent turn away tons of people who'd found a parking place and walked all the way up to the front door of this Deer Valley monstrosity. People from Warner Brothers. People from HBO, people who managed other people—she didn't care who they knew or who they were, she wasn't going to let them in. In the most nasally whine I've ever heard, she'd say, "I'm so sorry, you guys," and then they'd walk away really ticked off.

I watched this little escapade for about ten minutes, puffing away into the night. When things slowed down, she asked me if I wanted to go in, and I said, "Not really." But I did offer a bit of advice. I said she'd be wise just to go into the party and quit turning people away at the door because she was making way too many enemies—people who knew her name and weren't afraid to use it. This hit her like a snowslide off the roof. "Oh my God, you're right. Why didn't I think of that?" she gasped. She disappeared into the bowels of her condo, and I'm sure wherever she is now, she appreciates my little observation. I was happy to stay on the front porch, smoking contentedly and listening to the cacophony of all the people working the party in a box.

THE TYPICAL FILM FESTIVAL DIET.

By the arrival of the 1999 Sundance Film Festival, or what should have been the twentieth anniversary festival, I was feeling rather despondent about the whole thing. I had been removed from the selection committee the previous year, ostensibly to make room for "new voices." I had supposedly been invited to sit on the National Advisory Board for the film festival in a nice letter from Robert Redford and Geoff Gilmore, only to discover that I was never invited to the annual and altogether perfunctory meeting in New York, nor was I listed as being a member on that board. It was just a small slight but one I'd become accustomed to expect.

So as the 1999 festival started, I was feeling more like an outsider than ever. It got so bad, when I tried to be friendly with John Cooper, the associate programmer, he wouldn't even acknowledge me. And I knew, in my heart of hearts, I'd finally run my course with the organization. I'd made my contributions and this was in all probability the last Sundance Film Festival I would be attending. Even former assistant, R. J. Milliard, who had largely taken over press-office and media relations for Sundance in Saundra Saperstein's place, wouldn't or couldn't let me in early to one of the big parties being held for Sony Classics' *SLC Punk*, ironically a film I had worked on in production. Instead I was told I'd have to stand outside in the growing line to see the Violent Femmes perform. I was finally rescued from the cold by the director James Merendino's girlfriend when she recognized one of the film's coproducers, Tam Halling, and locations manager Arlene Sibley standing in line with me, and we were escorted into the party. Needless to say, I reflected long and hard on the juggernaut of a film festival we had all created. Ironically, I felt an odd sense of contentment waiting in line with all the other regular ticket holders. I realized that it had all come full circle as I tapped my toes together standing in the frozen Park City night. I was experiencing the festival in a unique way, given my background and position, and perhaps it was fitting. I tended to learn more about the festival from standing in lines and riding buses around town than I did from attending chichi parties. And I found that if I was outgoing and friendly with people, I ended up meeting the most fascinating folks. In my mind, that was one of the best parts of the festival experience.

SAUNDRA SAPERSTEIN BIDS HER FAREWELL AT CLOSING NIGHT.

I met Iris in a bar named Steeps during a rather mundane festival party. She was standing there in a full-length fur coat, looking a bit out of place. She was doing that head-turning maneuver where a person pretends to be looking for someone but has no idea who, when her eyes fell on me, standing equally uncomfortably and doing the same head-turning maneuver.

"So, you look like an interesting person to talk to," she said. "You look important."

"Hardly. Just hanging out," I lamely said as I took a long draw on a longneck.

"What's your story here?" I asked quickly, before she could ask me first.

She introduced herself and told me she had just sold her first screenplay to Miramax.

"I'm impressed. What's it about?" I asked.

"It's about the first female president. It's called *Madame President.*"

"That's great. My daughter wants to be the first female president," I said, always happy to introduce my children into a conversation with an attractive woman.

"She'd better hurry," she said with a laugh.

"So how did you come up with this idea?" I asked.

"Well, I'd been hanging around with Bill and Hilary," this got my attention, "and I'd been wanting to write a script, not to direct it or produce it or anything, but to write it. And I came up with this idea about what it would be like for the first female president. I told Bill about it, and he said he loved the idea and that I should get in touch with his friend Harvey. He meant Harvey Weinstein, the head of Miramax. So he made the call for me and they loved the idea. I wrote it, and they bought it. I guess it helps having the President call the head of the company for you."

By this point I was dying. All I could think was that I've been encouraged to keep writing, told that I do have a talent for it, and have even had offers to do scripts that failed to materialize. And here was this vivacious first-timer, a platinum blonde in a fur coat who sold an idea to Miramax because the President of the United States made the call for her!

Iris was a delightful new acquaintance, who insisted on exchanging all her telephone numbers with me, and we promised to get together in New York. "You'd really like my boyfriend," she said as we parted company, and I certainly wish her well. But in a funny way, my conversation with Iris, jammed into a loud Sundance Film Festival party was emblematic of just how clubby and kind of absurd the whole thing had become.

Even with my being frozen out in the cold, literally and figuratively, I felt an odd sense of vindication when the final awards were announced. Twenty-seven-year-old Tony Bui's visual feat *Three Seasons* was the top prizewinner, a strong ensemble piece about the disintegration and regeneration of three disparate stories set in current-day Vietnam. Headlined by a restrained performance from Harvey Keitel, who seems singularly distinguished as an actor willing to perform and support talented new directors, Tony Bui's film won both the grand prize and the Audience

Award, not to mention the Cinematography Award for director of photography Lisa Rinzler, a rarity bestowed on a very few films over the twenty-year history. The reason for my feeling vindicated was that I had been the first person to turn the festival programmers on to then twenty-four-year-old Tony Bui's work when I saw his beautiful short film, also set in Vietnam, *Yellow Lotus* at the 1996 Telluride Film Festival. When I got back to Utah, I immediately faxed Geoff a note with my recommendations out of Telluride, including a note that we had to play *Yellow Lotus* and that Tony Bui's work showed a directorial assurance that belied his age. He was clearly someone to watch. Sundance subsequently invited his next project to the June Lab. *Three Seasons* was the result.

Other highlights from the 1999 festival included James Merendino's outrageous acid romp through the 1980's punk scene in that center of punkdom, Salt Lake City, Utah. Based on his real-life experiences, the film was executive-produced by Jan de Bont, Michael Peyser, and Andrea Kreuzhage and starred Matthew Lillard, Michael Goorjian, and Annabeth Gish. *SLC Punk* had been picked up for North American distribution by Sony Pictures Classics when it had played the previous May in Cannes.

Mark Illsley's directorial debut *Happy, Texas* got some big laughs, especially after Miramax picked up the film for distribution at the rumored sum of $10 million, later denied. It turned out that the advance was more in the $3 million range but with a potentially more lucrative back-end deal should the film do some real numbers. The story involves two escapees from a West Texas chain gang who get mistaken for an out-of-town gay couple there to put on a beauty pageant. The film should help to dispel the notion that Sundance is an elitist event! The British film *Lock, Stock and Two Smoking Barrels* also received rave notices and quickly went into national release, having already been a box-office hit in Great Britain. Eric Mendelshon's first feature *Judy Berlin* also received strong notices, a dreamy black-and-white film about a young man's search for meaning amidst the circumvented lives of friends and neighbors in Babylon, New York. He finally comes to an understanding and a direction during a solar eclipse after he runs into an old friend from high school, the title character, who is about to leave town. She is on her way to Los Angeles to pursue her dream of becoming an actress. It is a wonderfully poetic and metaphorical film where hope finally triumphs over alienation, and despair must give in to wonderment. Although the film was not an obvious choice for most distributors, it was clear to everyone that the director has a lot on his mind and the requisite cinematic tools to communicate complicated ideas. We'll see if he is able to use what will surely come his way from Hollywood to his own artistic advantage. Certainly audiences deserve an opportunity to see *Judy Berlin*. The film has a fascinating and experienced ensemble cast in Barbara Barrie, Bob Dishy, Edie Falco, Madeline Kahn (who is especially stellar), Julie Kavner, and Anne Meara. One can only hope that this unique voice will be allowed to flourish.

Among the other films from the 1999 festival that were standouts in the documentary category was the documentary grand-prize winner, Chris Smith's *American Movie*, about the real-life ambitions and obsessions of an archetypical low-budget independent filmmaker, Mark Borchardt, who lives in Wisconsin with the burning passion to make a horror film that will propel him into stardom. Of questionable talent and even more questionable thinking, Borchardt nonetheless possesses heart. As he and Chris Smith trekked through the soggy streets of Park City, it was apparent that he was only too happy to have his moment in the sun, even though it was clearly Chris Smith who will benefit most from the relationship. It is often a fine line between empathy and exploitation.

No one understands that idea better than documentary demigod Errol Morris, who returned to the 1999 film festival with yet another odd masterpiece. *Dr. Death: The Rise and Fall of Fred A. Leuchter Jr.*, a film about the self-styled "execution technologist," who is hired by anti-Semites to prove the holocaust could not possibly have happened because of his failure to find traces of poison gases in stolen fragments of mortar from a gas chamber. Instead of this delusional pseudoscientist's finding becoming the crowning achievement of his life, as he thought it would, it became his downfall.

Errol Morris's sardonic sense of humor was in evidence once again in Park City. As he told *Los Angeles Times* film critic Kenneth Turan, he prepared for his arrival at Sundance by "spending seventy-two hours in a meat locker with people I don't like, and all of them have cell phones." Hilariously, he recounted his earliest experience at Sundance in 1981 when I had programmed his fabulous *Gates of Heaven*, the film about pet cemeteries, which remains one of my all-time favorite films. Reminiscing fondly, Morris told Turan:

> There was a snowstorm, I was staying in a godforsaken condo, and I only had an idea of where it was located. I had to hitchhike back there, and I was picked up by people who'd been in the theater and had hated the movie. They asked me what I thought, and since I had no alternative means of transportation, I said I, too, was extremely disappointed.

Self-deception seemed to be a running theme in many of the more noteworthy or at least notorious documentary films. Allen and Albert Hughes, the creators of *Menace II Society* and *Dead Presidents,* arrived with their unlikely documentary *American Pimp*. The film examines the men behind the world's oldest profession and the popular misconceptions surrounding them. With monikers like Filmore Slim, C-Note, Gorgeous Dre, and Rosebudd, these men are all too happy to share the secrets of their stock and trade. As Geoff Gilmore wrote (one can only assume tongue-in-cheek) in the program note, ". . . [an] incredibly straightforward and cooly unexploitative examination of a universe that is really virgin territory for documentary film."

The second controversial film, some questioned as pornography posing as political discourse, was Gough Lewis's *Sex: The Annabel Chong Story*. This was an incredibly graphic and sordid tale in which self-promotion meets self-loathing in the form of twenty-two-year-old graduate student and porn star Annabel Chong, who decided in 1995 to break a rather perverse world record formerly held by a sex worker from Amsterdam when she engaged in the world's largest gang bang by having continuous sex over a ten-hour period with 251 men. Many people expressed their outrage with this Caligula-like film by walking out in droves—this of course after they'd all fought to get into the screening in the first place. As a furious Gary Pollard, who heads up the Documentary Festival Program in New York, stated to me, "The festival should never have played that film. It was made to be a porn film. It isn't a documentary. The whole thing was set up." With the petite Annabel Chong roaming about the festival like some sort of automaton, one can only wonder what she was thinking. Rebecca Yeldham suggested in her program note that the act and the film had some sort of higher moral purpose. "For Chong, pornography is a vehicle by which she can exert her will, state her rampant sexual cravings, and assert her repugnance for societal repression and the 'politically correct' constructs of sexual normalcy." Did I mention she doubled the previous record?

Documentarian master and good friend of the festival, Jon Else arrived with another stylish and unique film, which won the Filmmaker's Trophy, *Sing Faster: The Stagehand's Ring Cycle*. This staging of Richard Wagner's mammoth opera *Ring Cycle*, with its seventeen-hour presentation of four separate operas, is a behemoth undertaking. Else takes his cameras behind the scenes and shows the entire production from the standpoint of the stagehands who are put through their paces by the sheer physical rigors of the fog, fire, thunder, earthquake, dragon, and immense scenery. Of course, this doesn't prevent them from maintaining an ongoing poker game throughout the opera, replete with a blow-by-blow account of the libretto. The result is an endearing artistic expression of people in various positions, all contributing to a common goal, not unlike the film festival itself.

On a sad note, midway through the festival, one of the key technical advisors, longtime Sundance projectionist Ron Montgomery, went back to his condo to catch a nap and died of a heart attack. His death cast a sad and somber reality on the staff of the festival who had long appreciated his sense of professionalism and easygoing manner. As in any death, especially one so sudden and premature (he was only forty-eight), it causes everyone in its shadow to pause and reflect on the nature of life and mortality. To the technical staff's credit, despite their personal feelings of loss, they didn't miss a beat, and the festival went on as it has for twenty years.

By 1999, the festival was a thriving success that had been instrumental in creating a market for a whole new kind of American movie, the independent film. Hundreds of talented people have contributed in so many creative ways. We have helped to create an identity and a level of consciousness, even internationally, that didn't exist prior to our articulation of the idea. We have all succeeded in adding a new level of cultural opportunity and human expression in the most dynamic artistic medium known to mankind. Yet, as the critical reviews of the 1999 festival trickled in, it was apparent there are still many battles to be won.

As David Denby noted in his piece for the *New Yorker* magazine:

> It is not unusual for a Sundance favorite to open theatrically, get good reviews, and then earn less than a million dollars at the box office. Sundance, I suspect, both creates and destroys the independent cinema, which turns out to be a much publicized "movement" without a sufficiently articulated culture of its own. The independent cinema still lacks certain obvious elements that would help to build a bigger college and young-adult audience—an aboveground, central, but hip and intellectually ambitious magazine, rather than another trade journal; a few arrogant critical texts that filmmakers and movie lovers could gather around; a set of aesthetic (rather than financial) criteria; and theaters offering the kind of status-creating social atmosphere that might reward audiences for supporting a true adversarial film movement. Redford himself is developing such theaters with the General Cinema chain, but one would hate to see the proposed new showplaces become an adjunct of the festival. Sundance has been so effective that it has made many other people lazy.

Geoffrey Gilmore would try to hedge such criticism. In his comments to Janet Maslin in the *New York Times* at the conclusion of the festival, "There's a lot of doubt right now in this community about how well independent film is surviving. But I think the festival defies that once again."

As David Denby went on in the *New Yorker* to rally behind the festival:

> Attending the festival seriously is rather like shacking up with an extremely energetic woman. One races about in a state of exhilaration and near exhaustion. It isn't possible to see more than a fraction of the movies, so one follows a figure in the carpet—say, the movies about searching for lost or unknown parties, or the movies about the aftermath of the Vietnam War. . . .
>
> Whatever one's grumblings, the Sundance movies offer subjects that Hollywood won't touch, made by directors Hollywood won't hire, who then create images that Hollywood would leave on the cutting-room floor.

But Tom Bernard, copresident of Sony Pictures Classics and longtime supporter of the film festival saw it differently. As he stated to John Clark in the *Los Angeles Times*, "I am very disappointed in Sundance, because to me it's become a festival of commerce. Years ago it used to be the festival of discovering new talent and new films, almost a convention of people who were in the grassroots movement of the American independent-film scene. I think the people in the film schools and out in the field are now looking at Sundance as a stepping-stone to get rich and to get into Hollywood." Young directors, such as Tony Bui and Eric Mendelsohn, have a lot of responsibility riding on their shoulders.

The tension between art and commerce, the push and pull of it, is no more pronounced in any other form of human expression as it is in movies. To my way of thinking, no matter how one feels about Sundance, it has all been for the good. We are a much healthier film culture with independent films serving as a vital source of subject matter and artistic expression than if these kinds of films had never existed. Can one even contemplate what the film-going landscape might look like as we move into the twenty-first century if independent films didn't exist and our cinematic cultural identity was entirely defined by Hollywood? One shudders at the thought and one takes immense pleasure and pride that, for myriad reasons, it hasn't been the case. In my mind, the artistic ambitions of creators of deep stories in our culture committed to film, has been met equally and enthusiastically by an intense intellectual and emotional hunger on the part of audiences. The trick is in bringing these simultaneous circumstances together so that people are willing to plunk down their money to sit in a darkened theater and experience something unique, informative, and perhaps even challenging. It is all about the dance between art and commerce. And no place is that physical dialogue more tangible than at Sundance.

ANOTHER PARTY IN ANOTHER BOX.

CHAPTER 12

Where Do We Go From Here

I am often asked my feelings about how different Sundance is now from when I helped to start it in 1978. My standard response is: The biggest problem with Sundance is that there aren't enough of them. At first, people aren't sure what I mean. Simply put, we need more festivals around the country dedicated to screening these kinds of films in their own towns, ultimately helping to build a groundswell of support for largely unknown works, by *developing audiences*!

By any yardstick, Sundance has been a major influence in establishing the direction of our national cinema today, both domestically and even around the world. But for this idea of a diverse national cinema to succeed so that people can actually make a living at it without having to move to Los Angeles or New York, we need more film festivals willing to take the chances we did in the early years. I like to remind people that if they truly believe in something, they should be willing to go into debt for it. There are other important and emerging film festivals, including Los Angeles Independent Film Festival, South By Southwest, Aspen Film Fest, Austin, New Directors, and the more established Telluride, Toronto, New York, Seattle, and Cannes. All of these need to be supported, and new regional festivals should sprout up in their shadow. But the trick is not just to recycle the same films to all these events. Distributors won't stand for it, and neither will filmmakers and audiences. Film festivals must offer something of genuine value to their constituencies.

Despite Sundance's cable channel and the Independent Film Channel, broadcast outlets for most independent films are difficult to come by, often dictated by the support of a theatrical release. And that's where the challenge for the vast majority of filmmakers lies. How does one get a film in front of audiences? I am increasingly convinced that independent filmmakers who do not play at Sundance, and even some who do, need to take control of their film's futures and, if all else fails, be prepared to self-distribute. And these words are discouraging for many people.

John Pierson estimates that of the roughly 1,000 independent films made during each of the past several years, nearly 60 percent have been financed on personal credit cards amassed by filmmakers before preproduction. This can be a dangerous game for many people. I've known about many filmmakers who have ruined their credit rating by making these movies, having them not work out, then declaring bankruptcy. This is the dirty little secret of independent filmmaking. A large portion of films being made are also taking advantage of probably the single largest transfer of wealth from one generation to the next ever to take place in the history of civilization. Trust funds across America are being burned up in film stock, equipment rental, cast and crew salaries, lab costs, and postproduction, only to discover at the end of the road, making movies that companies are willing to spend money to advertise and people are willing to pay money to see is harder than it looks. In a sense, I think events like Sundance and the attendant press attention overhype the idea of making a successful film and can lead filmmakers down the primrose path to financial ruin.

So I advocate filmmakers putting together their own damned film festivals. Take a lesson from guys like Jay Craven in Vermont, whose film *Where The River Flows North* couldn't get an acceptable advance from an interested distributor despite a stellar cast, a strong story, and a screening at Sundance. Jay decided to four-wall the film all through Vermont, where the story took place. He ended up playing the film anywhere he could—in church halls, Foreign Legion basements, mom-and-pop movie houses—and he set house records throughout the Northeast. By proving that the film worked with audiences, he was able to secure a much more lucrative cable and video deal, which largely paid off investors. Without Jay Craven's resourcefulness, the film would never have repaid investors much beyond twenty cents on the dollar. But I do think, if a person is hell-bent on making a movie and just cannot help him or herself, there are ways to improve the odds.

LORY SMITH IN HIS OFFICE.

I have a little theory about the way people come to the idea of desperately wanting, in fact needing, to make a film, be it a short, a feature, or a documentary. The first thing they do is immerse themselves in the movies. Not just endlessly watching films, all kinds of films, but becoming conversant with the language of cinema: pans, dolly moves, smash cuts, close-ups, masters, lighting for certain kinds of effects, sound design, and special effects, not to mention piquant writing and performance, characterization, setup and payoff, conflict and resolution, plot twists and points—the list goes on and on. After prospective filmmakers have acquired a thorough knowledge of the language, they can start to talk about how great it would be to make a film. This part of the process might go on for a long period of time. Eventually everyone gets sick and tired of hearing just talk about making a movie, and the only alternatives are to either make the damned film or shut up about it and do something else with one's life. I call it the "paint yourself into a corner" theory of film production. To keep the respect of family and friends, the filmmaker has to go ahead and make the film.

When we started this whole film-festival exercise, I wanted to empower people to make their own films about their own stories from their own regions and to develop audiences for these kinds of stories and cinematic experiences. It was a way to break down the very closed Hollywood system, a world in which not so much studios anymore but guilds and unions, not to mention the sheer physical requirements of film production, dominated and controlled the access of normal people who might have interesting stories to tell. Hollywood is a place where, if a person doesn't have a friend or relative working in the system of one of the guilds or unions, he or she has a very difficult time gaining entry. I used to joke that if I could only get my father a job in "the industry," as it is often called, I, too, might have a chance to succeed. Nepotism has long been rife in this line of work, and I was excited from the beginning to help provide an alternative to the way people come up through the system to reach the pinnacle of their profession. It is a great and rare privilege to work in the film industry, but that doesn't have to be the case. I wanted to physically blow open the doors to the ways and means of making films in our culture.

I think in some profound way we actually succeeded, but one of the problems I have with the current management of Sundance is that it, too, has been co-opted by the very system we set out to change. To be certain, Hollywood, the press, and audiences have come to embrace these different kinds of films, but these filmmakers and storytellers have also embraced, to a very large degree, the system we hoped to radically alter. Perhaps my private and political ambitions exceeded our ability to make changes in a system where distribution is still controlled by a very small cadre of companies increasingly owned and operated by corporate conglomerates.

Perhaps one of the best models to use for comparison is the music industry. The advent of rock and roll, in all its manifestations, really is a very good parallel to independent filmmaking. Garage bands were formed by people who just wanted to pick up an instrument and begin to explore avenues of self-expression, much in the same way people in the 1960s wanted to pick up 16 mm cameras and express themselves visually and emotionally. Both have had profound effects on our mass culture, a fact that hasn't been lost on the corporate entities poised with distribution outlets to take advantage of changing tastes and make a great deal of money on them. I suppose that is the way of capitalism, the dynamics of a free market, and the unique qualities inherent in mass-producing ideas that previously were the exclusive domain of artists and iconoclasts. The challenge facing both filmmakers and music makers is to retain some sense of the radical, to position oneself against established forms and then take advantage of the network of suppliers and consumers to broadcast one's creation. I suppose that must be a classic model of artistic growth, achievement, and ultimate survival.

Despite the substantial inroads we have made, many challenges remain. The uncomfortable reality is that it is as difficult today to make an artistically and commercially successful film as it was twenty years ago when we started this journey. In fact, sadly, it is even more difficult in some ways because the blush is off the rose, and the days of entrepreneurial people willing to take up the challenge of distributing such material may be over. Ancillary foreign markets are susceptible to the vagaries of their economies. Cable and home-video markets are dominated by major studio and mini-major releases. Celebrity worship, marquee value, and television Q-ratings drive movie financing today. Unless you are repped by a major talent agency in Hollywood, what's a poor filmmaker to do?

Increasingly, I'm convinced that new forms of technology can help formulate new strategies for disseminating material efficiently, but I'm concerned that they have also cluttered the cultural landscape with so many options for entertainment and information that we have lost sight of the goals of artistic endeavor and achievement. Digital technologies are changing the technical landscape, but no matter what format the material originates in, the rules of engagement with an audience remain fundamentally unchanged. People need to feel genuine emotion from the art they encounter. We want all to be moved on profound levels, to connect to stimulating ideas and other people.

That is why I continue to insist on audience development, with a particular emphasis on youth, as the key to sustaining the advances we have made. Otherwise, we run the risk of participating in the "golden era" of independent filmmaking and watching all the inroads get sucked up by corporations interested only in short-term results. We, as audiences, as filmmakers, as storytellers, and as a culture at large, vote each time we go see a movie on the kind of movies we hope to see in the future—high art versus low culture. It is all in our hands, our heads, our hearts, and our pocketbooks.

People who have been particularly successful have a special responsibility to assure that the future of independent filmmaking is as vital as the past. Despite Robert Redford's tendency to "brand" Sundance's name on so many aspects of the independent-film movement, I hold him in the highest esteem for his heartfelt commitment to offering divergent voices the opportunities for success. Certainly, he is unique among his peers for his dedication to the idea of independent-film production and his influence over the artistic means of its creation. Someone in his position didn't have to take on the challenge he has willingly accepted, sometimes even at the cost of his career, particularly in the middle years of the institute's history. It became much more of a lifelong commitment than I'm sure he ever imagined, but we are all the richer for it. Culturally and artistically, we all owe him a debt of gratitude for having the vision, guts, stature, heart, mind, and soul to recognize what is at stake for the industry that has treated him so kindly.

Many others in similar positions of success and influence would do themselves a lot of karmic good to look to Bob as a cultural model. No matter what minor disagreements we may have, I immensely respect what he has done. No matter his response to the gentle prodding of this book, I will always admire his tenacity and willingness to share his formidable intelligence and insight about the artistry and passion of making films. A profound coincidence of circumstances pointed the way and he was smart and passionate enough to recognize he could make a unique contribution to sustaining the industry he cares so much about. He has set high standards for himself and those around him and his influence will last long after we've all departed. What we need are others who have the wherewithal to contribute in their unique ways to the process.

One of my continuing gripes with distributors and exhibitors is that they fail in the marketplace to emphasize the distinctions unique to this kind of filmmaking. Instead, they lump all film together, as though it all speaks the same language and seeks out the same audience. In my opinion, they'd be wiser to exploit the differences than homogenize the similarities. And why is it that every movie trailer seems to use the same voice over and over? I'm sure it has tested well, but really, can't audiences expect more respect than that? I've had a lot of distributors tell me I should put my money where my mouth is and become one if I am so convinced I'm right. If I had any money, I might take them up on the challenge. But I'm an artist, not a businessman. That much seems clear to me.

Having spent twenty years of my life developing these ideas, having seen literally thousands of films and read hundreds of scripts, having worked on over eighty-five major film projects, having made a few films myself and written dozens of scripts with varying degrees of success, I can say that a life in film is one of the most difficult and competitive endeavors a person can ever embark on. The amount of rejection one must contend with, without letting it sap enthusiasm and life force, is at times overwhelming. Yet, there are some things I have learned over the course of twenty years that might help someone determined to work in this field to improve the odds of success.

The first consistent problem in independent films is lax writing. Being a writer, I know how it works. I slave to write a script I think is pretty good. I rewrite it a few more times, sometimes incorporating some of the suggestions from a small but trusted collection of honest readers, who include friends, family, and colleagues. They may even be local actors who want to be in it. Come to think of it, maybe they aren't so honest. After exhaustive rewrites, the script often sits while the focus shifts to financing, preproduction, and a lot of telephone calls. Once the financing is secured, often years later, the script may get some attention with the help of casting and interpretation, but by then the time for futzing is largely over. I think independent filmmakers often make the mistake of thinking the script is totally sacrosanct. They fail to keep adapting and improving it all the way through the process, even up to the shoot day.

Which leads me to the idea of a second act. Many independent films fail to understand the idea of a real second act. They set up the premise, establish the characters, and set the world of the story in place. Then they stall around until the conclusion. Sure there are episodes along the way, but they amount to a stall until the filmmaker can find a way to wrap it all together. When something does occur in the second act, it is often weak and unconvincing. In fact, it seems like it was arbitrarily placed there *simply as an impediment* in the story. Independent filmmakers consistently fail to develop characters fully enough to make the second-act conflict emerge from character instead of plot. I consistently feel cheated in the middle of an independent film.

Often combined with dinner and a few drinks, this is the reason why during home-video rentals so many independent films, even successful ones, get turned off in the middle. The setup is usually interesting enough, and the ending is at least an ending, but the middle consistently lacks sufficient believable conflict, based on the character's moral dilemmas, inner delusions, and first decisions. Independent films often skate through the second act.

In my opinion *all* movies skate through the third act. As director Arthur Penn once said at Sundance, "When the final shot of your movie is a crane up over the scene at the end, you really don't have an ending." But films have to end somewhere. And those crane shots are so damned easy, if expensive, and the unfailingly signal to the audience that the story has run its course.

The other consistent misstep for many independents is poor casting and uneven performance. So many films I've seen have moments and characters and dialogue to recommend them, but they have miscast one or two people who have successfully dragged the whole production down. Clever filmmakers can edit around these performances, but by that point, usually the filmmaker has got to live with what he or she has gotten. Casting is one of the most critical steps in the entire filmmaking process. The actors in the movie are the movie. One stumble here can kill the whole damn thing. And the problem is, once one has crossed the casting Rubicon, he or she is really down the road. To recast someone in rehearsal is one thing; to have to recast after production has started would be a nightmare.

The other thing I think is helpful is to adapt the script to the extent possible to capture the personal strengths of the performers. Rather than try to get them to adapt to the material, why shouldn't the material try to at least meet them halfway. Some of the strongest moments in my films came from suggestions from the actors trying to come to terms with their characters' situations. I immediately incorporated their comments into the script, and the lines suggested by the actors consistently were the ones that got the biggest laughs in the film. As a director and storyteller, one has to remain open to these rich suggestions, to be as good of a listener on the set as a leader.

The other area I find consistently problematic in many independent films is their editing. Part of the problem, I know, is coverage. That is, they often don't have much great footage they can cut to. Or if they do, the shots are clumsy attempts at close-ups without an understanding of where the real meat and potatoes of a scene lie; they lack any sense of pace and, the key to editing, anticipation. So many films I've watched just need a lot of smart cutting to play as more effective and well-paced dramas. They consistently linger for the visuals at the expense of the flow of the picture.

Inadequate editing is often the result of money constraints unless someone is doing the editing themselves, in which case their need for another set of eyes is even more important. The tendency is to hold onto a shot longer than necessary, or sometimes even comfortable. This consistent flaw can be found in dramatic moments as well as action and beauty shots. The ultimate goal is tight editing that anticipates the next shot, so that to the viewer's eye the transition is mostly seamless.

Another problem independent filmmakers have is their inability to describe their own films, and especially to write about them. After they've made the film, they really should think about hiring marketing experts to write the description of the story.

The best independent films succeed on all these levels and more. If filmmakers study the successful independent films of the past twenty years, they will discover that the films share many attributes, best summed up as an audacity of subject matter and execution. Independent filmmakers should strive toward an authentic weirdness. Outrageousness will help set a film apart from the pack. One should not attempt to duplicate what others have done before, especially what has come out of Hollywood's dream factory. He or she must find his or her own genuine voice and stick to it. An original voice is what everyone is looking for, one that helps us, the audience, connect to the characters and material on an emotional, intellectual, and visceral level.

As my good friend Jeff Dowd said to Anne Thompson in *L.A. Weekly,* back during the 1994 festival, "No one really knows anything. I'm supposed to be an expert at marketing and distribution. But I don't know anything. All any of us do is sit and listen to what works for an audience. Ultimately, all we do is sell emotion." As filmmakers and storytellers, we've got to go deeply enough into ourselves, into our points of view, to find the emotional chords that connect with audiences. It is a wonderful, heady, scary exercise in the ultimate creative experiment of the modern age.

Everyone loves movies. They hold a clout in our culture that is probably way out of proportion to their actual value, but that is because they have become the artistic instruments through which we model ourselves and come to an understanding of what it is to be human. When they work, they are a glorious illumination of the human spirit. I applaud each and every person who is driven to make the attempt to communicate his or her strongest feelings in little pieces of celluloid. When the lamp pushes light through the image, what we see on the screen is ultimately a reflection of who we are as a people. It has been a life-changing experience for me to have had the honor and privilege to be associated with so many talented and passionate individuals. May we all go on making films, combining words and images, until the last light of day slips past the horizon.

As for me, I hope to continue to write scripts, make films, and work in the realm of the senses most precious to me—as an artist and painter. In a sense, that is the completion of the circle for me, the rounding of the square. In my mind, there can be no greater endeavor than to live in the present and be deeply involved in the pursuit of self-expression. May your life be as full as you can make it. Embrace the future and please don't forget to have fun. Remind yourself that, in the end, the struggle to succeed may be the best part of the process, far more invigorating than success itself. We are all standing on each other's shoulders, reaching for the stars. May your reach always exceed your grasp. And may your life, as well as your bank account, always be balanced. Party on.

Index